LUDWIG WITTGENSTEIN

PHILOSOPHICAL
REMARKS

LUDWIG WITTGENSTEIN

PHILOSOPHICAL REMARKS

Edited from his posthumous
writings by Rush Rhees
and translated into English
by Raymond Hargreaves and
Roger White

The University of Chicago Press
Chicago

The editor was enabled to prepare this
volume for publication through the generosity of
the Nuffield Foundation. He owes it particular
gratitude. R. R.

The University of Chicago Press, Chicago 60637
Basil Blackwell, Oxford

ISBN: 0-226-90431-8
LCN: 80-14296

Et multi ante nos vitam istam agentes, praestruxerant aerumnosas vias, per quas transire cogebamur multiplicato labore et dolore filiis Adam.

Augustine

FOREWORD

This book is written for such men as are in sympathy with its spirit. This spirit is different from the one which informs the vast stream of European and American civilization in which all of us stand. That spirit expresses itself in an onwards movement, in building ever larger and more complicated structures; the other in striving after clarity and perspicuity in no matter what structure. The first tries to grasp the world by way of its periphery – in its variety; the second at its centre – in its essence. And so the first adds one construction to another, moving on and up, as it were, from one stage to the next, while the other remains where it is and what it tries to grasp is always the same.

I would like to say 'This book is written to the glory of God', but nowadays that would be chicanery, that is, it would not be rightly understood. It means the book is written in good will, and in so far as it is not so written, but out of vanity, etc., the author would wish to see it condemned. He cannot free it of these impurities further than he himself is free of them.

November 1930   *L. W.*

ANALYTICAL TABLE OF CONTENTS

I

8 The kind of co-ordination on the basis of which a heard or seen language functions would be, say: 'If you hear a shot or see me wave, run.'   55

9 Have philosophers hitherto always spoken nonsense?   55

II

10 Thinking of propositions as instructions for making models. For it to be possible for an expression to guide my hand, it must have the same multiplicity as the action desired. And this must also explain the nature of negative propositions.   57

11 How do I know that I can recognize red when I see it? How do I know it is the colour that I *meant*?   57

12 If the image of the colour is not identical with the colour that is really seen, how can a comparison be made?   58

13 Language must have the same multiplicity as a control panel that sets off the actions corresponding to its propositions.   58

14 Only the application makes a rod into a lever. – Every instruction can be construed as a description, every description as an instruction.   59

15 What does it mean, to understand a proposition as a member of a system of propositions? Its complexity is only to be explained by the use for which it is intended.   59

16 How do I know that *that* was what I expected? How do I know that the colour which I now call 'white' is the same as the one I saw here yesterday? By recognizing it again.   59

17 Should Logic bother itself with the question whether the

proposition was merely automatic or thoroughly *thought*? It is interested in the proposition as part of a language system.   60

18 I do not believe that logic can talk about sentences [propositions] in any other than the normal sense in which we say, 'There's a sentence written here'.   61

19 Agreement of a proposition with reality. We can look at recognition, like memory, in two different ways: as a source of the concepts of the past and of identity, or as a way of checking what happened in the past, and on identity.   61

III

20 If you exclude the element of intention from language, its whole function then collapses.   63

21 The essential difference between the picture conception (of intention) and Russell's conception is that the former regards recognition as seeing an internal relation. The causal connection between speech and action is an external relation.   63

22 I believe Russell's theory amounts to the following: if I give someone an order and I am happy with what he then does, then he has carried out my order.   64

23 If, when learning a language, speech, as it were, is connected up to action, can these connections possibly break down? If so, what means have I for *comparing* the original arrangement with the subsequent action?   64

24 The intention is already expressed in the way I *now* compare the picture with reality.   65

25 Expecting that *p* will be the case must be the same as expecting the fulfilment of this expectation.   65

26 If there were only an external connection, no connection could be described at all, since we only describe the external connection by means of the internal one.   66

27 The meaning of a question is the method of answering it. Tell me *how* you are searching, and I will tell you *what* you are searching for.   66

28 Expecting is connected with looking for. I know what I am looking for, without what I am looking for having to exist. The event that replaces an expectation is the reply to it. That of course implies that the expectation must be in the same space as what is expected.   67

29 Expectation is not given an *external* description by citing what is expected; describing it by means of what is expected is giving an internal description.   68

30 If I say 'This is the same event as I expected' and 'This is the same event as also happened on that occasion', then the word 'same' has a different meaning in each case.   68

31 Language and intention. If you say, 'That's a brake lever, but it doesn't work', you are speaking of intention.   69

32 I only use the terms expectation, thought, wish, etc. of something which is articulated.   69

33 *How* you search in one way or another expresses what you expect. Expectation prepares a yardstick for measuring the event. If there were no connection between expectation and reality, you could expect a nonsense.   70

34 If I say that the representation must treat of my world, then I cannot say 'since otherwise I could not verify it', but 'since otherwise it wouldn't even begin to make sense to me'.   71

35 The strange thing about expectation is that we know it is an

expectation. And *that* is what shows expectation is immediately connected with reality. We have to be able to give a description comparing expectation with the present.   72

36 What I once called 'objects' were simply that which we can speak about *no matter what may be the case*. 'I expect three knocks on the door.' What if I replied, 'How do you know three knocks *exist*?'   72

37 Is a man who cannot see any red around him at present in the same position as someone incapable of seeing red? If one of them imagines red, that is not a red he sees.   73

38 The memory and the reality must be in *one* space. Also: the image and the reality are in *one* space.   73

IV

39 If I can only see something black and say it isn't red, how do I know that I am not talking nonsense – i.e. that it could be red, that there is red – if red weren't just another graduation mark on the same scale as black?   75

40 If there is a valid comparison with a ruler, the word 'blue' must give the direction in which I go from black to blue. But how do these different directions find expression in grammar?   75

41 A man with red/green colour blindness has a different colour system from a normal man. Is the question then 'Can someone who doesn't know what red and green are like really see what we call "blue" and "yellow"?'   76

42 Grey must already be conceived as being in lighter/darker space. The yardstick must already be applied: I cannot *choose* between *inner* hearing and *inner* deafness.   76

43 For any question there is always a corresponding *method* of finding. You cannot compare a picture with reality unless you can set it against it as a yardstick.   77

44 How is a 'formally certified proposition' possible? The application of a yardstick doesn't presuppose any particular length for the object to be measured. That is why I can learn to measure in general.   78

45 But are the *words* in the same space as the object whose length is described? The unit length is part of the symbolism, and *it* is what contains the specifically spatial element.   78

46 A language using a co-ordinate system. The written sign without the co-ordinate system is senseless.   79

V

47 It doesn't strike us at all when we look round us, move about in space, feel our own bodies, etc., etc., because there is nothing that contrasts with the form of our world. The self-evidence of the world expresses itself in the very fact that language can and does only refer to it.   80

48 The stream of life, or the stream of the world, flows on and our propositions are so to speak verified only at instants. Then they are commensurable with the present.   80

49 Perhaps the difficulty derives from taking the time concept from time in physics and applying it to the course of immediate experience. We don't speak of present, past and future images. 81

50 'I do not see the past, only a *picture* of the past.' But how do I know it's a picture of the *past*?   82

51   On the film strip there is a present picture and past and future pictures: but on the screen there is only the present.   83

52   We cannot say 'time flows' if by time we mean the possibility of change. – It also appears to us as though memory were a faint picture of what we originally had before us in full clarity. And in the language of physical objects that is so.   83

53   But it can also be put *differently*; and that is important. The phrase 'optical illusion', for example, gives the idea of a mistake, even when there is none. One could imagine an absolutely *impartial* language.   84

54   Language can only say those things that we can also imagine otherwise. That everything flows must be expressed in the *application* of language. And if someone says only the present *experience* has reality, then the word 'present' must be redundant here.   84

55   Certain important propositions describing an experience which might have been otherwise: such as the proposition that my visual field is almost incessantly in a state of flux.   86

56   If I make a proposition such as 'Julius Caesar crossed the Alps', do I merely describe my present mental state? – The proposition states what I believe. If I wish to know what that is, the best thing to do is to ask *why* I believe it.   86

VI

57   One misleading representational technique in our language is the use of the word "I", particularly when it is used in representing immediate experience. How would it be if such experience were represented without using the personal pronoun?   88

58   Like this, say: If I, L. W., have toothache, that is expressed as 'There is toothache'. In other cases: '*A* is behaving as L. W. does when there is toothache'. Language can have anyone as its centre. That it has me as its centre lies in the application. This privileged status cannot be expressed. Whether I say that what is represented is *not* one thing among others; or that I cannot express the advantage of *my* language – both approaches lead to the same result.   88

59   It isn't possible to believe something for which you cannot find some kind of verification. In a case where I believe someone is sad I can do this. But I cannot *believe* that *I* am sad.   89

60   Does it make *sense* to say two people have the same body? 90

61   What distinguishes *his* toothache from *mine*?   90

62   'When I say he has toothache, I mean he now has what I once had.' But is this a relation toothache once had to me and now has to him?   91

63   I could speak of toothache (datum of feeling) in someone else's tooth in the sense that it would be possible to feel pain in a tooth in someone else's mouth.   92

64   If I say '*A* has toothache', I use the image of feeling pain in the same way as, say, the concept of flowing when I talk of an electric current flowing. – The hypotheses that (1) other people have toothache and that (2) they behave just as I do but don't have toothache – possibly have identical senses.   93

65   Our language employs the phrases 'my pain' and 'his pain' and also 'I have (or feel) a pain', but 'I feel my pain' or 'I feel his pain' is

nonsense.   94

66 What would it be like if I had two bodies, i.e. my body were composed of two separate organisms? – Philosophers who believe you can, in a manner of speaking, extend experience by thinking, ought to remember you can transmit speech over the telephone, but not measles.   95

VII

67 Suppose I had such a good memory that I could remember all my sense impressions. I could then describe them, e.g. by representing the visual images plastically, only finishing them so far as I had actually seen them and moving them with a mechanism. 97

68 If I describe a language, I am describing something that belongs to physics. But how can a physical language describe the phenomenal?   97

69 A phenomenon (specious present) contains time, but isn't in time. Whereas language unwinds in time.   98

70 We need a way of speaking with which we can represent the phenomena of visual space, isolated as such.   98

71 Visual space is called subjective only in the language of physical space. The essential thing is that the representation of visual space is the representation of an object and contains no suggestion of a subject.   99

72 How can I tell that I see the world through the pupil of my eyeball? Surely not in an essentially different way from that of my seeing it through the window.   100

73 In visual space there isn't an eye belonging to me and eyes

belonging to others. Only the space itself is asymmetrical.   102

74   The exceptional position of my body in visual space derives from other feelings, and not from something purely visual.   102

75   Is the time of isolated 'visual' phenomena the time of our ordinary idioms of physics? I imagine the changes in my visual space are discontinuous and in time with the beats of a metronome. I can then describe them and compare the description with what actually happens. A delusion of memory? No, a delusion that, *ex hypothesi*, cannot be unmasked isn't a delusion. And here the time of my memory is precisely the time I'm describing.   103

VIII

76   Incompatible for red and green to be in *one* place at the same time. What would a mixed colour of red and green be? And different degrees of red are also incompatible with one another. – And yet I can say: 'There's an even redder blue than the redder of these two'. That is, from the given I can construct what is not given. – Is a construction possible within the elementary proposition which doesn't work by means of truth functions and also has an effect on one proposition's following logically from another? In that case, two elementary propositions can contradict one another.   105

77   This is connected with the idea of a *complete description*.   106

78   That r and g completely occupy the f – that doesn't show itself in our signs. But it must show itself if we look, not at the sign, but at the symbol. For since this includes the form of the objects, then the impossibility of '$f(r) \cdot f(g)$' must show itself there in this form.   106

79 That would imply I can write down two particular propositions, but not their logical product? We can say that the '·' has a different meaning here.   107

80 A mixed or intermediate colour of blue and red is such in virtue of an internal relation to the structures of red and blue. But this internal relation is *elementary*. That is, it doesn't consist in the proposition '*a* is blue-red' representing a logical product of '*a* is blue' and '*a* is red'.   107

81 As with colours, so with sounds or electrical charges. It's always a question of the complete description of a certain state at *one* point or at the same time. But how can I express the fact that e.g. a colour is definitively described? How can I bring it about that a second proposition of the same form contradicts the first? – Two elementary propositions can't contradict one another.   108

82 There are rules for the truth functions which also deal with the elementary part of the proposition. In which case propositions become even more like yardsticks. The fact that *one* measurement is right automatically excludes all others. It isn't a proposition that I put against reality as a yardstick, it's a system of propositions. Equally in the case of negative description: I can't be given the zero point without the yardstick.   109

83 The concept of the independent co-ordinates of description. The propositions joined e.g. by 'and' are not independent of one another, they form *one* picture and can be tested for their compatibility or incompatibility.   111

84 In that case every assertion would consist in setting a number of scales (yardsticks), and it's impossible to set one scale simultaneously at two graduation marks.   112

85 That all propositions contain time appears to be accidental when compared with the fact that the truth functions can be applied to any proposition.   112

86   Syntax prohibits a construction such as '*a* is green and *a* is red', but for '*a* is green' the proposition '*a* is red' is not, so to speak, *another* proposition, but another form of the same proposition. In this way syntax draws together the propositions that make *one* determination.   113

IX

87   The general proposition 'I see a circle on a red background' – a proposition which leaves possibilities open. What would this generality have to do with a totality of objects? Generality in this sense, therefore, enters into the theory of elementary propositions.   115

88   If I describe only a part of my visual field, my description must necessarily include the whole visual space. The form (the logical form) of the patch in fact presupposes the whole space.   115

89   Can I leave some determination in a proposition open, *without* at the same time specifying precisely what possibilities are left open? 'A red circle is situated in the square.' How do I know such a proposition? Can I ever know it as an endless disjunction?   116

90   Generality and negation. 'There is a red circle that is not in the square.' I cannot express the proposition 'This circle is not in the square' by placing the 'not' *at the front of* the proposition. That is connected with the fact that it's nonsense to give a circle a name.   116

91   'All circles are in the square' can mean either 'A certain number of circles are in the square' or: 'There is no circle outside it'. But the last proposition is again the negation of a generalization and not the generalization of a negation.   117

92   The part of speech is only determined by *all* the grammatical

rules which hold for a word, and seen from this point of view our language contains countless different parts of speech.   118

93   The subject-predicate form does not in itself amount to a logical form. The forms of the propositions: 'The plate is round', 'The man is tall', 'The patch is red', have nothing in common. – Concept and object: but that is subject and predicate.   118

94   Once you have started doing arithmetic, you don't bother about functions and objects. – The description of an object may not express what would be essential for the existence of the object.   119

95   If I give names to three visual circles of equal size – I always name (directly or indirectly) a *location*. What characterizes propositions of the form 'This is . . .' is only the fact that the reality outside the so-called system of signs somehow enters into the symbol.   119

96   What remains in this case, if form and colour alter? For position is part of the form. It is clear that the phrase 'bearer of a property' conveys a completely wrong – an impossible – picture.

    120

97   Roughly speaking, the equation of a circle is the sign for the concept 'circle'. So it is as if what corresponds with the objects falling under the concept were here the co-ordinates of the centres. In fact, the number pair that gives the co-ordinates of the centre is not just anything, but characterizes just what in the symbol constitutes the 'difference' of the circles.   121

98   The specification of the 'here' must not prejudge *what* is here. $F(x)$ must be an *external* description of x. – but if I now say 'Here is a circle' and on another occasion 'Here is a sphere', are the two 'here's' of the same kind?   122

equally it is not an examination of concepts which tells us that A is a tautology. Numbers must be of a kind with what we use to represent them.   129

108   Arithmetic is the grammar of numbers.   129

109   Every mathematical calculation is an application of itself and only as such does it have a sense. *That* is why it isn't necessary to speak about the general form of logical operation here. – Arithmetic is a more general kind of geometry.   130

110   It's as if we're surprised that the numerals cut adrift from their definitions function so unerringly; which is connected with the internal consistency of geometry. The general form of the application of arithmetic seems to be represented by the fact that *nothing* is said about it.   131

111   Arithmetical constructions are autonomous, like geometrical ones, and hence they guarantee their own applicability.   132

112   If 3 strokes on paper are the sign for the number 3, then you can say the number 3 is to be applied in the way in which 3 strokes can be applied. (Cf. §107)   133

113   A statement of number about the extension of a concept is a proposition, but a statement of number about the range of a variable is not, since it can be derived from the variable itself.

133

114   Do I know there are 6 permutations of 3 elements in the same way in which I know there are 6 people in this room? No. Therefore the first proposition is of a different *kind* from the second.   134

XI

115   A statement of number doesn't always contain something general or indefinite. For instance, 'I see 3 equal circles equidistant from one another'. Something indefinite would be, say: I know that three things have the property φ, but I don't know *which*.

Here it would be nonsense to say I don't know *which* circles they are.   136

116   There is no such concept as 'pure colour'. Similarly with permutations. If we say that $A\ B$ admits of two permutations, it sounds as though we had made a general assertion. But 'Two permutations are possible' cannot say any less – i.e. something more general – than the schema $A\ B$, $B\ A$. They are not the extension of a concept: they are the concept.   137

117   There is a mathematical question: 'How many permutations of 4 elements are there?' which is the same kind as 'What is 25×18?' For in both cases there is a general method of solution.

139

118   In Russell's theory only an *actual* correlation can show the "similarity" of two classes. Not the *possibility* of correlation, for this consists precisely in the numerical equality.   140

119   What sort of an *impossibility* is the impossibility of a 1-1 correlation between 3 circles and 2 crosses? – It is nonsense to say of an extension that it has such and such a number, since the number is an *internal* property of the extension.   140

120   Ramsey explains the sign ' $=$ ' like this: $x = x$ is taut.; $x = y$ is cont. What then is the relation of ' $\overset{\text{Def}}{=}$ ' to ' $=$ '? – You may compare mathematical equations only with significant propositions, not with tautologies.   141

121   An equation is a rule of syntax. You may construe sign-rules as propositions, but you don't *have to* construe them so. The 'heterological' paradox.   143

122   The generality of a mathematical assertion is different from the generality of the proposition proved. A mathematical proposition is an allusion to a proof. A generalization only makes sense if it – i.e. all values of its variables – is completely determined.

143

131   Generality in Euclidean geometry. Strange that what holds for one triangle should therefore hold for every other. But once more the construction of a proof is not an experiment; no, a description of the construction must suffice. – What is demonstrated can't be expressed by a proposition.   152

132   'The world will *eventually* come to an end' means nothing at all, for it's compatible with this statement that the world should still exist on any day you care to mention. 'How many 9s immediately succeed one another after 3.1415 in the development of π?' If this question is meant to refer to the extension, then it doesn't have the sense of the question which interests us. ('I grasp an infinite stretch in a different way from an endless one.')   153

133   The difficulty in applying the simple basic principles shakes our confidence in the principles themselves.   153

134   'I saw the ruler move from t_1 to t_2, *therefore* I must have seen it at t.' If in such a case I appear to infer a particular case from a general proposition, then the general proposition is never derived from experience, and the proposition isn't a real proposition.   154

135   'We only know the infinite by description.' Well then, there's just the description and nothing else.   155

136   Does a notation for the infinite presuppose infinite space or infinite time? Then the possibility of such a hypothesis must surely be prefigured somewhere. The problem of the smallest visible distinction.   155

137   If I cannot visibly bisect the strip any further, I can't even *try* to, and so can't see the failure of such an attempt. Continuity in our visual field consists in our not seeing discontinuity.   156

138 Experience as experience of the facts gives me the finite; the objects *contain* the infinite. Of course, not as something rivalling finite experience, but in intension. (Infinite possibility is *not* a quantity.) Space has no extension, only spatial objects are extended, but infinity is a property of space.   157

139 Infinite divisibility: we can conceive of *any* finite number of parts but not of an infinite number; but that is precisely what constitutes infinite divisibility. – That a patch in visual space can be divided into three parts means that a proposition describing a patch divided in this way makes sense. Whereas infinite divisibility doesn't mean there's a proposition describing a line divided into infinitely many parts. Therefore this possibility is not brought out by any reality of the signs, but by a possibility of a *different* kind in the signs themselves.   158

140 Time contains the possibility of all the future *now*. The space of human movement is infinite in the same way as time.   160

141 The rules for a number system – say, the decimal system – contain everything that is infinite about the numbers. – It all hangs on the syntax of reality and possibility. $m = 2n$ contains the *possibility of correlating any number* with another, *but doesn't correlate all numbers with others*.   161

142 The propositions 'Three things can lie in this direction' and 'Infinitely many things can lie in this direction' are only apparently formed in the same way, but are in fact different in structure: the 'infinitely many' of the second structure doesn't play the same role as the 'three' of the first.   162

143 Empty infinite time is only the possibility of facts which alone are the realities. – If there is an infinite reality, then there is also contingency in the infinite. And so, for instance, also an

infinite decimal that isn't given by a law. – Infinity lies in the nature of time, it isn't the extension it happens to have.   163

144 The infinite number series is only the infinite possibility of finite series of numbers. The signs themselves only contain the possibility and not the reality of their repetition. Mathematics can't even try to speak about their possibility. If it tries to *express* their possibility, i.e. when it confuses this with their reality, we ought to cut it down to size.   164

145 An infinite decimal not given by a rule. 'The number that is the result when a man endlessly throws a die', appears to be nonsense. – An infinite row of trees. If there is a law governing the way the trees' heights vary, then the series is defined and can be imagined by means of this law. If I now assume there could be a random series, then that is a series about which, by its very nature, nothing can be known apart from the fact that I can't know it.   165

146 The multiplicative axiom. In the case of a finite class of classes we can in fact make a selection. But in the case of infinitely many sub-classes I can only know the law for making a selection. Here the infinity is only in the rule.   167

147 What makes us think that perhaps there are infinitely many things is only our confusing the things of physics with the elements of knowledge. 'The patch lies somewhere between *b* and *c*': the infinite possibility of positions isn't expressed in the analysis of this. – The illusion of an infinite hypothesis in which the parcels of matter are confused with the simple objects. What we can imagine multiplied to infinity are the combinations of the things in accordance with their infinite possibilities, never the things themselves.   168

148 While we've as yet no idea how a certain proposition is to be proved, we still ask 'Can it be proved or not?' You cannot have a logical plan of search for a *sense* you don't know. Every proposition teaches us through its sense how we are to convince ourselves whether it is true or false. 170

149 A proof of relevance would be a proof which, while yet not proving the proposition, showed the form of a method for testing the proposition. 170

150 I can assert the general (algebraic) proposition just as much or as little as the equation $3 \times 3 = 9$ or $3 \times 3 = 11$. The general method of solution is in itself a clarification of the nature of the equation. Even in a particular case I see only the rule. 'The equation yields a' means: if I transform the equation in accordance with certain rules I get a. But these rules must be given to me before the word 'yields' has a meaning and before the question has a sense. 172

151 We may only put a question in mathematics where the answer runs: 'I must work it out'. The question 'How many solutions are there to this equation?' is the holding in readiness of the general method for solving it. And that, in general, is what a question is in mathematics: the holding in readiness of a general method. 175

152 I can't ask whether an angle can be trisected until I can see the system 'Ruler and Compasses' embedded in a larger one, where this question has a sense. – The system of rules determining a calculus thereby determines the 'meaning' of its signs too. If I change the rules, then I change the form, the meaning. – In mathematics, we cannot talk of systems in general, but only within systems. 177

153 A mathematical proof is an analysis of a mathematical

proposition. It isn't enough to say that p is provable, we have to say: provable according to a particular system. Understanding p means understanding its system.   179

154   I can ask 'What is the solution of this equation?', but not 'Has it a solution?' – It's impossible for us to discover rules of a new type that hold for a form with which we are familiar. – The proposition: 'It's possible – though not necessary – that p should hold for all numbers' is nonsense. For 'necessary' and 'all' belong together in mathematics.   181

155   Finding a new system (Sheffer's discovery, for instance). You can't say: I already had all these results, now all I've done is find a better way that leads to all of them. The new way amounts to a new system.   182

156   Unravelling knots in mathematics. We may only speak of a genuine attempt at a solution *to the extent* that the structure of the knot is clearly seen.   184

157   You can't write mathematics, you can only do it. – Suppose I hit upon the right way of constructing a regular pentagon by accident. If I don't understand this construction, as far as I'm concerned it doesn't even begin to be the construction of a pentagon. The way I have arrived at it vanishes in what I understand.
                                    186

158   Where a connection is now known to exist which was previously unknown, there wasn't a gap before, something incomplete which has now been filled in. – Induction: if I know the law of a spiral, that's in many respects analogous with the case in which I know all the whorls. Yet not completely analogous – and that's all we can say.   187

159   But doesn't it still count as a question, whether there is a finite number of primes or not? Once I can write down the general form of primes, e.g. 'dividing . . . by smaller numbers leaves a

remainder' – there is no longer a question of 'how many' primes there are. But since it was possible for us to have the phrase 'prime number' before we had the strict expression, it was also possible for people to have wrongly formed the question. Only in our verbal language are there in mathematics 'as yet unsolved problems'. 188

160 A consistency proof can't be essential for the application of the axioms. For these are propositions of syntax. 189

161 A polar expedition and a mathematical one. How can there be conjectures in mathematics? Can I make a hypothesis about the distribution of primes? What kind of verification do I then count as valid? I can't conjecture the proof. And if I've got the proof it doesn't prove what was conjectured. 189

162 Sheffer's discovery. The systems are certainly not in *one* space, so that I could say: there are systems with 3 and 2 logical constants, and now I'm trying to reduce the number of constants *in the same way*. – A mathematical proposition is only the immediately visible surface of a whole body of proof and this surface is the boundary facing us. 191

XIV

163 A proof for the associative law? As a basic rule of the system it cannot be proved. The usual mistake lies in confusing the extension of its application with what the proof genuinely contains. – Can one prove that by addition of forms ((1 + 1) + 1) etc. numbers of this form would always result? The proof lies in the rule, i.e. in the definition and in nothing else. 193

164 A recursive proof is only a general guide to arbitrary special proofs: the general form of continuing along this series. Its

generality is not the one we desire but consists in the fact that we can repeat the proof. What we gather from the proof we cannot represent in a proposition at all. 196

165 The correct expression for the associative law is not a proposition, but precisely its 'proof', which admittedly doesn't state the law. I know the specific equation is correct just as well as if I had given a complete derivation of it. That means it really is proved. The *one* whorl, in conjunction with the numerical forms of the given equation, is enough. 198

166 One says an induction is a sign that such and such holds for all numbers. But an induction isn't a sign for anything but itself. – Compare the generality of genuine propositions with generality in arithmetic. It is differently verified and so is of a different kind. 200

167 An induction doesn't prove an algebraic equation, but it justifies the setting up of algebraic equations from the standpoint of their application to arithmetic. That is, it is only through the induction that they gain their sense, not their truth. An induction is related to an algebraic proposition not as proof is to what is proved, but as what is designated to a sign. 201

168 If we ask 'Does $a + (b + c) = (a + b) + c$?', what could we be after? – An algebraic proposition doesn't express a generality; this is shown, rather, in the formal relation to the substitution, which proves to be a term of the inductive series. 202

169 One can prove any arithmetical equation of the form $a \times b = c$ or prove its opposite. A proof of this provability would be the exhibition of an induction from which it could be seen what sort of propositions the ladder leads to. 204

170 The theory of aggregates says that you can't grasp the actual infinite by means of arithmetical symbolism at all, it can therefore only be described and not represented. So one could talk about a logical structure without reproducing it in the proposition itself. A method of wrapping a concept up in such a way that its form disappears. 206

171 Any proof of the continuity of a function must relate to a number system. The numerical scale, which comes to light when calculating a function, should not be allowed to disappear in the general treatment. – Can the continuum be described? A form cannot be described: it can only be presented. 207

172 'The highest point of a curve' doesn't mean 'the highest point among all the points of the curve'. In the same way, the maximum of a function isn't the largest value among all its values. No, the highest point is something I *construct*, i.e. derive from a law. 208

173 The expression '(n) . . .' has a sense if nothing more than the unlimited possibility of going on is presupposed. – Brouwer –. The explanation of the Dedekind cut as if it were clear what was meant by: either R has a last member and L a first, or, etc. In truth none of these cases can be conceived. 209

174 Set theory builds on a fictitious symbolism, therefore on nonsense. As if there were something in Logic that could be known, but not by us. If someone says (as Brouwer does) that for $(x) \cdot f_1 x = f_2 x$ there is, as well as yes and no, also the case of undecidability, this implies that '(x) . . .' is meant extensionally and that we may talk of all x happening to have a property. 211

175 If one regards the expression 'the root of the equation $\varphi x = 0$' as a Russellian description, then a proposition about the

root of the equation $x + 2 = 6$ must have a different sense from one saying the same about 4. 213

176 How can a purely internal generality be refuted by the occurrence of a single case (and so by something extensional)? But the particular case refutes the general proposition from within – it attacks the internal proof. – The difference between the two equations $x^2 = x \cdot x$ and $x^2 = 2x$ *isn't* one consisting in the extensions of their validity. 214

XVI

177 That a point in the plane is represented by a number-pair, and in three-dimensional space by a number-triple, is enough to show that the object represented isn't the point at all but the point-network. 216

178 Geometry as the syntax of the propositions dealing with objects in space. Whatever is arranged in visual space stands in this *sort* of order *a priori*, i.e. in virtue of its logical nature, and geometry here is simply grammar. What the physicist sets into relation with one another in the geometry of physical space are instrument readings, which do not differ in their *internal* nature whether we live in a linear space or a spherical one. 216

179 I can approach any point of an interval indefinitely by always carrying out the bisection prescribed by tossing a coin. Can I divide the rationals into two classes in a similar way, by putting either o or 1 in an infinite binary expansion according to the way the coin falls (heads or tails)? No law of succession is described by the instruction to toss a coin; and infinite indefiniteness does not define a number. 218

180 Is it possible within the law to abstract from the law and see the extension presented as what is essential? – If I cut at a place

34

where there is no rational number, then there must be approximations to this cut. But closer to what? For the time being I have nothing in the domain of number which I can approach. – All the points of a line can actually be represented by arithmetical rules. In the case of approximation by repeated bisection we approach *every* point via *rational* numbers. 221

XVII

181 What criterion is there for the irrational numbers being *complete*? Every irrational number runs through a series of rational approximations, and never leaves this series behind. If I have the totality of all irrational numbers except π, and now insert π, I cannot cite a point at which π is really needed; at every point it has a companion agreeing with it. This shows clearly that an irrational number isn't the extension of an infinite decimal fraction, it's a law. If π were an extension, we would never feel the lack of it – it would be impossible for us to detect a gap. 223

182 $'\sqrt{2}$: a rule with an exception. – There must first be the rules for the digits, and then – e.g. – a root is expressed in them. But this expression in a sequence of digits only has significance through being the expression for a real number. If someone subsequently alters it, he has only succeeded in distorting the expression, but not in obtaining a new number. 224

183 If $'\sqrt{2}$ is anything at all, then it is the same as $\sqrt{2}$, only another expression for it; the expression in another system. It doesn't measure until it is in a system. You would no more say of $'\sqrt{2}$ that it is a limit towards which the sums of a series are tending than you would of the instruction to throw dice. 225

184 That we can apply the law holds also for the law to throw digits like dice. And what distinguishes π' from this can only consist in our knowing that there must be a law governing the occurrences

of the digit 7 in π, even if we don't yet know what the law is. π′
alludes to a law which is as yet unknown.   227

185   Only a law approaches a value.   228

186   The letter π stands for a law which has its position in arithmetical space. Whereas π′ doesn't use the idioms of arithmetic and
so doesn't assign the law a place in this space. For substituting 3 for
7 surely adds absolutely nothing to the law and in this system isn't
an arithmetical operation at all.   228

187   To determine a real number a rule must be completely
intelligible *in itself*. That is to say, it must not be essentially undecided whether a part of it could be dispensed with. If the extensions of two laws coincide as far as we've gone, and I cannot
compare the laws as such, then the numbers defined cannot be
compared.   230

188   The expansion of π is simultaneously an expression of the
nature of π *and of the nature of the decimal system*. Arithmetical operations only use the decimal system as a means to an end. They can
be translated into the language of any other number system, and
do not have any of them as their *subject matter*. – A general rule of
operation gets its generality from the generality of the change it
effects in the numbers. π′ makes the decimal system into its subject
matter, and for that reason it is no longer sufficient that we can use
the rule to form the extension.   231

189   A law where *p* runs through the series of whole numbers
except for those for which Fermat's last theorem doesn't hold.
Would this law define a real number? The number *F* wants to use
the spiral . . . and choose sections of this spiral according to a
principle. But this principle doesn't belong to the spiral. There is
admittedly a law there, but it doesn't refer directly to the number.
The number is a sort of lawless by-product of the law.   232

36

190 In this context we keep coming up against something that could be called an 'arithmetical experiment'. Thus the primes come out from the method for looking for them, as the results of an experiment. I can certainly see a law in the rule, but not in the numbers that result. 235

191 A number must measure in and of itself. If it doesn't do that but leaves it to the rationals, we have no need of it. – The true expansion is the one which evokes from the law a comparison with a rational number. 235

192 A real number can be compared with the fiction of an infinite spiral, whereas structures like F, P or π' only with finite sections of a spiral. 237

193 To compare rational numbers with $\sqrt{2}$, I have to square them. – They then assume the form $\sqrt{a}$, where $\sqrt{a}$ is now an arithmetical operation. Written out in this system, they can be compared with $\sqrt{2}$, and it is for me as if the spiral of the irrational number had shrunk to a point. 237

194 Is an arithmetical experiment still possible when a recursive definition has been set up? No, because with the recursion each stage becomes arithmetically comprehensible. 238

195 Is it possible to prove a greater than b, without being able to prove at which place the difference will come to light? 1.4 – Is that the square root of 2? No, it's the root of 1.96. That is, I can immediately write it down as an approximation to $\sqrt{2}$. 238

196 If the real number is a rational number a, a comparison of its law with a must show this. That means the law must be so formed as to 'click into' the rational number when it comes to the appro-

priate place. It wouldn't do, e.g., if we couldn't be sure whether $\sqrt{25}$ really breaks off at 5. 240

197 Can I call a spiral a number if it is one which, for all I know, comes to a stop at a rational point? There is a lack of a method for comparing with the rationals. Expanding indefinitely isn't a method, even when it leads to a result of the comparison. 241

198 If the question how F compares with a rational number has no sense, since all expansion still hasn't given us an answer, then this question also had no sense before we tried to settle the matter at random by means of an extension. 242

199 It isn't only necessary to be able to say whether a given rational number is the real number: we must also be able to say how close it can possibly come to it. An order of magnitude for the distance apart. Decimal expansion doesn't give me this, since I cannot know e.g. how many 9s will follow a place that has been reached in the expansion. – 'e isn't this number' means nothing; we have to say 'It is at least this interval away from it'. 243

Appendix: From F. Waismann's shorthand notes of a conversation on 30 December 1930 245

XIX

200 It appears to me that negation in arithmetic is interesting only in conjunction with a certain generality. – Indivisibility and inequality. – I don't write '$\sim (5 \times 5 = 30)$', I write $5 \times 5 \neq 30$, since I'm not negating anything but want to establish a relation between 5×5 and 30 (and hence something positive). Similarly, when I exclude divisibility, this is equivalent to establishing indivisibility. 247

201   There is something recalcitrant to the application of the law of the excluded middle in mathematics – Looking for a law for the distribution of primes. We want to replace the negative criterion for a prime number by a positive one – but this negation isn't what it is in logic, but an indefiniteness. – The negation of an equation is as like and as unlike the denial of a proposition as the affirmation of an equation is as like or unlike the affirmation of a proposition.   248

202   Where negation essentially – on logical grounds – corresponds to a disjunction or to the exclusion of one part of a logical series in favour of another – then here it must be one and the same as those logical forms and therefore only apparently a negation.
                                                                              249

203   Yet what is expressed by inequalities is *essentially* different from what is expressed by equations. And so you can't immediately compare a law yielding places of a decimal expansion which works with inequalities, with one that works with equations. Here we have completely different methods and consequently different kinds of arithmetical structure.   250

204   Can you use the prime numbers to define an irrational number ? As far as you can foresee the primes, and no further.   251

XX

205   Can we say a patch is simpler than a larger one ? – It seems as if it is impossible to see a uniformly coloured patch as composite. – The larger *geometrical* structure isn't composed of smaller *geometrical* structures. The 'pure geometrical figures' are of course only logical possibilities.   252

206   Whether it makes sense to say 'This part of a red patch is red' depends on whether there is absolute position. It's possible to

establish the identity of a position in the visual field, since we would otherwise be unable to distinguish whether a patch always stays in the same place. In visual space there is absolute position, absolute direction, and hence absolute motion. If this were not so, there would be *no sense* in speaking in this context of the same or different places. This shows the structure of our visual field: for the criterion for its structure is what propositions make sense for it.

253

207   Can I say: 'The top half of my visual field is red'? – There isn't a relation of 'being situated' which would hold between a colour and a position.   257

208   It seems to me that the concept of distance is given immediately in the structure of visual space. Measuring in visual space. Equal in length, unequal in parts. Can I be sure that what I count is really the number I see?   257

209   But if I can't say there is a definite number of parts in *a* and *b*, how in that case am I to describe the visual image? – 'Blurred' and 'unclear' are relative expressions. – If we were really to *see* 24 and 25 parts in *a* and *b*, we couldn't then see *a* and *b* as equal. The word 'equal' has a meaning even for visual space which stamps this as a contradiction.   260

210   The question is, how to explain certain contradictions that arise when we apply the methods of inference used in Euclidean space to visual space. This happens because we can only see the construction piecemeal and not as a whole: because there's no visual construction that could be composed of these individual visual pieces.   261

211   The moment we try to apply exact concepts of measurement to immediate experience, we come up against a peculiar vagueness in this experience. – The words 'rough', 'approximate', etc. have

only a relative sense, but they are still needed and they characterize the nature of our experience. – Problem of the heap of sand. – What corresponds in Euclidean geometry to the visual circle isn't a circle, but a class of figures. – Here it seems as though an exact *demarcation* of the inexactitude is impossible. We border off a swamp with a wall, and the wall is not *the* boundary of the swamp.

263

212 The correlation between visual space and Euclidean space. *If* a circle is at all the sort of thing we see, then we must be able to see *it* and not merely something like it. If I cannot see an exact circle then in this sense neither can I see approximations to one.

265

213 We need new concepts and we continually resort to those of the language of physical objects. For instance 'precision'. If it is right to say 'I do not see a sharp line', then a sharp line *is* conceivable. If it makes sense to say 'I never see an exact circle', then this implies: an exact circle is conceivable in visual space. – The word 'equal' used with quite different meanings. – Description of colour patches close to the boundary of the visual field. Clear that the lack of clarity is an internal property of visual space.   266

214 What distinctions are there in visual space? The fact that you see a physical hundred-sided polygon as a circle implies nothing as to the *possibility* of seeing a hundred-sided polygon. Is there a *sense* in speaking of a visual hundred-sided polygon?   268

215 Couldn't I say, 'Perhaps I see a perfect circle, but can never know it'? Only if it is established in what cases one calls one measurement more precise than another. It means nothing to say the circle is only an ideal to which reality can only approximate. But it may also be that we call an infinite possibility itself a circle. As with an irrational number. – Now, is the imprecision of measurement the same concept as the imprecision of visual images? Certainly not. – 'Seems' and 'appears' ambiguous: in one

case it is the result of measurement, in another a further appearance.   269

216 'Sense datum' contains the idea: if we talk about 'the
appearance of a tree' we are either taking for a tree something
which is one, or something which is not. But this connection isn't
there.   270

217 *Can* you try to give 'the right model for visual space'? You
cannot translate the blurredness of phenomena into an imprecision
in the drawing. That visual space isn't Euclidean is already shown
by the occurrence of two different kinds of lines and points.   271

XXI

218 Simple colours – simple as psychological phenomena. I
need a purely phenomenological colour theory in which mention
is only made of what is actually perceptible and no hypothetical
objects – waves, rods, cones and all that – occur. Can I find a
metric for colours? Is there a sense in saying, e.g., that with respect
to the amount of red in it, one colour is *halfway* between two other
colours?   273

219 Orange is a mixture of red and yellow in a sense in which
yellow isn't a mixture of red and green although yellow comes
between red and green in the colour circle. – If I imagine mixing a
blue-green with a yellow-green I see straightaway that it can't
happen, that a component part would first have to be 'killed'.   273

220 I must know what in general is meant by the expression
'mixture of colours *A* and *B*'. If someone says to me that the colour
of a patch lies between violet and red, I understand this and can
imagine a redder violet than the one given. But: 'The colour lies

between this violet and an orange'? The way in which the mixed colour lies between the others is no different here from the way red comes between blue and yellow. – 'Red and yellow make orange' doesn't speak of a quantity of components. It means nothing to say this orange and this violet contain the same amount of red. – False comparison between the colour series and a system of two weights on a balance. 274

221   The position here is just as it is with the geometry of visual space as compared with Euclidean geometry. There are here quantities of a different sort from that represented by our rational numbers. – If the expression 'lie between' on one occasion designates a mixture of two simple colours, and on another a simple component common to two mixed colours, the multiplicity of its application is different in the two cases. – You can also arrange all the shades along a straight line. But then you have to introduce rules to exclude certain transitions, and in the end the representation on the lines has to be given the same kind of topological structure as the octahedron has. Completely analogous to the relation of ordinary language to a 'logically purified' mode of expression. 276

222   We can't say red has an orange tinge in the same sense as orange has a reddish tinge. 'x is composed of y and z' and 'x is the common component of y and z' are not interchangeable here. 278

223   When we see dots of one colour intermingled with dots of another we seem to have a different sort of colour transition from that on the colour-circle. Not that we establish experimentally that certain colours arise in this way from others. For whether or not such a transition is *possible* (or conceivable) is an internal property of the colours. 279

224   The danger of seeing things as simpler than they really are. – Understanding a Gregorian mode means hearing something new; analogous with suddenly seeing 10 strokes, which I had hitherto only been able to see as twice five strokes, as a characteristic whole. 281

225 A proposition, an hypothesis, is coupled with reality – with varying degrees of freedom. All that matters is that the signs in the end still refer to immediate experience and not to an intermediary (a thing in itself). A proposition construed in such a way that it can be uncheckably true or false is completely detached from reality and no longer functions as a proposition. 282

226 An hypothesis is a symbol for which certain rules of representation hold. The choice of representation is a process based on so-called induction (not mathematical induction). 283

227 We only give up an hypothesis for an even higher gain. The question, how simple a representation is yielded by assuming a particular hypothesis, is connected with the question of probability. 284

228 What is essential to an hypothesis is that it arouses an expectation, i.e., its confirmation is never completed. It has a different formal relation to reality from that of verification. – Belief in the uniformity of events. An hypothesis is a law for forming propositions. 285

229 The probability of an hypothesis has its measure in how much evidence is needed to make it profitable to throw it out. If I say: I assume the sun will rise again tomorrow, because the opposite is so unlikely, I here mean by 'likely' and 'unlikely' something completely different from 'It's equally likely that I'll throw heads or tails'. – The expectation must make sense *now*; i.e. I must be able to compare it with how things stand at present. 286

230 Describing phenomena by means of the hypothesis of a

world of material things compared with a phenomenological description. – Thus the theory of Relativity doesn't represent the logical multiplicity of the phenomena themselves, but that of the regularities observed. This multiplicity corresponds not to *one* verification, but to a *law* by verifications. 286

231 Hypothesis and postulate. No conceivable experience can refute a postulate, even though it may be extremely inconvenient to hang on to it. Corresponding to the greater or slighter convenience, there is a greater or slighter probability of the postulate. It is senseless to talk of a measure for this probability. 288

232 If I say 'That will probably occur', this proposition is neither verified by the occurrence nor falsified by its non-occurrence. If we argue about whether it is probable or not, we shall always adduce arguments from the past only. – It's always as if the same state of affairs could be corroborated by experience, whose existence was evident *a priori*. But that's nonsense. If the experience agrees with the computation, that means my computation is justified by the experience – not its *a priori* element, but its bases, which are *a posteriori*: certain natural laws. In the case of throwing a die the natural law takes the form that it is equally likely for any of the six sides to be the side uppermost. It's this law that we test. 289

233 Certain possible events must contradict the law if it is to be one at all; and should these occur, they must be explained by a different law. – The prediction that there will be an equal distribution contains an assumption about those natural laws that I don't know precisely. 290

234 A man throwing dice every day for a week throws nothing but ones – and not because of any defect in the die. Has he grounds

for thinking that there's a natural law at work here which makes him throw nothing but ones? – When an insurance company is guided by probability, it isn't guided by the probability calculus but by a frequency actually observed.   291

235 'Straight line with deviations' is only one form of description. If I state 'That's the rule', that only has a sense as long as I have determined the maximum number of exceptions I'll allow before knocking down the rule.   292

236 It only makes sense to say of the stretch you actually see that it gives the general impression of a straight line, and not of an hypothetical one you assume. An experiment with dice can only give grounds for expecting things to go in the same way.   293

237 Any 'reasonable' expectation is an expectation that a rule we have observed up to now will continue to hold. But the rule must have been observed and can't, for its part too, be merely expected. – Probability is concerned with the form and a standard of expectation.   294

238 A ray of light strikes two different surfaces. The centre of each stretch seems to divide it into equally probable possibilities. This yields apparently incompatible probabilities. But the assumption of the probability of a certain event is verified by a frequency experiment; and, if confirmed, shows itself to be an hypothesis belonging to *physics*. The geometrical construction merely shows that the equal lengths of the sections was *no* ground for assuming equal likelihood. I can arbitrarily lay down a law, e.g. that if the lengths of the parts are equal, they are equally likely; but any other law is just as permissible. Similarly with further examples. It is from experience that we determine these possibilities as equally likely. But logic gives this stipulation no precedence.   295

First Appendix

Second Appendix (from *F. Waismann's shorthand notes on Wittgenstein's talks and conversation between December 1929 and September 1931*)

PHILOSOPHICAL REMARKS

1 A proposition is completely logically analysed if its grammar is made completely clear: no matter what idiom it may be written or expressed in.

I do not now have phenomenological language, or 'primary language' as I used to call it, in mind as my goal. I no longer hold it to be necessary. All that is possible and necessary is to separate what is essential from what is inessential in *our* language.

That is, if we so to speak describe the class of languages which serve their purpose, then in so doing we have shown what is essential to them and given an immediate representation of immediate experience.

Each time I say that, instead of such and such a representation, you could also use this other one, we take a further step towards the goal of grasping the essence of what is represented.

A recognition of what is essential and what inessential in our language if it is to represent, a recognition of which parts of our language are wheels turning idly, amounts to the construction of a phenomenological language.

Physics differs from phenomenology in that it is concerned to establish laws. Phenomenology only establishes the possibilities. Thus, phenomenology would be the grammar of the description of those facts on which physics builds its theories.

To explain is more than to describe; but every explanation contains a description.

An octahedron with the pure colours at the corner-points e.g. provides a *rough* representation of colour-space, and this is a grammatical representation, not a psychological one. On the other hand, to say that in such and such circumstances you can see a red after-image (say) is a matter of psychology. (*This* may, or may not, be the case – the other is *a priori*; we can establish the one by experiment but not the other.)

Using the octahedron as a representation gives us a *bird's-eye view* of the grammatical rules [1].

The chief trouble with our grammar is that we don't have a *bird's-eye view* of it [2].

What Mach calls a thought experiment is of course not an experiment at all [3]. At bottom it is a grammatical investigation.

2   Why is philosophy so complicated? It ought, after all, to be *completely* simple. – Philosophy unties the knots in our thinking, which we have tangled up in an absurd way; but to do that, it must make movements which are just as complicated as the knots. Although the *result* of philosophy is simple, its methods for arriving there cannot be so.
The complexity of philosophy is not in its matter, but in our tangled understanding.

3   How strange if logic were concerned with an 'ideal' language and not with *ours*. For what would this ideal language express? Presumably, what we now express in our ordinary language; in that case, this is the language logic must investigate. Or something else: but in that case how would I have any idea what that would be? – Logical analysis is the analysis of something we have, not of something we don't have. Therefore it is the analysis of propositions *as they stand*. (It would be odd if the human race had been speaking all this time without ever putting together a genuine proposition.)

When a child learns 'Blue is a colour, red is a colour, green, yellow – all are colours', it learns nothing new about the colours,

---

1] German: Die Oktaeder-Darstellung ist eine *übersichtliche* Darstellung der grammatischen Regeln.
2] German: Unserer Grammatik fehlt es vor allem an *Übersichtlichkeit*.
3] E. Mach, *Erkenntnis und Irrtum*, 2nd ed., Leipzig 1906. p. 186, 191.

but the meaning of a variable in such propositions as: 'There are beautiful colours in that picture' etc. The first proposition tells him the values of a variable.

The words 'Colour', 'Sound', 'Number' etc. could appear in the chapter headings of our grammar. They need not occur within the chapters but that is where their structure is given.

4   Isn't the theory of harmony at least in part phenomenology and therefore grammar?
The theory of harmony isn't a matter of taste.

If I could describe the point of grammatical conventions by saying they are made necessary by certain properties of the colours (say), then that would make the conventions superfluous, since in that case I would be able to say precisely that which the conventions exclude my saying. Conversely, if the conventions were necessary, i.e. if certain combinations of words had to be excluded as nonsensical, then for that very reason I cannot cite a property of colours that makes the conventions necessary, since it would then be conceivable that the colours should not have this property, and I could only express that by violating the conventions.

It cannot be proved that it is nonsense to say of a colour that it is a semitone higher than another. I can only say 'If anyone uses words with the meanings that I do, then he can connect no sense with this combination. If it makes sense to him, he must understand something different by these words from what I do.'

5   The arbitrariness of linguistic expressions: might we say: A child must of course learn to speak a particular language, but doesn't have to learn to think, i.e. it would think spontaneously, even without learning any language?
But in my view, if it thinks, then it forms for itself pictures and in a certain sense these are arbitrary, that is to say, in so far as other

pictures could have played the same role. On the other hand, language has certainly also come about naturally, i.e. there must presumably have been a first man who for the first time expressed a definite thought in spoken words. And besides, the whole question is a matter of indifference because a child learning a language only learns it by beginning to think in it. Suddenly beginning; I mean: there is no preliminary stage in which a child already uses a language, so to speak uses it for communication, but does not yet think in it.

Of course, the thought processes of an ordinary man consist of a medley of symbols, of which the strictly linguistic perhaps form only a small part.

6   If I explain the meaning of a word 'A' to someone by pointing to something and saying 'This is A', then this expression may be meant in two different ways. Either it is itself a proposition already, in which case it can only be understood once the meaning of 'A' is known, i.e. I must now leave it to chance whether he takes it as I meant it or not. Or the sentence is a definition. Suppose I have said to someone 'A is ill', but he doesn't know who I mean by 'A', and I now point at a man, saying 'This is A'. Here the expression is a definition, but this can only be understood if he has already gathered what kind of object it is through his understanding of the grammar of the proposition 'A is ill'. But this means that any kind of explanation of a language presupposes a language already. And in a certain sense, the use of language is something that cannot be taught, i.e. I cannot use language to teach it in the way in which language could be used to teach someone to play the piano. – And that of course is just another way of saying: I cannot use language to get outside language.

7   Grammar is a 'theory of logical types'.

I do not call a rule of representation a convention if it can be justified in propositions: propositions describing what is represented and showing that the representation is adequate. Grammatical conventions cannot be justified by describing what is represented. Any such description already presupposes the grammatical rules. That is to say, if anything is to count as nonsense in the grammar which is to be justified, then it cannot at the same time pass for sense in the grammar of the propositions that justify it (etc.).

You cannot use language to go beyond the possibility of evidence.

The possibility of explaining these things always depends on someone else using language in the same way as I do. If he states that a certain string of words makes sense to him, and it makes none to me, I can only suppose that in this context he is using words with a different meaning from the one I give them, or else is speaking without thinking.

8   Can anyone believe it makes sense to say 'That's not a noise, it's a colour'?

On the other hand, you can of course say 'It's not the noise but the colour that makes me nervous', and here it might look as if a variable assumed a colour and a noise as values. ('Sounds and colours can be used as vehicles of communication.') It is clear that this proposition is of the same kind as 'If you hear a shot or see me wave, run.' For this is the kind of co-ordination on the basis of which a heard or seen language functions.

9   Asked whether philosophers have hitherto spoken nonsense, you could reply: no, they have only failed to notice that they are using a word in quite different senses. In this sense, if we say it's nonsense to say that one thing is as identical as another, this needs qualification, since if anyone says this with conviction, then at that

moment he means something by the word 'identical' (perhaps 'large'), but isn't aware that he is using the word here with a different meaning from that in $2 + 2 = 4$.

II

10 If you think of propositions as instructions for making models, their pictorial nature becomes even clearer.

Since, for it to be possible for an expression to guide my hand, it *must* have the same multiplicity as the action desired.

And this must also explain the nature of negative propositions. Thus, for example, someone might show his understanding of the proposition 'The book is not red' by throwing away the red when preparing a model.

This and the like would also show in what way the negative proposition has the multiplicity of the proposition it denies and *not* of those propositions which could perhaps be true in its stead.

11 What does it mean to say 'Admittedly I can't see any red, but if you give me a paint-box, I can point it out to you'? How can you *know* that you will be able to point it out if . . .; and so, that you will be able to recognize it when you see it?

This might mean two different kinds of things: it might express the expectation that I shall recognize it if I am shown it, in the same sense that I expect a headache if I'm hit on the head; then it is, so to speak, an expectation that belongs to physics, with the same sort of grounds as any other expectation relating to the occurrence of a physical event. – Or else it has nothing to do with expecting a physical event, and for that reason neither would my proposition be falsified if such an event should fail to occur. Instead, it's as if the proposition is saying that I possess a paradigm that I could at any time compare the colour with. (And the 'could' here is logical possibility.)

Taking the first interpretation: if, on looking at a certain colour, I in fact do give a sign of recognition, how do I know it is the colour that I *meant*?

The propositions of our grammar are always of the same sort as propositions of physics and not of the same sort as the 'primary' propositions which treat of what is immediate.

12 The idea that you 'imagine' the meaning of a word when you hear or read it, is a naïve conception of the meaning of a word. And in fact such imagining gives rise to the same question as a word meaning something. For if, e.g., you imagine sky-blue and are to use this image as a basis for recognizing or looking for the colour, we are still forced to say that the image of the colour isn't the same as the colour that is really seen; and in that case, how can one compare these two?

Yet the naïve theory of *forming-an-image* can't be utterly wrong.

If we say 'A word only has meaning in the context of a proposition', then that means that it's only in a proposition that it functions as a word, and this is no more something that can be said than that an armchair only serves its purpose when it is in space. Or perhaps better: that a cogwheel only functions as such when engaged with other cogs.

13 Language must have the same multiplicity as a control panel that sets off the actions corresponding to its propositions.

Strangely enough, the problem of *understanding* language is connected with the problem of the Will.

Understanding a command before you obey it has an affinity with willing an action before you perform it.

Just as the handles in a control room are used to do a wide variety of things, so are the words of language that correspond to the handles. One is the handle of a crank and can be adjusted continuously; one belongs to a switch and is always either on or off; a third to a switch which permits three or more positions; a fourth is the handle of a pump and only works when it is being moved up and down, etc.; but all are handles, are worked by hand.

14 A word only has meaning in the context of a proposition: that is like saying only in use is a rod a lever. Only the application makes it into a lever.

Every instruction can be construed as a description, every description as an instruction.

15 What does it mean, to understand a proposition as *a* member of a system of propositions? (It's as if I were to say: the use of a word isn't over in an instant, any more than that of a lever).

Imagine a gearbox whose lever can take four positions. Now of course it can only take these positions in succession, and that takes time; and suppose it happened that it only ever occupied one of these positions, since the gearbox was then destroyed. Wasn't it still a gearbox with *four* positions? Weren't the four possible?

Anyone who saw it would have seen its complexity, and its complexity is only to be explained by the use for which it was intended, to which in fact it was not put. Similarly I would like to say in the case of language: What's the point of all these preparations; they only have any meaning if they find a use.

You might say: The sense of a proposition is its purpose. (Or, of a word 'Its meaning is its purpose'.)

But the natural history of the use of a word can't be any concern of logic.

16 If I expect an event and that which fulfils my expectation occurs, does it then make sense to ask whether that really is the

event I expected? i.e. how would a proposition that asserted this be verified? It is clear that the *only* source of knowledge I have here is a comparison of the *expression* of my expectation with the event that has occurred.

How do I know that the colour of this paper, which I call 'white', is the same as the one I saw here yesterday? By recognizing it again; and recognizing it again is my only source of knowledge here. In that case, 'That it is the same' *means* that I recognize it again.

Then of course you also can't ask whether it really is the same and whether I might not perhaps be mistaken; (whether it *is* the same and doesn't just *seem* to be.)

Of course, it would also be possible to say that the colour is the same because chemical investigations do not disclose any change. So that if it doesn't look the same to me then I am mistaken. But even then there must still be something that is immediately recognized.

And the 'colour' I can recognize immediately and the one I establish by chemical investigation are two different things.

One source only yields *one* thing.

17   Is it an objection to my view that we often speak half or even entirely automatically? If someone asks me 'Is the curtain in this room green?' and I look and say, 'No, red', I certainly don't have to hallucinate green and compare it with the curtain. No, just looking at the curtain can automatically produce the answer, and yet this answer is of interest to Logic, whereas a whistle, say, that I make automatically on seeing red is not. Isn't the point that Logic is only interested in this answer as a part of a language system? The system our books are written in. Could we say Logic considers language *in extenso*? And so, in the same way as grammar.

Could you say that Logic has nothing to do with that utterance if it was merely automatic? For should Logic bother itself with the question whether the proposition was also really thoroughly *thought?* And what would the criterion for that be? Surely not the lively play of images accompanying its expression! It is plain that here we have got into a region that is absolutely no concern of ours and from which we should retire with the utmost alacrity.

18   Here we come to the apparently trivial question, what does Logic understand by a word – is it an ink-mark, a sequence of sounds, is it necessary that someone should associate a sense with it, or should have associated one, etc., etc.? – And here, the crudest conception must obviously be the only correct one.

And so I will again talk about 'books'; here we have words; if a mark should happen to occur that looks like a word, I say: that's not a word, it only looks like one, it's obviously unintentional. This can only be dealt with from the standpoint of normal common sense. (It's extraordinary that that in itself constitutes a change in perspective.)

I do not believe that Logic can talk about sentences [1] in any other than the normal sense in which we say, 'There's a sentence written here' or 'No, that only looks like a sentence, but isn't', etc., etc.

The question 'What is a word?' is completely analogous with the question 'What is a chessman?'

19   Isn't it agreement and disagreement that is primary, just as recognition is what is primary and identity what is secondary? If we see a proposition verified, what higher court is there to which we could yet appeal in order to tell whether it *really* is true?

The agreement of a proposition with reality only resembles the agreement of a picture with what it depicts to the same extent as the agreement of a memory image with the present object.

1] The German word here is 'Satz', which spans both 'proposition' and 'sentence': in English the translation 'sentence' would frequently become intolerably strained and we have therefore normally rendered 'Satz' by 'proposition': in this context 'sentence' is clearly required and yet this passage should link with those other passages in the book where we have adopted 'proposition' as our translation. [trans.]

But we can look at recognition, like memory, in two different ways: as a source of the concepts of the past and of identity, or as a way of checking what happened in the past, and on identity.

If I can see two patches of colour alongside one another and say that they have the same colour, and if I say that this patch has the same colour as one I saw earlier, the identity assertion means something different in the two cases, since it is differently verified.

To know that it *was* the same colour is something different from knowing that it *is* the same colour.

III

20 You can draw a plan from a description. You can translate a description into a plan.

The rules of translation here are not essentially different from the rules for translating from one verbal language into another.

A wrong conception of the way language functions destroys, of course, the *whole* of logic and everything that goes with it, and doesn't just create some merely local disturbance.

If you exclude the element of intention from language, its whole function then collapses.

21 What is essential to intention is the picture: the picture of what is intended.

It may look as if, in introducing intention, we were introducing an uncheckable, a so-to-speak metaphysical element into our discussion. But the essential difference between the picture conception and the conception of Russell, Ogden and Richards, is that it regards recognition as seeing an internal relation, whereas in their view this is an external relation.

That is to say, for me, there are only two things involved in the fact that a thought is true, i.e. the thought and the fact; whereas for Russell, there are three, i.e. thought, fact and a third event which, if it occurs, is just recognition. This third event, a sort of satisfaction of hunger (the other two being hunger and eating a particular kind of food), could, for example, be a feeling of pleasure. It's a matter of complete indifference here how we describe this third event; that is irrelevant to the essence of the theory.

The causal connection between speech and action is an external relation, whereas we need an internal one.

22   I believe Russell's theory amounts to the following: if I give someone an order and I am happy with what he then does, then he has carried out my order.

(If I wanted to eat an apple, and someone punched me in the stomach, taking away my appetite, then it was this punch that I originally wanted.)

The difficulty here in giving an account of what's going on is that if someone makes false assumptions about the way language works and tries to give an account of something with language conceived as functioning in this way, the result is not something false but nonsense.

Thus in terms of Russell's theory I could not express things by saying that the order is carried out *if* I am made happy by what happens, because I have also to recognise my being made happy, and this requires that something *else* should happen which I cannot describe in advance.

23   Suppose you were now to say: pictures do occur, but they are not what is regular; but how strange then, if they happen to be there and a conflict were now to arise between the two criteria of truth and falsity. How should it be adjudicated?

In that case, there would, of course, be no distinction between a command and its countermand, since both could be obeyed in the same way.

If when a language is first learnt, speech, as it were, is connected up to action – i.e. the levers to the machine – then the question arises, can these connections possibly break down? If they can't, then I have to accept any action as the right one; on the other hand if they can, what criterion have I for their having broken down? For what means have I for *comparing* the original arrangement with the subsequent action?

It is such *comparison* which is left out in Russell's theory. And comparison doesn't consist in confronting the representation with what it represents and through this confrontation experiencing a phenomenon, which, as I have said, itself could not be described in advance.

(Experience decides whether a proposition is true or false, but not its sense.)

24 How is a picture meant? The intention never resides in the picture itself, since, no matter how the picture is formed, it can always be meant in different ways. But that doesn't mean that the way the picture is meant only emerges when it elicits a certain reaction, for the intention is already expressed in the way I *now* compare the picture with reality.

In philosophy we are always in danger of giving a mythology of the symbolism, or of psychology: instead of simply saying what everyone knows and must admit.

What if someone played chess and, when he was mated, said, 'Look, I've won, for *that* is the goal I was aiming at'? We would say that such a man simply wasn't trying to play chess, but another game; whereas Russell would have to say that if anyone plays with the pieces and is satisfied with the outcome, then he has won at chess.

I expect that the rod will be 2 m high *in the same sense* in which it is now 1 m 99 cm high.

25 The fulfilment of an expectation doesn't consist in a third thing happening which you could also describe in another way than just as 'the fulfilment of the expectation', thus for example as a feeling of satisfaction or pleasure or whatever.

For expecting that *p* will be the case must be the same as expecting that this expectation will be fulfilled; whereas, if I am wrong, expecting *p* would be different from expecting that this expectation will be fulfilled.

Isn't it like this: My theory is completely expressed in the fact that the state of affairs satisfying the expectation of *p* is represented by the proposition *p*? And so, not by the description of a *totally* different event.

26 I should like to say, if there were only an external connection no connection could be described at all, since we only describe the external connection by means of the internal one. If this is lacking, we lose the footing we need for describing anything at all – just as we can't shift anything with our hands unless our feet are planted firmly.

Causality rests on an observed uniformity. Now, that doesn't mean that a uniformity we have observed until now will go on for ever, but it must be an established fact that events have been uniform until now; *that* cannot in turn be the insecure result of a series of observations which again is itself not a datum, but depends on another equally insecure series, etc. *ad inf.*

If I wish that *p* were the case, then of course *p* is not the case and there must be a surrogate for *p* in the state of wishing, just as, of course, in the expression of the wish.

There's nothing left for me, in answer to the question, 'What does *p* instruct you to do?', but to say it, i.e. to give another sign.

But can't you give someone an instruction by showing him how to do something? Certainly: and then you have to tell him 'Now copy that'. Perhaps you have already had examples of this before but now you have to say to him that what happened then should happen now. That still means: sooner or later there is a leap from the sign to what is signified.

27 The meaning of a question is the method of answering it: then what is the meaning of 'Do two men really mean the same by the word "white"?'

Tell me *how* you are searching, and I will tell you *what* you are searching for.

If I understand an order but do not carry it out, then understanding it can only consist in a process which is a *surrogate* for its execution, and so in a *different* process from its execution.

I should like to say, assuming the surrogate process to be a picture doesn't get me anywhere, since even that does not do away with the transition from the picture to what is depicted.

If you were to ask: 'Do I expect the future itself, or only something similar to the future?', that would be nonsense. Or, if you said, 'We can never be certain that *that* was what we really expected.'

Co-ordinating signals always contains something general, otherwise the co-ordination is unnecessary. It is a co-ordination which has to be understood in the particular case.

If I say to someone that it will be fine *tomorrow*, he gives evidence of his having understood by not trying to verify the proposition *now*.

28 Expecting is connected with looking for: looking for something presupposes that I know what I am looking for, without what I am looking for having to exist.

Earlier I would have put this by saying that searching presupposes the elements of the complex, but not *the* combination that I was looking for.

And that isn't a bad image: for, in the case of language, that would be expressed by saying that the sense of a proposition only presupposes the grammatically correct use of certain words.

How do I know that I have found *that* which I was looking for? (That what I expected has occurred, etc.)

I cannot confront the previous expectation with what happens.

The event that replaces the expectation, is a reply to it.

But for that to be so, necessarily *some* event must take its place, and that of course implies that the expectation must be in the same space as what is expected.

In this context I am talking about an expectation only as something that is necessarily either fulfilled or disappointed: therefore not of an expectation in the void.

29   The event which takes the place of an expectation, answers it: i.e. the replacement constitutes the answer, so that no question can arise whether it really is the answer. Such a question would mean putting the *sense* of a proposition in question.

'I expect to see a red patch' describes, let's say, *my present mental state*. 'I see a red patch' describes what I expect: a completely different event from the first. Couldn't you now ask whether the word 'red' has a different meaning in the two cases? Doesn't it look as if the first proposition uses an alien and inessential event to describe my mental state? Perhaps like this: I now find myself in a state of expectation which I characterize by saying that it is satisfied by the event of my seeing a red patch. That is, as though I were to say 'I am hungry and know from experience that eating a particular kind of food will or would satisfy my hunger.' But expectation isn't like that! Expectation is not given an external description by citing what is expected, as is hunger by citing what food satisfies it – in the last resort the appropriate food of course can still only be a matter of conjecture. No, describing an expectation by means of what is expected is giving an internal description.

The way the word 'red' is used is *such that* it has a use in all these propositions: 'I expect to see a red patch', 'I remember a red patch', 'I am afraid of a red patch', etc.

30   If I say 'This is the same event as I expected', and 'This is the same event as also happened on that occasion', then the word

'same' has two different meanings. (And you wouldn't normally say 'This is the same as I expected' but 'This is what I expected'.)

Could we imagine any language at all in which expecting p was described without using 'p'?

Isn't that *just as* impossible as a language in which $\sim p$ would be expressed without using 'p'?

Isn't this simply because *expectation* uses the same symbol as the thought of its fulfilment?

For if we think in signs, then we also expect and wish in signs.

(And you could almost say that someone could hope in German and fear in English, or vice versa.)

31   Another mental process belonging to this group, and which ties in with all these things, is *intention*. You could say that language is like a control room operated with a particular *intention* or built for a particular purpose.

If a mechanism is *meant* to act as a brake, but for some reason accelerates a machine then the purpose of the mechanism cannot be found out from it alone.

If you were then to say 'That's a brake lever but it doesn't work', you would be talking about intention. It is just the same as when we still call a broken clock a clock.

(Psychological – trivial – discussions of expectation, association, etc. always leave out what is really remarkable, and you notice that they talk all around, without touching on the vital point.)

32   I only use the terms the expectation, thought, wish, etc., that p will be the case, for processes having the multiplicity that finds

expression in *p*, and thus only if they are *articulated*. But in that case they are what I call the interpretation of signs.

I only call an *articulated* process a thought: you could therefore say 'only what has an articulated expression'.

(Salivation – no matter how precisely measured – is *not* what I call expecting.)

Perhaps we have to say that the phrase 'interpretation of signs' is misleading and instead we ought to say 'the use of signs'. For 'interpretation' makes it sound as if one were now to correlate the word 'red' with the colour (when it isn't even there), etc. And now the question again arises: what is the connection between sign and world? Could I look for something unless the space were there to look for it in?

Where does the sign link up with the world?

33   To look for something is, surely, an expression of expectation. In other words: How you search in one way or another expresses what you expect.

Thus the idea would be: what expectation has in common with reality is that it refers to another point in the *same* space. ('Space' in a completely general sense.)

I see a patch getting nearer and nearer to the place where I expect it.

If I say I remember a colour – say, the colour of a certain book – you could take as evidence for this the fact that I was in a position to mix this colour or recognize it again, or say of other colours that they are more like or less like the colour I remember.

Expectation, so to speak, prepares a yardstick for measuring the event when it comes and what's more, in such a way that it will necessarily be possible to measure the one with the other, whether the event coincides with the expected graduation mark or not.

It is, say, as if I guess a man's height by looking at him, saying

'I believe he's 5 ft 8 in' and then set about measuring him with a tape measure. Even if I don't know how tall he is, I still know that his height is measured with a tape measure and not a weighing machine.

If I expect to see red, then I *prepare* myself for red.

I can prepare a box for a piece of wood to fit in, just because the wood, whatever it's like, must have a volume.

If there were no connection between the act of expectation and reality, you could expect a nonsense.

34 The expectation of *p* and the occurrence of *p* correspond perhaps to the hollow shape of a body and the solid shape. Here *p* corresponds to the shape of the volume, and the different ways in which this shape is given correspond to the distinction between expectation and occurrence.

If I say 'I can make you a sketch of that any time you like', then that presupposes that I *am* in the same space as the business involved.

Our expectation anticipates the event. In this sense, it makes a model of the event. But we can only make a model of a fact in *the* world we live in, i.e. the model must be essentially related to the world we live in and what's more, independently of whether it's true or false.
If I say that the representation must treat of my world, then you cannot say 'since otherwise I could not verify it', but 'since otherwise it wouldn't even begin to make sense to me'.

35 In expecting, the part corresponding to searching in a space is the directing of one's attention.

Surely the strange thing about expectation is that we know that it is an *expectation*. For we couldn't, e.g., imagine the following situation: I have some image or other before me and say: 'Now, I don't know whether it's an expectation or a memory, or an image without any relation to reality.'

And *that* is what shows that expectation is immediately connected with reality.

For of course you couldn't say that the future the expectation speaks of – I mean the concept of the future – was also only a surrogate for the real future.

For I await in just as real a sense as I *wait*.

Could you also say: You cannot describe an expectation unless you can describe the present reality; or, you cannot describe an expectation unless you can give a description *comparing* the expectation with the present, of the form: *Now* I see a red circle *here,* and expect a blue square *there later on.*

That is to say the yardstick of language must be applied at the point which is present and then points out beyond it – roughly speaking, in the direction of the expectation.

36   It only makes sense to give the length of an object if I have a method for finding the object – since otherwise I cannot apply a yardstick to it.

What I once called 'objects', simples, were simply what I could refer to without running the risk of their possible non-existence; i.e. that for which there is neither existence nor non-existence, and that means: what we can speak about *no matter what may be the case.*

The visual table is not composed of electrons.

What if someone said to me 'I expect three knocks on the door' and I replied 'How do you know *three knocks* exist?' – Wouldn't that be just like the question 'How do you know six feet exist?' after someone has said 'I believe A is 6 feet high'?

37   Can absolute silence be confused with inner deafness, meaning having no acquaintance with the concept of sound? If that were so, you couldn't distinguish lacking the sense of hearing from lacking any other sense.

But isn't this exactly the same question as: 'Is a man who cannot see any red around him at present, in the same position as someone incapable of seeing red?'

You could of course say: The one can still imagine red, but the red we imagine is not the same as the red we see.

38   Our ordinary language has no means for describing a particular shade of a colour, such as the brown of my table. Thus it is incapable of producing a picture of this colour.

If I want to tell someone what colour some material is to be, I send him a sample, and obviously this sample belongs to language; and equally the memory or image of a colour that I conjure by a word, belongs to language.

The memory and the reality must be in *one* space.
I could also say: the image and the reality are in *one* space.

If I compare two colour samples in front of me with one another, and if I compare a colour sample with my image of a sample, that is similar to comparing, on the one hand, the lengths of two rods standing up against each other and on the other of two that are apart. In that case, I can say perhaps, they are the same height, if, turning my gaze horizontally, I can glance from the tip of the one to the tip of the other.

As a matter of fact I have never seen a black patch become gradually lighter and lighter until it is white and then redden until it is red; but I know that this would be possible because I can imagine it; i.e. I operate with my images in colour space and do with them what would be possible with the colours. And my words take their sense from the fact that they more or less completely reflect the operations of the images perhaps in the way in which a score can be used to describe a piece of music that has been played, but for example, does *not* reproduce the emphasis on each individual note.

Grammar gives language the necessary degrees of freedom.

IV

39   The colour octahedron is grammar, since it says that you can speak of a reddish blue but not of a reddish green, etc.

If I can only see something black and say it isn't red, how do I know that I am not talking nonsense, i.e. that it could be red, that there is red? Unless red is just another graduation mark on the same scale as black. What is the difference between 'That is not red' and 'That is not abracadabra'? Obviously I need to know that 'black', which describes the actual state of affairs (or is used in describing it), is that in whose place 'red' stands in the description.

But what does that mean? How do I know it isn't 'soft' in whose place 'red' stands? Can you say red is less different from black than from soft? That would of course be nonsense.

40   How far can you compare the colours with points on a scale?
    Can you say that the direction leading from black to red is a different one from the one you must take from black to blue?
    For, if there is black in front of me and I am expecting red, that's different from having black in front of me and expecting blue. And if there is a valid comparison with a ruler, the word 'blue' must so to speak give me the direction in which I go from black to blue; so to speak the method by which I reach blue.
    Couldn't we also say: 'The proposition must give a construction for the position of blue, the point the fact must reach if such and such is to be blue'?
    The fact that I can say that one colour comes closer to what I expected than another belongs here.

But how do these different directions find expression in grammar? Isn't it the same case as my seeing a grey and saying 'I expect this grey to go darker'? How does grammar deal with the distinction between 'lighter' and 'darker'? Or, how can the ruler going from white to black be applied to grey in a particular direction?

It's still as if grey were only *one* point; and how can I see the two *directions* in that? And yet I should be able to do so somehow or other if it is to be possible for me to get to a particular place in these directions [1].

41   The feeling is as if, for it to negate p, $\sim p$ has in a certain sense first to make it true. One asks '*What* isn't the case?' This must be represented but cannot be represented in such a way that p is actually made true.

A man with red/green colour blindness has a different colour system from a normal man. He will be like a man whose head was fixed in one position and so had a different kind of space, since for him there would only be visual space and therefore, e.g., no 'behind'. That wouldn't of course mean that Euclidean space was bounded for him. But that – at least as far as seeing things was concerned – he wouldn't acquire the concept of Euclidean space. Is the question then: can someone who doesn't know what red and green are like, really see what we (or I) call 'blue' and 'yellow'?

This question must, of course, be just as nonsensical as the question whether someone else with normal vision really sees the same as I do.

42   Grey must already be conceived as being in lighter/darker space if I want to talk of its being possible for it to get darker or lighter.

So you might perhaps also say: the yardstick must already be applied, I cannot apply it how I like; I can only pick out a point on it.

This amounts to saying: if I am surrounded by absolute silence,

---

1] Cf. diagram on p. 278.

I cannot join (construct) or not join auditory space on to this silence as I like, i.e. either it is for me 'silence' as opposed to a sound, or the word 'silence' has no meaning for me, i.e. I cannot *choose* between inner hearing and *inner* deafness.

And in just the same way, I cannot while I am seeing greyness *choose* between normal inner vision and partial or complete colour-blindness.

Suppose we had a device for completely cutting out our visual activity so that we could lose our sense of sight; and suppose I had so cut it out: could I say in such circumstances 'I can see a yellow patch on a red background'? Could this way of talking make *sense* to me?

43   I should like to say: for any question there is always a corresponding *method* of finding.

Or you might say, a question *denotes* a method of searching.

You can only search in a *space*. For only in space do you stand in a relation to where you are not.

To understand the sense of a proposition means to know how the issue of its truth or falsity is to be decided.

The essence of what we call the will is immediately connected with the continuity of the given.

You must find the way from where you are to where the issue is decided.

You cannot search wrongly; you *cannot* look for a visual impression with your sense of touch.

You cannot compare a picture with reality, unless you can set it against it as a yardstick.

You must be able to fit the proposition on to reality.

The reality that is perceived takes the place of the picture.

If I am to settle whether two points are a certain distance apart, I must look at the distance that *does* separate them.

44   How is a 'formally certified proposition' possible? It would be a proposition that you could tell was true or false by looking at it. But how can you discover by inspecting the proposition or thought that it is true? The thought is surely something quite different from the state of affairs asserted by the proposition.

The method of taking measurements, e.g. spatial measurements, is related to a particular measurement in precisely the same way as the sense of a proposition is to its truth or falsity.

The use, the application, of a yardstick doesn't presuppose any particular length for the object to be measured.

That is why I can learn how to measure in general, without measuring *every* measurable object. (This isn't simply an analogy, but is in fact an example.)

All that I need is: I must be able to be certain I can apply my yardstick.

Thus if I say 'Three more steps and I'll see red', that presupposes that at any rate I can apply the yardsticks of length and colour.

Someone may object that a scale with a particular height marked on it can say that something has that height, but not *what* has it.

I would then perhaps reply that all I can do is say that something 3 m away from me in a certain direction is 2 m high.

45   I will count any fact whose obtaining is a presupposition of a proposition's making sense, as belonging *to language*.

It's easy to understand that a ruler is and must be in the same space as the object measured by it. But in what sense are *words* in the same space as an object whose length is described in words, or, in the same space as a colour, etc.? It sounds absurd.

A black colour can become lighter but not louder. That means that it is in light/dark space but not loud/soft space. – But surely the object just stops being black when it becomes lighter. But in that case it was black and just as I can see movement (in the ordinary sense), I can see a colour movement.

The unit length is part of the symbolism. It belongs to the method of projection. Its length is arbitrary, but *it* is what contains the specifically spatial element.

And so if I call a length '3', the 3 signifies via the unit length presupposed in the symbolism.

You can also apply these remarks to time.

46 When I built language up by using a coordinate system for representing a state of affairs in space, I introduced into language an element which it doesn't normally use. This device is surely permissible. And it shows the connection between language and reality. The written sign without the coordinate system is senseless. Mustn't we then use something similar for representing colours?

If I say something is three feet long, then that presupposes that somehow or other I am given the foot length. In fact it is given by a description: in such and such a place there is a rod one foot long. The 'such and such a place' indirectly describes a method for getting there; otherwise the specification is senseless. The place name 'London' only has a sense if it is possible to *try to find* London.

A command is only then complete, when it makes sense no matter what may be the case. We might also say: That is when it is completely analysed.

V

47 That it doesn't strike us at all when we look around us, move about in space, feel our own bodies, etc., etc., shows how natural these things are to us. We do not notice that we see space perspectively or that our visual field is in some sense blurred towards the edges. It doesn't strike us and never can strike us because it is *the* way we perceive. We never give it a thought and it's impossible we should, since there is nothing that contrasts with the form of our world.

What I wanted to say is it's strange that those who ascribe reality only to things and not to our ideas [1] move about so unquestioningly in the world as idea [1] and never long to escape from it.

In other words, how much of a matter of course the given is. It would be the very devil if this were a tiny picture taken from an oblique, distorting angle.

This which we take as a matter of course, *life,* is supposed to be something accidental, subordinate; while something that normally never comes into my head, reality!

That is, what we neither can nor want to go beyond would not be the world.

Time and again the attempt is made to use language to limit the world and set it in relief – but it can't be done. The self-evidence of the world expresses itself in the very fact that language can and does only refer to it.

For since language only derives the way in which it means from its meaning, from the world, no language is conceivable which does not represent this world.

48 If the world of data is timeless, how can we speak of it at all?

1] ideas = Vorstellungen; the world as idea = Vorstellungswelt. [trans.]

The stream of life, or the stream of the world, flows on and our propositions are so to speak verified only at instants.

Our propositions are only verified by the present.

So they must be so constructed that they can be verified by it. And so in some way they must be commensurable with the present; and they cannot be so *in spite of* their spatio-temporal nature; on the contrary this must be related to their commensurability as the corporeality of a ruler is to its being extended – which is what enables it to measure. In this case, too, you cannot say: 'A ruler does measure in spite of its corporeality; of course a ruler which only has length would be the Ideal, you might say the *pure* ruler'. No, if a body has length, there can be no length without a body – and although I realize that in a certain sense only the ruler's length measures, what I put in my pocket still remains the ruler, the body, and isn't the length.

49 Perhaps this whole difficulty stems from taking the time concept from time in physics and applying it to the course of immediate experience. It's a confusion of the time of the film strip with the time of the picture it projects. For 'time' has one meaning when we regard memory as the source of time, and another when we regard it as a picture preserved from a past event.

If we take memory as a picture, then it's a picture of a physical event. The picture fades, and I notice how it has faded when I compare it with other evidence of what happened. In this case, memory is not the source of time, but a more or less reliable custodian of what 'actually' happened; and this is something we can know about in other ways, a physical event. – It's quite different if we now take memory to be the source of time. Here it isn't a picture, and cannot fade either – not in the sense in which a picture fades, becoming an ever less faithful representation of its object. Both ways of talking are in order, and are equally legitimate, but cannot be mixed together. It's clear of course that speaking of memory as a picture is only a metaphor; just as the way of speaking of images as 'pictures of objects in our minds' (or some such phrase) is a metaphor. We know what a picture is, but images are surely no kind of picture at all. For, in the first case I can see the picture and the object of which it is a picture. But in the other, things are obviously quite different. We have just used a metaphor and now the metaphor tyrannizes us. While in the language of the metaphor, I am unable to move outside of the metaphor. It must lead to nonsense if you try to use the language of this metaphor to talk about memory as the source of our knowledge, the verification of our propositions. We can speak of present, past and future events in the physical world, but not of present, past and future images, if what we are calling an image is not to be yet another kind of physical object (say, a physical picture which takes the place of the body), but precisely that which is present. Thus we cannot use the concept of time, i.e. the syntactical rules that hold for the names of physical objects, in the world of the image [1], that is, not where we adopt a radically different way of speaking.

50   If memory is *no* kind of seeing into the past, how do we know at all that it is to be taken as referring to the past? We could then remember some incident and be in doubt whether in our memory image we have a picture of the past or of the future.

We can of course say: I do not see the past, only a *picture* of the past. But how do I know it's a picture of the *past* unless this belongs to the essence of a memory-image? Have we, say, learnt from experience to interpret these pictures as pictures of the past? But in this context what meaning would 'past' have at all?

Yet it contradicts every concept of physical time that I should have perception into the past, and that again seems to mean nothing

---

1] world of the image = Welt der Vorstellung. [trans.]

else than that the concept of time in the first system must be radically different from that in physics.

Can I conceive the time in which the experiences of visual space occur without experiences of sound? It appears so. And yet how strange that something should be able to have a form, which would also be conceivable without *this* content. Or does a man who has been given hearing also learn a new time along with it?

The traditional questions are not suited to a logical investigation of phenomena. These generate their own questions, or rather, give their own answers.

51   If I compare the facts of immediate experience with the pictures on the screen and the facts of physics with pictures in the film strip, on the film strip there is a present picture and past and future pictures. But on the screen, there is only the present.

What is characteristic about this image is that in using it I regard the future as pre-formed.

There's a point in saying future events are pre-formed if it belongs to the *essence* of time that it does not break off. For then we can say: something will happen, it's only that I don't know what. And in the world of physics we can say that.

52   It's strange that in ordinary life we are not troubled by the feeling that the phenomenon is slipping away from us, the constant flux of appearance, but only when we philosophize. This indicates that what is in question here is an idea suggested by a misapplication of our language.

The feeling we have is that the present disappears into the past without our being able to prevent it. And here we are obviously using the picture of a film strip remorselessly moving past us, that we are unable to stop. But it is of course just as clear that the picture is misapplied: that we cannot say 'Time flows' if by time we mean the possibility of change. What we are looking at here is really the possibility of motion: and so the logical form of motion.

In this connection it appears to us as if memory were a somewhat secondary sort of experience, when compared with experience of the present. We say 'We can *only* remember that'. As though in a primary sense memory were a somewhat faint and uncertain picture of what we originally had before us in full clarity.

In the language of physical objects, that's so: I say: 'I *only* have a *vague* memory of this house.'

53   And why not let matters rest there? For this way of talking surely says everything we want to say, and everything that can be said. But we wish to say that it can also be put *differently*; and that is important.

It is as if the emphasis is placed elsewhere in this other way of speaking: for the words 'seem', 'error', etc., have a certain emotional overtone which doesn't belong to the essence of the phenomena. In a way it's connected with the will and not merely with cognition.

We talk for instance of an optical illusion and associate this expression with the idea of a mistake, although of course it isn't essential that there should be any mistake; and if appearance were normally more important in our lives than the results of measurement, then language would also show a different attitude to this phenomenon.

There is not – as I used to believe – a primary language as opposed to our ordinary language, the 'secondary' one. But one could speak of a primary language as opposed to ours in so far as the former would not permit any way of expressing a preference for certain phenomena over others; it would have to be, so to speak, absolutely *impartial*.

54   What belongs to the essence of the world cannot be expressed by language.

For this reason, it cannot *say* that everything flows. Language can only say those things that we can also imagine otherwise.

That everything flows must be expressed in the application of language, and in fact not in one kind of application as opposed to another but in *the* application. In anything we would ever call the application of language.

By application I understand what makes the combination of sounds or marks into a language at all. In the sense that it is the application which makes the rod with marks on it into a *measuring rod* [1]: *putting* language *up against* reality.

We are tempted to say: only the experience of the present moment has reality. And then the first reply must be: As opposed to what?

Does it imply I didn't get up this morning? (For if so, it would be dubious.) But that is not what we mean. Does it mean that an event that I'm not remembering at this instant didn't occur? Not that either.

The proposition that only the present experience has reality appears to contain the last consequence of solipsism. And in a sense that is so; only what it is able to say amounts to just as little as can be said by solipsism. – For what belongs to the essence of the world simply *cannot* be said. And philosophy, if it were to say anything, would have to describe the essence of the world.

But the essence of language is a picture of the essence of the world; and philosophy as custodian of grammar can in fact grasp the essence of the world, only not in the propositions of language, but in rules for this language which exclude nonsensical combinations of signs.

If someone says, only the *present experience* has reality, then the word 'present' must be redundant here, as the word 'I' is in other contexts. For it cannot mean *present* as opposed to past and future. – Something else must be meant by the word, something that isn't *in* a space, but is itself a space. That is to say, not something bordering on something else (from which it could therefore be limited off). And so, something language cannot legitimately set in relief.

1] Maßstab (usually rendered 'yardstick'). [trans.]

The present we are talking about here is not the frame in the film reel that is in front of the projector's lens at precisely this moment, as opposed to the frames before and after it, which have already been there or are yet to come; but the picture on the screen which would illegitimately be called present, since 'present' would not be used here to distinguish it from past and future. And so it is a meaningless epithet.

55 There are, admittedly, very interesting, completely general propositions of great importance, therefore propositions describing an actual experience which might have been otherwise, but just *is as it is*. For instance, that I have only *one* body. That my sensations never reach out beyond this body (except in cases where someone has had a limb, e.g. an arm, amputated, and yet feels pain in his fingers). These are remarkable and interesting facts.

But it does *not* belong in this category, if someone says I cannot remember the future. For that means nothing, and, like its opposite, is something inconceivable.

That I always see with my *eyes* when I am awake is on the other hand a remarkable and interesting fact. Equally, it is important that my visual field is almost incessantly in a state of flux.

'I' clearly refers to my body, for *I* am in this room; and 'I' is essentially something that is in a place, and in a place belonging to the same space as the one the other bodies are in too.

From the very outset 'Realism', 'Idealism', etc., are names which belong to metaphysics. That is, they indicate that their adherents believe they can say something specific about the essence of the world.

56 Anyone wishing to contest the proposition that only the present experience is real (which is just as wrong as to maintain it) will perhaps ask whether then a proposition like 'Julius Caesar crossed the Alps' merely describes my present mental state which is occupied with the matter. And of course the answer is: no, it

describes an event which we believe happened ca. 2,000 years ago. That is, if the word 'describes' is construed in the same way as in the sentence 'The proposition "I am writing" *describes* what I am at present doing'. The name Julius Caesar designates a person. But what does all that amount to? I seem to be fighting shy of the genuinely philosophical answer! Propositions dealing with people, i.e. containing proper names, can be verified in very different ways. – We still might find Caesar's corpse: that this is thinkable is directly connected with the sense of the proposition about Caesar. But also that a manuscript might be found from which it emerged that such a man never lived and that the accounts of his existence were concocted for particular purposes. Propositions about Julius Caesar must, therefore, have a sense of a sort that covers this possibility. If I utter the proposition: I can see a red patch crossing a green one, the possibilities provided for in 'Julius Caesar crossed the Alps' are not present here, and to that extent I can say that the proposition about Caesar has its sense in a more indirect way than this one.

Everything which, if it occurred, would legitimately confirm a belief, determines logically the nature of this belief. That is, it shows something about the logical nature of the belief.

The proposition about Julius Caesar is simply a framework (like that about any other person) that admits of widely differing verifications, although not all those it would allow in speaking of other people – of living people, for instance.

Isn't all that I mean: between the proposition and its verification there is no go-between negotiating this verification?

Even our ordinary language has of course to provide for all cases of uncertainty, and if we have any philosophical objection to it, this can only be because in certain cases it gives rise to misinterpretations.

VI

57   One of the most misleading representational techniques in our language is the use of the word 'I', particularly when it is used in representing immediate experience, as in 'I can see a red patch'.

It would be instructive to replace this way of speaking by another in which immediate experience would be represented without using the personal pronoun; for then we'd be able to see that the previous representation wasn't essential to the facts. Not that the representation would be in any sense more correct than the old one, but it would serve to show clearly what was logically essential in the representation.

The worst philosophical errors always arise when we try to apply our ordinary – physical – language in the area of the immediately given.

If, for instance, you ask, 'Does the box still exist when I'm not looking at it?', the only right answer would be 'Of course, unless someone has taken it away or destroyed it'. Naturally, a philosopher would be dissatisfied with this answer, but it would quite rightly reduce his way of formulating the question *ad absurdum*.

All our forms of speech are taken from ordinary, physical language and cannot be used in epistemology or phenomenology without casting a distorting light on their objects.

The very expression 'I can perceive x' is itself taken from the idioms of physics, and x ought to be a physical object – e.g. a body – here. Things have already gone wrong if this expression is used in phenomenology, where x must refer to a datum. For then 'I' and 'perceive' also cannot have their previous senses.

58   We could adopt the following way of representing matters: if I, L. W., have toothache, then that is expressed by means of the proposition 'There is toothache'. But if that is so, what we now

express by the proposition 'A has toothache', is put as follows: 'A is behaving as L. W. does when there is toothache'. Similarly we shall say 'It is thinking' [1] and 'A is behaving as L. W. does when it is thinking'. (You could imagine a despotic oriental state where the language is formed with the despot as its centre and his name instead of L. W.) It's evident that this way of speaking is equivalent to ours when it comes to questions of intelligibility and freedom from ambiguity. But it's equally clear that this language could have anyone at all as its centre.

Now, among all the languages with different people as their centres, each of which I can understand, the one with me as its centre has a privileged status. This language is particularly adequate. How am I to express that? That is, how can I rightly represent its special advantage in words? This can't be done. For, if I do it in the language with me as its centre, then the exceptional status of the description of this language in its own terms is nothing very remarkable, and in the terms of another language my language occupies no privileged status whatever. – The privileged status lies in the application, and if I describe this application, the privileged status again doesn't find expression, since the description depends on the language in which it's couched. And now, which description gives just that which I have in mind depends again on the application.

Only their application really differentiates languages; but if we disregard this, all languages are equivalent. All these languages only describe one single, incomparable thing and *cannot* represent anything else. (Both these approaches must lead to the same result: first, that what is represented is not one thing among others, that it is not capable of being contrasted with anything; second, that I cannot express the advantage of *my* language.)

59   It isn't possible to believe something for which you cannot imagine some kind of verification.

If I say I believe that someone is sad, it's as though I am seeing his behaviour through the medium of sadness, from the viewpoint

---

1] To be construed by analogy with 'It is snowing'. [trans.]

of sadness. But could you say: 'It looks to me as if I'm sad, my head is drooping so'?

60   Not only does epistemology pay no attention to the truth or falsity of genuine propositions, it's even a philosophical method of focusing on precisely those propositions whose content seems to us as physically impossible as can be imagined (e.g. that someone has an ache in someone else's tooth). In this way, epistemology highlights the fact that its domain includes everything that can possibly be thought.

Does it make *sense* to say that two people have the same body? That is an uncommonly important and interesting question. If it makes no sense, then that means – I believe – that only our bodies are the principle of individuation. It is clearly imaginable that I should feel a pain in the hand of a different body from the one called my own. But suppose now that my old body were to become completely insensible and inert and from then on I only felt my pains in the other body?

You could say: Philosophy is constantly gathering a store of propositions without worrying about their truth or falsity; only in the cases of logic and mathematics does it have to do exclusively with the 'true' propositions.

61   In the sense of the phrase 'sense data' in which it is inconceivable that someone else should have them, it cannot, for this very reason, be said that someone else does not have them. And by the same token, it's senseless to say that *I*, as opposed to someone else, *have* them.

We say, 'I *cannot* feel your toothache'; when we say this, do we only mean that so far we have never as a matter of fact felt someone else's toothache? Isn't it, rather, that it's logically impossible?

What distinguishes *his* toothache from *mine*? If the word 'toothache' means the same in 'I have toothache' and 'He has toothache', what does it then mean to say he can't have the same toothache as I do? How are toothaches to be distinguished from one another? By intensity and similar characteristics, and by location. But suppose these are the same in the two cases? But if it is objected that the distinction is simply that in the one case *I* have it, in the other *he*; then the owner is a defining mark of the toothache itself; but then what does the proposition 'I have toothache' (or someone else does) assert? Nothing at all.

If the word 'toothache' has the same meaning in both cases, then we must be able to compare the toothaches of the two people; and if their intensities, etc. coincide, they're the same. Just as two suits have the *same* colour, if they match one another in brightness, saturation, etc.

Equally, it's nonsense to say two people can't have the same sense datum, if by 'sense datum' what is *primary* is really intended.

62   In explaining the proposition 'He has toothache', we even say something like: 'Quite simple, I know what it means for *me* to have toothache, and when I say he has toothache, I mean he now has what I once had.' But what does 'he' mean and what does '*have* toothache' mean? Is this a relation toothache once had to me and now has to him? So in that case I would also be conscious of toothache now and of his having it now, just as I can now see a wallet in his hand that I saw earlier in mine.

Is there a sense in saying 'I have a pain, only I don't notice it'? For I could certainly substitute 'he has' for 'I have' in this proposition. And conversely, if the propositions 'He has a pain' and 'I have a pain' are logically on a par, I must be able to substitute 'I have' for 'he has' in the proposition 'He has a pain that I can't feel'. – I might also put it like this: only in so far as I can have a pain I don't feel can he have a pain I don't feel. Then it might still be the case that in fact I always feel the pain I have, but it must make sense to deny that I do.

'I have no pain' means: if I compare the proposition 'I have a pain' with reality, it turns out false – so I must be in a position to compare the proposition with what is in fact the case. And the possibility of such a comparison – even though the result may be negative – is what we mean when we say: what is the case must happen in the same space as what is denied; only it must be *otherwise*.

63   Admittedly the concept of toothache as a datum of feeling can be applied to someone else's tooth just as readily as it can to mine, but only in the sense that it might well be perfectly possible to feel pain in a tooth in someone else's mouth. According to our present way of speaking we wouldn't, however, express this fact in the words 'I feel his toothache' but by saying 'I've got a pain in his tooth'. – Now we may say: Of course you haven't got his tooth-ache, for it is now more than possible that he will say, 'I don't feel anything in this tooth'. And in such a situation, am I supposed to say 'You're lying, I can feel how your tooth is aching'?

When I feel sorry for someone with toothache, I put myself in his place. But I put *myself* in his place.

The question is, whether it makes sense to say: 'Only A can verify the proposition "A is in pain", I can't'. But what would it be like if this were false, and *I* could verify it: can that mean anything other than that I'd have to feel pain? But would that be a verification? Let's not forget: it's nonsense to say I must feel *my* or *his* pain.

We might also put the question like this: What in my experience justifies the 'my' in 'I feel *my* pain'? Where is the multiplicity in the feeling that justifies this word? And it can only be justified if we could also replace it by another word.

64 'I have a pain' is a sign of a completely different kind when I am using the proposition, from what it is to me on the lips of another; the reason being that it is senseless, as far as I'm concerned, on the lips of another until I know through which mouth it was expressed. The propositional sign in this case doesn't consist in the sound alone, but in the fact that the sound came out of this mouth. Whereas in the case in which I say or think it, the sign is the sound itself.

Suppose I had stabbing pains in my right knee and my right leg jerked with every pang. At the same time I see someone else whose leg is jerking like mine and he complains of stabbing pains; and while this is going on my left leg begins jerking like the right although I can't feel any pain in my left knee. Now I say: the other fellow obviously has the same pains in his knee as I've got in my right knee. But what about my left knee, isn't it precisely the same case here as that of the other's knee?

If I say 'A has toothache', I use the image of feeling pain in the same way as, say, the concept of flowing when I talk of an electric current flowing.

The two hypotheses that other people have toothache and that they behave just as I do but don't have toothache, possibly have identical senses. That is, if I had, for example, learnt the second form of expression, I would talk in a pitying tone of voice about people who don't have toothache, but are behaving as I do when I have.

Can I imagine pains in the tips of my nails, or in my hair? Isn't that just as possible or impossible as it is to imagine a pain in any part of the body whatever in which I have none at the moment, and cannot remember having had any?

65   The logic of our language is so difficult to grasp at this point: our language employs the phrases 'my pain' and 'his pain', and also the expressions 'I have (or feel) a pain' and 'He has (or feels) a pain'. An expression 'I feel my pain' or 'I feel his pain' is nonsense. And it seems to me that, at bottom, the entire controversy over behaviourism turns on this.

The experience of feeling pain is not that a person 'I' has something.
I distinguish an intensity, a location, etc. in the pain, but not an owner.
What sort of a thing would a pain be that no one *has*? Pain belonging to no one at all?

Pain is represented as something we can perceive in the sense in which we perceive a matchbox. What is unpleasant is then naturally not the pain, only perceiving it.

When I am sorry for someone else because he's in pain, I do of course imagine the pain, but I imagine that *I* have it.

Is it also to be possible for me to imagine the pain of a tooth lying on the table, or a teapot's pain? Are we perhaps to say: it merely isn't true that the teapot is in pain, but I can imagine it being so?!

The two hypotheses, that others have pain, and that they don't and merely behave as I do when I have, must have identical senses if every *possible* experience confirming the one confirms the other as well. In other words, if a decision between them on the basis of experience is inconceivable.

To say that others have no pain, presupposes that it makes sense to say they do have pains.

I believe it's clear we say other people have pains in the same sense as we say a chair has none.

66   What would it be like if I had two bodies, i.e. my body were composed of two separate organisms?

Here again, I think, we see the way in which the self is not on a par with others, for if everyone else had two bodies, I wouldn't be able to tell that this was so.

Can I imagine experience with two bodies? Certainly not visual experience.

The phenomenon of feeling toothache I am familiar with is represented in the idioms of ordinary language by 'I *have* a pain in such-and-such a tooth'. Not by an expression of the kind 'In this place there is a feeling of pain'. The *whole* field of this experience is described in this language by expressions of the form 'I have . . .'. Propositions of the form 'N has toothache' are reserved for a totally different field. So we shouldn't be surprised when for propositions of the form 'N has toothache', there is nothing left that links with experience in the same way as in the first case.

Philosophers who believe you can, in a manner of speaking, extend experience by thinking, ought to remember that you can transmit speech over the telephone, but not measles.

Similarly I cannot at will experience time as bounded, or the visual field as homogeneous, etc.

Visual space and retina. It's as if you were to project a sphere orthogonally on to a plane, for instance in the way in which you represent the two hemispheres of the globe in an atlas, and now someone might believe that what's on the page surrounding the two projections of the sphere somehow still corresponds to a possible extension of what is to be found on the sphere. The point is that here a *complete space* is projected onto a *part* of another space; and it is like this with the limits of language in a dictionary.

If someone believes he can imagine four-dimensional space, then why not also four-dimensional colours – colours which in addition to the degree of saturation, hue and intensity of light, are susceptible of being determined in yet a fourth way.

VII

67 Suppose I had such a good memory that I could remember all my sense impressions. In that case, there would, *prima facie*, be nothing to prevent me from describing them. This would be a biography. And why shouldn't I be able to leave everything hypothetical out of this description?

I could, e.g., represent the visual images plastically, perhaps with plaster-cast figures on a reduced scale which I would only finish as far as I had actually seen them, designating the rest as inessential by shading or some other means.

So far everything would be fine. But what about the time I take to make this representation? I'm assuming I'd be able to keep pace with my memory in 'writing' this language – producing this representation. But if we suppose I then read the description through, isn't it now hypothetical after all?

Let's imagine a representation such as this: the bodies I seem to see are moved by a mechanism in such a way that they would give the visual images to be represented to two eyes fixed at a particular place in the model. The visual image described is then determined from the position of the eyes in the model and from the position and motion of the bodies.

We could imagine that the mechanism could be driven by turning a crank and in that way the description 'read off'.

68 Isn't it clear that this would be the most immediate description we can possibly imagine? That is to say, that anything which tried to be more immediate still would inevitably cease to be a description.

Instead of a description, what would then come out would be

that inarticulate sound with which many writers would like to begin philosophy. ('I have, knowing of my knowledge, consciousness of something.')

You simply can't begin before the beginning.

Language itself belongs to the second system. If I describe a language, I am essentially describing something that belongs to physics. But how can a physical language describe the phenomenal?

69   Isn't it like this: a phenomenon (specious present) contains time, but isn't in time?

Its form is time, but it has no place in time.

Whereas language unwinds in time.

What we understand by the word 'language' unwinds in physical time. (As is made perfectly clear by the comparison with a mechanism.)

Only what corresponds to this mechanism in the primary world could be the primary language.

I mean: what I call a sign must be what is called a sign in grammar; something on the film, not on the screen.

'I cannot tell whether . . .' only makes sense if I *can* know, not when it's inconceivable.

70   With our language we find ourselves, so to speak, in the domain of the film, not of the projected picture. And if I want to make music to accompany what is happening on the screen, whatever produces the music must again happen in the sphere of the film.

On the other hand, it's clear we need a way of speaking with which we can represent the phenomena of visual space, isolated as such.

'I can see a lamp standing on the table', says, in the way in which it has to be understood in our ordinary language, more than a description of visual space. 'It seems to me as if I were seeing a lamp standing on a table' would certainly be a correct description: but this form of words is misleading since it makes it look as though nothing actual were being described, but only something whose nature was unclear.

Whereas 'it seems' is only meant to say that something is being described as a special case of a general rule, and all that is uncertain is whether further events will be capable of being described as special cases of the same rule.

It seems as if there is a sine curve on the film, of which we can see particular parts.

That is to say, what we see can be described by means of a sine curve on the film, when the light projecting it has been interrupted at particular points.

A concentric circle seems to have been drawn round the circle K and a, b, c, d, e, f to have been drawn as tangents to it.

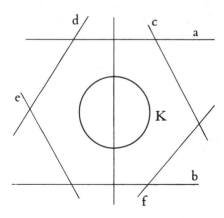

71 It could, e.g., be practical under certain circumstances to give proper names to my hands and to those of other people, so that you

wouldn't have to mention their relation to somebody when talking about them, since that relation isn't essential to the hands themselves; and the usual way of speaking could create the impression that its relation to its owner was something belonging to the essence of the hand itself.

Visual space has essentially no owner.

Let's assume that, with all the others, I can always see one particular object in visual space – viz my nose –. Someone else naturally doesn't see this object in the same way. Doesn't that mean, then, that the visual space I'm talking about *belongs to me*? And so is subjective? No. It has only been construed subjectively here, and an objective space opposed to it, which is, however, only a construction with visual space as its basis. In the – secondary – language of 'objective' – physical – space, visual space is called subjective, or rather, whatever in this language corresponds directly with visual space is called subjective. In the same way that one might say that in the language of real numbers whatever in their domain corresponds directly with the cardinal numbers is called the 'positive integers'.

In the model described above neither the two eyes that see the objects, nor their position need be included. That's only *one* technique of representation. It does just as well if e.g. the part of the objects that is 'seen', is indicated by shading it in. Of course you can always work out the position of two eyes from the boundaries of this shaded area; but that only corresponds to translation from one way of speaking into another.

The essential thing is that the representation of visual space is the representation of an object and contains no suggestion of a subject.

72   Suppose all the parts of my body could be removed until only one eyeball was left; and this were to be firmly fixed in a certain position, retaining its power of sight. How would the world appear to me? I wouldn't be able to perceive any part of myself,

and supposing my eyeball to be transparent for me, I wouldn't be able to see myself in the mirror either. One question arising at this point is: would I be able to locate myself by means of my visual field? 'Locate myself', of course here only means to establish a particular structure for the visual space.

Does anything now force me into interpreting the tree I see through my window as larger than the window? If I have a sense for the distance of objects from my eye, this is a justified interpretation. But even then it's a representation in a different space from visual space, for what corresponds to the tree in visual space is, surely, obviously smaller than what corresponds to the window.

Or ought I to say: Well, that all depends on how you're using the words 'larger' and 'smaller'?

And that's right: in visual space I can use the words 'larger' and 'smaller' both ways. And in one sense the visual mountain is smaller, and in the other larger, than the visual window.

Suppose my eyeball were fixed behind the window, so that I would see most things through it. In that case this window could assume the role of a part of my body. What's near the window is near me. (I'm assuming I can see three-dimensionally with one eye.) In addition, I assume that I'm in a position to see my eyeball in the mirror, and perceive similar eyeballs on the trees outside, say.

How can I in this case tell, or arrive at the assumption, that I see the world through the pupil of my eyeball? Surely not in an essentially different way from that of my seeing it through the window, or, say, through a hole in a board that my eye is directly behind.

In fact, if my eye were in the open stuck on the end of a branch, my position could be made perfectly clear to me by someone bringing a ring closer and closer until in the end I could see everything through it. They could even bring up the old surroundings of my eye: cheek bones, nose, etc., and I would know where it all fits in.

73   Does all this mean then that a visual image does essentially contain or pre-suppose a subject after all?

Or isn't it rather that these experiments give me nothing but purely geometrical information?

That is to say information that constantly only concerns the object.

Objective information about reality.

There isn't an eye belonging to me and eyes belonging to others in visual space. Only the space itself is asymmetrical, the objects in it are on a par. In the space of physics however this presents itself in such a way that one of the eyes which are on a par is singled out and called *my* eye.

I want to know what's going on behind me and turn round. If I were prevented from doing this, wouldn't the idea that space stretches out around me remain? And that I could manage to see the objects now behind me by turning around. *Therefore* it's the possibility of turning around that leads me to this idea of space. The resulting space around me is thus a mixture of visual space and *the space of muscular sensation*.

Without the feeling of the ability 'to turn around', my idea of space would be *essentially* different.

Thus the detached, immovable eye wouldn't have the idea of a space all around it.

74   Immediate experience cannot contain any contradiction. If it is beyond all speaking and contradicting, then the demand for an explanation cannot arise either: the feeling that there must be an explanation of what is happening, since otherwise something would be amiss.

What about when we close our eyes: we don't stop seeing. But what we see in this case surely can't have any relation to an eye. And it's the same with a dream image. But even in the case of normal seeing, it's clear that the exceptional position of my body in visual space only derives from other feelings that are located in my body, and not from something purely visual.

Even the word 'visual space' is unsuitable for our purpose, since it contains an allusion to a sense organ which is as inessential to the space as it is to a book that it belongs to a particular person; and it could be very misleading if our language were constructed in such a way that we couldn't use it to designate a book without relating it to an owner. It might lead to the idea that a book can only exist in relation to a person.

75   If, now, phenomenological language isolates visual space and what goes on in it from everything else, how does it treat time? Is the time of 'visual' phenomena the time of our ordinary idioms of physics?

It's clear we're able to recognize that two time intervals are equal. I could, e.g., imagine what happens in visual space being accompanied by the ticking of a metronome or a light flashing at regular intervals.

To simplify matters, I'm imagining the changes in my visual space to be discontinuous, and, say, in time with the beats of the metronome. Then I can give a description of these changes (in which I use numbers to designate the beats).

Suppose this description to be a prediction, which is now to be verified. Perhaps I know it by heart and now compare it with what actually happens. Everything hypothetical is avoided here, apart from what is contained in the presupposition that the description is given to me independently of the question of which elements in it are before me at precisely this moment.

The whole is a talking film, and the spoken word that goes with the events on the screen is just as fleeting as those events and not the same as the sound track. The sound track doesn't accompany the scenes on the screen.

Does it now make any sense to say I could have been deceived by a demon and what I took for a description wasn't one at all, but a memory delusion? No, that can have no sense. A delusion that, *ex hypothesi, cannot* be unmasked isn't a delusion.

And this means no more and no less than that the time of my memory is, in this instance, precisely the time which I'm describing.

This isn't the same as time as it's usually understood: for that, there are any number of possible sources, such as the accounts other people give, etc. But here it is once again a matter of isolating the one time.

If there are three pipes in which a black liquid, a yellow liquid and a red liquid are flowing respectively, and these combine at some point to make a brown, then the resulting liquid has its own way of flowing too; but all I want to say is that each of the liquids with a simple colour also has a way of flowing, and I wish to examine this at a point before the three have run into one another.

Of course the word 'present' is also out of place here. For to what extent can we say of reality that it is present? Surely only if we embed it once more in a time that is foreign to it. In itself it isn't present. Rather, on the contrary, it contains a time.

VIII

76 One's first thought is that it's incompatible for two colours to be in *one* place at the same time. The next is that two colours in one place simply combine to make another. But third comes the objection: how about the complementary colours? What do red and green make? Black perhaps? But do I then see green in the black colour? – But even apart from that: how about the mixed colours, e.g. mixtures of red and blue? These contain a greater or lesser element of red: what does that mean? It's clear what it means to say that something *is red*: but that it *contains* more or less red? – And different degrees of red are incompatible with one another. Someone might perhaps imagine this being explained by supposing that certain small quantities of red added together would yield a specified degree of red. But in that case what does it mean if we say, for example, that five of these quantities of red are present? It cannot, of course, be a logical product of quantity no. 1 being present, and quantity no. 2 etc., up to 5; for how would these be distinguished from one another? Thus the proposition that 5 degrees of red are present can't be analysed like this. Neither can I have a concluding proposition that this is all the red that is present in this colour: for there is no sense in saying that no more red is needed, since I can't add quantities of red with the 'and' of logic.

Neither does it mean anything to say that a rod which is 3 yards long is 2 yards long, because it is 2 + 1 yards long, since we can't say it is 2 yards long and that it is 1 yard long. The length of 3 yards is something new.

And yet I can say, when I see two different red-blues: there's an even redder blue than the redder of these two. That is to say, from the given I can construct what is not given.

You could say that the colours have an elementary affinity with one another.

That makes it look as if a construction might be possible within the elementary proposition. That is to say, as if there were a construction in logic which didn't work by means of truth functions.

What's more, it also seems that these constructions have an effect on one proposition's following logically from another.

For, if different degrees exclude one another it follows from the presence of one that the other is not present. In that case, two elementary propositions can contradict one another.

77   How is it possible for $f(a)$ and $f(b)$ to contradict one another, as certainly seems to be the case? For instance, if I say 'There is red here now' and 'There is green here now'?

This is connected with the idea of *a complete description*: 'The patch is green' describes the patch completely, and there's no room left for another colour.

It's no help either that red and green can, in a manner of speaking, pass one another by in the dimension of time: for, suppose I say that throughout a certain period of time a patch was red and that it was green?

If I say for example that a patch is simultaneously light red and dark red, I imagine as I say it that the one shade covers the other. But then is there still a sense in saying the patch has the shade that is invisible and covered over?

Does it make any sense at all to say that a perfectly black surface is white, only we don't see the white because it is covered by the black? And why does the black cover the white and not vice versa?

If a patch has a visible and an invisible colour, then at any rate it has these colours in quite different senses.

78   If $f(r)$ and $f(g)$ contradict one another, it is because r and g completely occupy the f and cannot both be in it. But that doesn't show itself in our signs. But it must show itself if we look, not at

the sign, but at the symbol. For since this includes the form of the objects, then the impossibility of '$f(r) \cdot f(g)$' must show itself there, in this form.

It must be possible for the contradiction to show itself entirely in the symbolism, for if I say of a patch that it is red and green, it is certainly at most only one of these two, and the contradiction must be contained in the *sense* of the two propositions.

That two colours won't fit at the same time in the same place must be contained in their form and the form of space.

But the symbols do contain the form of colour and of space, and if, say, a letter designates now a colour, now a sound, it's a *different* symbol on the two occasions; and this shows in the fact that different syntactical rules hold for it.

Of course, this doesn't mean that inference could now be not only formal, but also material. – Sense follows from sense and so form from form.

'Red and green won't both fit into the same place' doesn't mean that they are as a matter of fact never together, but that you can't even say they are together, or, consequently, that they are never together.

79 But that would imply that I can write down two particular propositions, but not their logical product.

The two propositions collide in the object.

The proposition $f(g) \cdot f(r)$ isn't nonsense, since not *all* truth possibilities disappear, even if they are all rejected. We can, however, say that the '$\cdot$' has a different meaning here, since '$x \cdot y$' usually means (TFFF); here, on the other hand, it means (FFF). And something analogous holds for '$x \, v \, y$', etc.

80 A yellow tinge is not the colour yellow.

Strictly, I cannot *mix* yellow and red, i.e. not strictly see them at the same time, since if I want to see yellow in this place, the red must leave it and vice versa.

It's clear, as I've said, that the proposition that a colour contains five tints of yellow cannot say it contains tint no. 1 and it contains tint no. 2 etc. On the contrary the addition of the tints must occur within the elementary proposition. But what if these tints are objects lined up like links in a chain in a certain way; and now in one proposition we are speaking of five such links, and in another proposition of three. All right, but these propositions must exclude one another, while yet not being analysable. – But then do $F5$ and $F6$ have to exclude each other? Can't I say, Fn doesn't mean that the colour contains *only* n tints, but that it contains *at least* n tints? It contains *only* n tints would be expressed by the proposition $F(n) \cdot \sim F(n + 1)$. But even then the elementary propositions aren't independent of one another, since $F(n - 1)$ at any rate still follows from $F(n)$, and $F(5)$ contradicts $\sim F(4)$.

The proposition asserting a certain degree of a property contradicts on the one interpretation the specification of any other degree and on the other interpretation it follows from the specification of any higher degree.

A conception which makes use of a product $aRx \cdot xRy \cdot yRb$ is inadequate too, since I must be able to distinguish the things x, y, etc., if they are to yield a distance.

A mixed colour, or better, a colour intermediate between blue and red is such in virtue of an internal relation to the structures of blue and red. But this internal relation is *elementary*. That is, it doesn't consist in the proposition '*a* is blue-red' representing a logical product of '*a* is blue' and '*a* is red'.

To say that a particular colour is now in a place is to describe that place *completely*.

81   Besides, the position is no different for colours than for sounds or electrical charges.

In every case it's a question of the complete description of a certain state at *one* point or at the same time.

Wouldn't the following schema be possible: the colour at a point isn't described by allocating *one* number to a point, but by allocating *several* numbers. Only a mixture of such numbers makes the colour; and to describe the colour in full I need the proposition that *this* mixture is the complete mixture, i.e. that nothing more can be added. That would be like describing the taste of a dish by listing its ingredients; then I must add at the end that these are *all* the ingredients.

In this way we could say the colour too is definitely described when all its ingredients have been specified, of course with the addition that these are all there are.

But how is such an addition to be made? If in the form of a *proposition*, then the incomplete description would already have to be one as well. And if not in the form of a proposition, but by some sort of indication in the first proposition, how can I then bring it about that a second proposition of the same form contradicts the first?

Two elementary propositions can't contradict one another.

What about all assertions which appear to be similar, such as: a point mass can only have *one* velocity at a time, there can only be *one* charge at a point of an electrical field, at one point of a warm surface only *one* temperature at one time, at one point in a boiler only *one* pressure etc.? No one can doubt that these are all self-evident and that their denials are contradictions.

82   This is how it is, what I said in the *Tractatus* doesn't exhaust the grammatical rules for 'and', 'not', 'or' etc.; there are rules for the truth functions which also deal with the elementary part of the proposition.

In which case, propositions turn out to be even more like yard-sticks than I previously believed. – The fact that *one* measurement is right automatically excludes all others. I say automatically: just as all the graduation marks are on *one* rod, the propositions corresponding to the graduation marks similarly belong together, and we can't measure with one of them without simultaneously measuring with all the others. – It isn't a proposition which I put against reality as a yardstick, it's a *system* of propositions [1].

We could now lay down the rule that the same yardstick may only be applied once in one proposition. Or that the parts corresponding to different applications of one yardstick should be collated.

'I haven't got stomach-ache' may be compared to the proposition 'These apples cost nothing'. The point is that they don't cost any money, not that they don't cost any snow or any trouble. The zero is the zero point of *one* scale. And since I can't be given any point on the yardstick without being given the yardstick, I can't be given its zero point either. 'I haven't got a pain' doesn't refer to a condition in which there can be no talk of pain, on the contrary we're talking about pain. The proposition presupposes the capacity for feeling pain, and this can't be a 'physiological capacity' – for otherwise how would we know what it was a capacity for – it's a logical possibility. – I describe my present state by alluding to something that isn't the case. If this allusion is needed for the description (and isn't merely an ornament), there must be something in my present state making it necessary to mention (allude to) this. I compare this state with another, it must therefore be comparable with it. It too must be located in pain-space, even if at a different point. – Otherwise my proposition would mean something like: my present state has *nothing to do* with a painful one; rather in the way I might say the colour of this rose has nothing to do with Caesar's conquest

---

1] cf. Appendix, p. 317.

of Gaul. That is, there's no connection between them. But I mean precisely that there is a connection between my present state and a painful one.

I don't describe a state of affairs by mentioning something that has nothing to do with it and stating it has nothing to do with it. That wouldn't be a negative description.

'The sense consists in the possibility of recognition', but this is a logical possibility. I must be in the space in which what is to be expected is located.

83   The concept of an 'elementary proposition' now loses all of its earlier significance.

The rules for 'and', 'or', 'not' etc., which I represented by means of the T-F notation, are *a part* of the grammar of these words, but not *the whole*.

The concept of independent co-ordinates of description: the propositions joined, e.g., by 'and' are not independent of one another, they form *one* picture and can be tested for their compatibility or incompatibility.

In my old conception of an elementary proposition there was no determination of the value of a co-ordinate; although my remark that a coloured body is in a colour-space, etc., should have put me straight on to this.

A co-ordinate of reality may only be determined *once*.

If I wanted to represent the general standpoint I would say: 'You should not say now one thing and now another about the same matter.' Where the matter in question would be the co-ordinate to which I can give *one* value and no more.

84　The situation is misrepresented if we say we may not ascribe to an object two incompatible attributes. For seen like that, it looks as if in every case we must first investigate whether two determinations are incompatible or not. The truth is, *two* determinations of the same kind (co-ordinate) are impossible.

What we have recognized is simply that we are dealing with yardsticks, and not in some fashion with isolated graduation marks.

In that case every assertion would consist, as it were, in setting a number of scales (yardsticks) and it's *impossible* to set one scale simultaneously at two graduation marks.

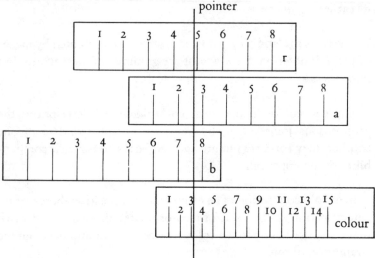

For instance, that would be the claim that a coloured circle, of colour . . . and radius . . . was located at . . . . We might think of signals on a ship: 'Stop', 'Full Speed Ahead', etc.

Incidentally, they don't have to be yardsticks. For you can't call a dial with two signals a yardstick.

85　That every proposition contains time in some way or other appears to us to be accidental, when compared with the fact that the truth-functions can be applied to any proposition.

The latter seems to be connected with their nature as propositions, the former with the nature of the reality we encounter.

True-false, and the truth functions, go with the representation of reality by propositions. If someone said: Very well, how do you know that the whole of reality can be represented by propositions?, the reply is: I only know that it can be represented by propositions in so far as it can be represented by propositions, and to draw a line between a part which can and a part which can't be so represented is something I can't do in language. Language *means* the totality of propositions.

We could say: a proposition is that to which the truth functions may be applied. – The truth functions are essential to *language*.

86 Syntax prohibits a construction such as '*A* is green and *A* is red' (one's first feeling is that it's almost as if this proposition had been done an injustice; as though it had been cheated of its rights as a proposition), but for '*A* is green', the proposition '*A* is red' is not, so to speak, *another* proposition – and that strictly is what the syntax fixes – but another form of the same proposition.

In this way syntax draws together the propositions that make *one* determination.

If I say I did *not* dream last night, I must still know where I would have to look for a dream (i.e. the proposition 'I dreamt', applied to this situation can at most be false, it cannot be nonsense).

I express the present situation by a setting – the negative one – of the signal dial 'dreams – no dreams'. But in spite of its negative setting I must be able to distinguish it from other signal dials. I must know that *this* is the signal dial I have in my hand.

Someone might now ask: Does that imply you have, after all, felt something, so to speak, the hint of a dream, which makes you conscious of the place where a dream would have been? Or if I say 'I haven't got a pain in my arm', does that mean I have a sort of shadowy feeling, indicating the place where the pain would be? No, obviously not.

In what sense does the present, painless, state contain the possibility of pain?

If someone says 'For the word pain to have a meaning, it's necessary that pain should be recognized as such when it occurs', we may reply 'It's no more necessary than that the absence of pain should be recognized as such'.

'Pain' means, so to speak, the whole yardstick and not one of its graduation marks. That it is set at one particular graduation mark can only be expressed by means of a *proposition*.

IX

87   The general proposition 'I see a circle on a red background' appears simply to be a proposition which leaves possibilities open.

A sort of incomplete picture. A portrait in which, e.g. the eyes have not been painted in.

But what would this generality have to do with a totality of objects?

There must be incomplete elementary propositions from whose application the concept of generality derives.

This incomplete picture is, if we compare it with reality, right or wrong: depending on whether or not reality agrees with what can be read off from the picture.

(The theory of probability is connected with the fact that the more general, i.e. the more incomplete, description is more likely to fit the facts than the more complete one.)

Generality in this sense, therefore, enters into the theory of elementary propositions, and not into the theory of truth functions.

88   If I do not completely describe my visual field, but only a part of it, it is obvious that there is, as it were, a gap in the fact. There is obviously something left out.

If I were to paint a picture of this visual image, I would let the canvas show through at certain places. But of course the canvas also has a colour and occupies space. I could not leave *nothing* in the place where something was missing.

My description must therefore necessarily include the whole visual space – and its being coloured, even if it does not specify what the colour is at every place.

That is, it must still say that there is a colour at every place.

Does that mean that the description, in so far as it does not exhaust the space with constants, must exhaust it with variables?

To this one might object that you cannot describe a part of the visual field separated from the whole at all, since it is not even conceivable *on its own.*

But the form (the logical form) of the patch in fact presupposes the whole space. And if you can only describe the whole visual field, then why not only the whole flux of visual experience; for a visual image *can only* exist in time.

89   The question is this: can I leave some determination in a proposition open, *without* at the same time specifying precisely what the possibilities left open are?

Is the case of the general proposition 'A red circle is situated in the square' essentially different from a general assertion of numerical equality, such as 'I have as many jackets as trousers'? and is not this proposition for its part completely on all fours with 'There is *a* number of chairs in this room'? Of course, in everyday life you would not need to develop the disjunction of numbers very far. But however far you go, you must stop somewhere. The question here is always: How do I know such a proposition? Can I ever know it as an endless disjunction?

Even if the first case is construed in such a way that we can establish the position and size of the circle by taking measurements, even then the general proposition cannot be construed as a disjunction (or if so, then just as a finite one). For what then is the criterion for the general proposition, for the circle's being in the square? Either, nothing that has anything to do with a set of positions (or sizes), or else something that deals with a finite number of such positions.

90   Suppose this is my incomplete picture: a red circle stands on a differently coloured background with colour x. It is clear that this picture can be used as a proposition in a positive sense, but also in a negative one. In the negative sense it says what Russell expresses as $\sim (\exists x)\, \varphi x$.

Now is there also in my account an analogue to Russell's

$(\exists x) \sim \varphi x$? That would mean: there is an x of which it is not true that a red circle stands on a background with this colour. Or in other words: there is a colour of the background on which there does not stand a red circle. And in this context that is nonsense!

But how about the proposition 'There is a red ball which is not in the box'? Or 'There is a red circle not in the square'? That is once more a general description of a visual image. Here negation seems to be used in a different way. For it certainly seems as if I could express the proposition 'This circle is not in the square' so that the 'not' is placed *at the front of* the proposition. – But that seems to be an illusion. If you mean by the words 'this circle', 'the circle that I am pointing at', then this case of course falls into line, for then it says 'It is not the case that I am pointing at a circle in the square', but it does not say that I am pointing at a circle outside the square.

This is connected with the fact that it's nonsense to give a circle a name. That is to say, I cannot say 'The circle A is not in the square'. For that would only make sense if it made sense to say 'The circle A is in the square' even when it wasn't.

91   If generality no longer combines with truth functions into a homogeneous whole, then a negation cannot occur *within* the scope of a quantifier.

Of course I could say: 'There is a red circle outside the square' means 'It is not the case that all red circles are in the square'. But what does 'all' refer to here?

'All circles are in the square' can only mean, either 'A certain number of circles are in the square', or 'There is no circle outside'. But the proposition 'There is no circle outside' is once again the negation of a generalization and not the generalization of a negation.

92   If someone confronts us with the fact that language can express everything by means of nouns, adjectives and verbs, we can only say that then it is at any rate necessary to distinguish between entirely different kinds of nouns etc., since different grammatical rules hold for them. This is shown by the fact that it is not permissible to substitute them for one another. This shows that their being nouns is only an external characteristic and that we are in fact dealing with quite different parts of speech. The part of speech is only determined by *all* the grammatical rules which hold for a word, and seen from this point of view our language contains countless different parts of speech.

If you give a body a name then you cannot in the same sense give names to its colour, its shape, its position, its surface. And vice versa.

'*A*' is the name of a shape, not of a cluster of graphite particles.

The different ways names are used correspond exactly to the different uses of the demonstrative pronoun. If I say: 'That is a chair', 'That is the place where it stood', 'That is the colour it had', the word '*that*' is used in that many different ways. (I cannot in the same sense point at a place, a colour, etc.)

93   Imagine two planes, with figures on plane *I* that we wish to map on to plane *II* by some method of projection. It is then open to us to fix on a method of projection (such as orthogonal projection) and then to interpret the images on plane *II* according to this method of mapping. But we could also adopt a quite different procedure: we might for some reason lay down that the images on plane *II* should all be circles no matter what the figures on plane *I* may be. That is, different figures on *I* are mapped on to *II* by different methods of projection. In order in this case to construe the circles in *II* as images, I shall have to say for each circle what

method of projection belongs to it. But the mere fact that a figure is represented on *II* as a circle will say nothing. – It is like this with reality if we map it onto subject-predicate propositions. The fact that we use subject-predicate propositions is only a matter of our notation. The subject-predicate form does not in itself amount to a logical form and is the way of expressing countless fundamentally different logical forms, like the circles on the second plane. The forms of the propositions: 'The plate is round', 'The man is tall', 'The patch is red', have nothing in common.

One difficulty in the Fregean theory is the generality of the words 'concept' and 'object'. For even if you can count tables and tones and vibrations and thoughts, it is difficult to bracket them all together.

Concept and object: but that is subject and predicate. And we have just said that there is not just one logical form which is *the* subject-predicate form.

94 That is to say, it is clear that once you have started doing arithmetic, you don't bother about functions and objects. Indeed, even if you decide only to deal with extensions, strangely enough you still ignore the form of the objects completely.

There is a sense in which an object may not be described.

That is, the description may ascribe to it no property whose absence would reduce the existence of the object itself to nothing, i.e. the description may not express what would be essential for the existence of the object.

95 I see three circles in certain positions; I close my eyes, open them again and see three circles of the same size in different positions. Does it make sense to ask whether these are the same circles and which is which? Surely not. However, *while* I can see

them, I can identify them (even if they move before my eyes, I can identify the circles in the new places with those that were in the earlier ones). If I give them names, close my eyes, open them again and see that the circles are in the same places, I can give to each its name once more. (I could still do this even if they had moved so as to exchange places.) In any case, I always name (directly or indirectly) a *location*.

Would it be possible to discover a *new* colour? (For the man who is colour-blind is of course in the same position as ourselves, his colours form just as complete a system as ours; he does not see gaps where the remaining colours fit in.)
(Comparison with mathematics.)

If someone says that substance is indestructible, then what he is really after is that it is senseless in any context to speak of 'the destruction of a substance' – either to affirm or deny it.

What characterizes propositions of the form 'This is . . .' is only the fact that the reality outside the so-called system of signs somehow enters into the symbol.

96   Russell and Frege construe a concept as a sort of property of a thing. But it is very unnatural to construe the words 'man', 'tree', 'treatise', 'circle' as properties of a substratum.

If a table is painted brown then it's easy to think of the wood as bearer of the property brown, and you can imagine what remains when the colour changes. Even in the case of *one* particular circle which appears now red, now blue. It is thus easy to imagine *what* is red, but difficult to imagine what is circular. What *remains* in this case, if form and colour alter? For position is part of the form, and it is arbitrary for me to lay down that the centre should stay fixed and the only changes in form be changes in the radius.

We must once more adhere to ordinary language and say that a *patch* is circular.

It is clear that the phrase 'bearer of a property' in this context conveys a completely wrong – an impossible – picture. If I have a lump of clay, I can consider it as the bearer of a form, and that, roughly, is where this picture comes from.

'The patch changes its form' and 'The lump of clay changes its form' are fundamentally different forms of proposition.

You can say 'Measure whether *that* is a circle' or 'See whether *that* over there is a hat'. You can also say 'Measure whether *that* is a circle or an ellipse', but not '. . . whether that is a circle or a hat'; not 'See whether that is a hat or red'.

If I point to a curve and say 'That is a circle', then someone can object that if it were not a circle, it would no longer be *that*. That is to say, what I mean by the word 'that' must be independent of what I assert about it.

('Was *that* thunder or gunfire?' Here you could not ask 'Was that a noise?')

97   Roughly speaking, the equation of a circle is the sign for the concept 'circle', if it does not have definite values substituted for the co-ordinates of its centre and for the radius, or even, if these are only given as lying within a certain range. The object falling under the concept is then a circle whose position and size have been fixed.

How are two red circles of the same size distinguished? This question makes it sound as if they were pretty nearly one circle, and only distinguished by a nicety.

In the technique of representation by equations, what is common is expressed by the form of the equation and the difference by the difference in the co-ordinates of the centres.

So it is as if what corresponds with the objects falling under the concept were here the co-ordinates of the centres.

Couldn't you then say, instead of 'This is a circle', 'This point is the centre of a circle'? For, to be the centre of a circle is an external property of the point.

For the number pair that gives the co-ordinates of the centre is in fact not just anything, any more than the centre is: the number pair characterizes just what in the symbol constitutes the 'difference' of the circles.

98 What is necessary to a description that – say – a book is in a certain position? The internal description of the book, i.e. of the concept, and a description of its place which it would be possible to give by giving the co-ordinates of three points. The proposition, 'Such a book is *here*', would then mean that it had *these* three triples of co-ordinates. For the specification of the 'here' must not pre-judge *what* is here.

But doesn't it come to the same thing whether I say '*This* is a book' or 'Here is a book'? The proposition would then amount to saying 'Those are three particular corners of such a book'.

Similarly you can also say 'This circle is the projection of a sphere' or 'This is a man's appearance'.

All that I am saying comes back to this: $F(x)$ must be an *external* description of x.

If in this sense I now say in three-dimensional space 'Here is a circle' and on another occasion 'Here is a sphere', are the two 'here's of the same type? Couldn't both refer to the three co-ordinates of the relevant centre-point? But, the position of the circle in three-dimensional space is not fixed by the co-ordinates of its centre.

Suppose my visual field consisted of two red circles of the same size on a blue background: what occurs twice here and what once? And what does this question mean in any case?

Here we have *one* colour, but *two* positions.

X

99 We can ask whether numbers are essentially concerned with concepts. I believe this amounts to asking whether it makes sense to ascribe a number to objects that haven't been brought under a concept. For instance, does it mean anything to say '*a* and *b* and *c* are three objects'? I think obviously not. Admittedly we have a feeling: Why talk about concepts; the number, of course, depends only on the *extension* of the concept, and once that has been determined, the concept may drop out of the picture. The concept is only a method for determining an extension, but the extension is autonomous and, in its essence, independent of the concept; for it's quite immaterial which concept we have used to determine the extension. That is the argument for the extensional viewpoint. The immediate objection to it is: if a concept is really only an expedient for arriving at an extension, then there is no place for concepts in arithmetic; in that case we must simply divorce a class completely from the concept which happens to be associated with it; but if it isn't like that, then an extension independent of a concept is just a chimera, and in that case it's better not to speak of it at all, but only of the concept.

How about the proposition '$(\exists x,y,z) \cdot aRx \cdot xRy \cdot yRz \cdot zRb . \mathrm{v} . aRy \cdot yRx \cdot xRz \cdot zRb . \mathrm{v} .$ etc.' (all combinations)? Can't I write this in the perfectly intelligible form: '$(\exists 3)_x \cdot aRxRb$' – say 'Three links are inserted between *a* and *b*'? Here we've formed the concept 'link between *a* and *b*'.

(Things between these walls.)

If I have two objects, then I can of course, at least hypothetically, bring them under one umbrella, but what characterizes the extension is still the class, and the concept encompassing it still only a makeshift, a pretext.

Now we could regard the extension of a concept as an object, whose name, like any other, has sense only in the context of a proposition. Admittedly, '*a* and *b* and *c*' has no sense, it isn't a proposition. But then neither is '*a*' a proposition.

$$(E1)_x \varphi x \cdot (E1)_x \psi x \cdot (x) \cdot \sim (\varphi x \cdot \psi x) \ . \ \supset \ . \ (E2)_x \varphi x \cdot \vee \cdot \psi x$$

If φ and ψ here are of the form $x = a \cdot \vee \cdot x = b$, etc., then the whole proposition has become a contrivance for ensuring that we add correctly.

In the symbolism there is an actual correlation, whereas at the level of meaning only the possibility of correlation is at issue.

The problem is: How can we make preparations for the reception of something that may happen to exist?

The axiom of infinity is nonsense if only because the possibility of expressing it would presuppose infinitely many things – i.e. what it is trying to assert. You can say of logical concepts such as that of infinity that their essence implies their existence.

101   $(3)_x \varphi x \cdot (4)_x \psi x \cdot \sim (\exists x) \varphi x \cdot \psi x \cdot \underset{\varphi \psi}{\supset} \cdot (3+4)_x \varphi x \cdot \vee \cdot \psi x$ [1]
This expression isn't equivalent to the substitution rule $3 + 4 = 7$.

We might also ask: Suppose I have four objects satisfying a function, does it always make sense to say that these 4 objects are $2 + 2$ objects? I certainly don't know whether there are functions grouping them into 2 and 2. Does it make sense to say of 4 objects taken at random that they are composed of 2 objects and 2 objects?

1] In the manuscript *W*. precedes this formula by the following definitions:

$$'(\exists x) \ \varphi x \overset{\mathbf{Def}}{=} (\exists 1)_x \ \varphi(x)$$

$$(\exists x, y) \ \varphi x \cdot \varphi y \overset{\mathbf{Def}}{=} (\exists 1 + 1)_x \ \varphi(x)$$

$$(\exists x, y, z) \ \varphi x \cdot \varphi y \cdot \varphi z \overset{\mathbf{Def}}{=} (\exists 1 + 1 + 1)_x \ \varphi(x)$$

etc.

further:

$$(\exists n)_x \ \varphi(x) \cdot \sim (\exists n + 1)_x \ \varphi(x) \overset{\mathbf{Def}}{=} (n)_x \ \varphi x'$$

and then leads into the formula in the text with the words 'Then you can e.g. write: . . .' ['Dann kann man z. B. schreiben: . . .'].

The notation I used above '$(3 + 4)_x$' etc. already contains the assumption that it always makes sense to construe 7 as $3 + 4$, since on the right hand side of the '$\underset{\varphi\psi}{\supset}$' ψ I have so to speak already forgotten where the 3 and 4 have come from. On the other hand: I can surely always distinguish 3 and 4 in the sign $1 + 1 + 1 + 1 + 1 + 1 + 1$.

Perhaps this provides the answer? What would it be like for me to have a sign for 7 in which I couldn't separate 3 and 4? Is such a sign conceivable?

Does it make sense to say a relation holds between 2 objects, although for the rest there is no concept under which they both fall?

102   I want to say numbers can only be defined from propositional *forms*, independently of the question which propositions are true or false.

Only 3 of the objects a, b, c, d have the property φ. That can be expressed through a disjunction. Obviously another case where a numerical assertion doesn't refer to a concept (although you could make it look as though it did by using an ' $=$ '.)

If I say: If there are 4 apples on the table, then there are $2 + 2$ on it, that only means that the 4 apples already contain the possibility of being grouped into two and two, and I needn't wait for them actually to be grouped by a concept. This '*possibility*' refers to the sense, not the truth of a proposition. $2 + 2 = 4$ may mean 'whenever I have four objects, there is the possibility of grouping them into 2 and 2'.

103   How am I to know that |||||||| and |||||||| are the *same* sign? It isn't enough that they look *alike*. For having roughly the same Gestalt can't be what is to constitute the identity of the signs, but just their being the same in number.

If you write (E |||||) etc. ·(E |||||||) etc. · ⊃ . (E |||||||||||||)———
A [1] you may be in doubt as to how I obtained the numerical sign
in the right-hand bracket if I don't know that it is the result of
adding the two left-hand signs. I believe that makes it clear that
this expression is only an application of $5 + 7 = 12$ but doesn't
represent this equation itself.

If we ask: But what then does '$5 + 7 = 12$' mean – what kind
of significance or point is left for this expression – the answer is, this
equation is a rule for signs which specifies which sign is the result
of applying a particular operation (addition) to two other particular
signs. The content of $5 + 7 = 12$ (supposing someone didn't know
it) is precisely what children find difficult when they are learning
this proposition in arithmetic lessons.

We can completely disregard the special structure of the proposition A and pay attention solely to the relation, the connection,
between the numerical signs in it. This shows that the relation
holds independently of the proposition – i.e. of the other features
of its structure which make it a tautology.

For if I look at it as a tautology I merely perceive features of its
structure and can now perceive the addition theorem *in* them,
while disregarding other characteristics that are essential to it as
a proposition.

The addition theorem is in this way to be recognized in it (among
other places), not *by means of* it.

This thought would of course be nonsense if it were a question
here of the *sense* of a proposition, and not of the way the structure
of a tautology functions.

1] In the manuscript Wittgenstein first wrote 'the proposition A' as follows:
'$(\exists 2x)\ \varphi x \cdot (\exists 2x) x \cdot \mathrm{Ind}..\supset. (\exists 4x)\ \varphi x v\ \psi x$ – – A. This proposition
doesn't – of course – say that $2 + 2 = 4$ but that the expression is a tautology
shows it. φ and ψ must be disjoint variables.'
  He also writes in this connection: 'For isn't '$(\exists 2x)\ \varphi x \cdot (\exists 2x)\psi x \cdot$ Ind.
$(\exists 4x)\ \varphi x v\ \psi x$' an application of $2 + 2 = 4$, *just as much as* '$(E2x)\ \varphi x$ etc., etc.'?
  By this stage he is using '$(E2x)\ \varphi x$' in contrast with '$(\exists 2x)\ \varphi x$' to mean
'There are exactly two φs', as opposed to 'There are at least two φs'.

104   You could reply: what I perceive in the sign A and call the relation between the numerical signs is once more only the bringing together of extensions of concepts: I combine the first five strokes of the right-hand bracket, which stand in 1–1 correspondence with the five in one of the left-hand brackets, with the remaining 7 strokes, which stand in 1–1 correspondence with the seven in the other left-hand bracket, to make 12 strokes which do one or the other. But even if I followed this train of thought, the fundamental insight would still remain, that the 5 strokes and the 7 combine *precisely to make 12* (and so for example to make the same structure as do 4 and 4 and 4). – It is always only insight into the internal relations of the structures and not some proposition or other or some logical consideration which tells us this. And, as far as this insight is concerned, everything in the tautology apart from the numerical structures is mere decoration; they are all that matters for the arithmetical proposition. (Everything else belongs to the *application* of the arithmetical proposition.)

Thus what I want to say is: it isn't what occasions our combining 5 and 7 that belongs to arithmetic, but the process of doing so and its outcome.

Suppose I wrote out the proposition A but put the wrong number of strokes in the right-hand bracket, then you would and could only come upon this mistake by comparing the structures, not by applying theorems of logic.

If asked how do you know that this number of strokes in the right-hand bracket is correct, I can only justify it by a comparison of the structures.

In this way it would turn out that what Frege called the 'ginger-snap standpoint' in arithmetic could yet have some justification.

105   And now – I believe – the relation between the extensional conception of classes and the concept of a number as a feature of a

logical structure is clear: an extension is a characteristic of the sense of a proposition.

106   Now if the transition in A were the only application of this arithmetical schema, wouldn't it then be possible or necessary to replace it or define it by the tautology?

That is to say, what would it be like for A to be the most general form of the application of the arithmetical schema?

If A were the only – and therefore *essentially* the only – application of the schema, then in the very nature of the case the schema couldn't mean anything other than just the tautology.

Or: the schema itself must then be the tautology and the tautology nothing other than the schema.

In that case, you also could no longer say A was an application of the schema – A would be the schema, only not as it were the implement on its own, but the implement with its handle, without which it is after all useless.

What A contains apart from the schema can then only be what is necessary in order to apply it.

But nothing at all is necessary, since we understand and apply the propositions of arithmetic perfectly well without adding anything whatever to them.

But forming a tautology is especially out of place here, as we can see perfectly well from the tautology itself, since otherwise in order to recognise it as a tautology we should have to recognise yet another one as a tautology and so on [1].

1] (Later marginal note): That we can make the calculus with strokes and without tautologies shows we do not need tautologies for it. Everything that does not belong to the number calculus is mere decoration.

107   Arithmetical propositions, like the multiplication table and things of that kind, or again like definitions which do not have whole propositions standing on both sides, are used in *application* to propositions. And anyhow I certainly can't apply them to anything else. (Therefore I don't first need some description of their application.)

No investigation of concepts, only direct insight can tell us [1] that $3 + 2 = 5$.

That is what makes us rebel against the idea that A could be the proposition $3 + 2 = 5$. For what enables us to tell that this expression is a tautology cannot itself be the result of an examination of concepts but must be immediately visible.

And if we say numbers are structures we mean that they must always be of a kind with what we use to represent them.

I mean: numbers are what I represent in my language by number schemata.

That is to say, I take (so to speak) the number schemata of the language as what I know, and say numbers are what these represent [2].

This is what I once meant when I said, it is with the calculus [system of calculation] that numbers enter into logic.

108   What I said earlier about the nature of arithmetical equations and about an equation's not being replaceable by a tautology explains – I believe – what Kant means when he insists that $7 + 5 = 12$ is not an analytic proposition, but synthetic *a priori*.

1] (Later correction): . . . only direct insight into the number calculus can tell us . . . (with a mark of dissatisfaction under the words 'direct insight').
2] (Later marginal note): Instead of a question of the definition of number, it's only a question of the grammar of numerals.

Am I using the same numbers when I count the horses in a stall and when I count the different species of animal in the stall? When I count the strokes in a line and the kinds of group (as defined by the different number of strokes)?

Whether they are cardinal numbers in the same sense depends on whether the same syntactical rules hold for them.

(It is conceivable that there should be no man in a room, but not that there should be a man of *no* race in it.)

Arithmetic is the grammar of numbers. Kinds of number can only be distinguished by the arithmetical rules relating to them.

109   One always has an aversion to giving arithmetic a foundation by saying something about its application. It appears firmly enough grounded in itself. And that of course derives from the fact that arithmetic is its own application.

Arithmetic doesn't talk about numbers, it works with numbers.

The calculus presupposes the calculus.

Aren't the numbers a logical peculiarity of space and time?

The calculus itself exists only in space and time.

Every mathematical calculation is an application of itself and only as such does it have a sense. *That* is why it isn't necessary to speak about the general form of logical operation when giving a foundation to arithmetic.

A cardinal number is applicable to the subject-predicate form, but not to every variety of this form. And the extent to which it is applicable simply characterizes the subject-predicate form.

On the one hand it seems to me that you can develop arithmetic completely autonomously and its application takes care of itself, since wherever it's applicable we may also apply it. On the other hand a nebulous introduction of the concept of number by means of the general form of operation – such as I gave – can't be what's needed.

You could say arithmetic is a kind of geometry; i.e. what in geometry are constructions on paper, in arithmetic are calculations (on paper). – You could say it is a more general kind of geometry.

And can't I say that in this sense chess (or any other game) is also a kind of geometry.
But in that case it must be possible to work out an *application* of chess that is completely analogous to that of arithmetic.

You could say: Why bother to limit the application of arithmetic, that takes care of itself. (I can make a knife without bothering which sorts of material it will cut: that will show soon enough.)
What speaks against our demarcating a region of application is the feeling that we can understand arithmetic without having any such region in mind. Or put it like this: instinct rebels against anything that isn't restricted to an analysis of the thoughts already before us.

110
$$2+3+4 = 2+4+3 = 4+3+2$$
$$\underbrace{}_{5}\overset{}{\diagup}_{9} \quad \underbrace{}_{6}\overset{}{\diagup}_{9} \quad \underbrace{}_{7}\overset{}{\diagup}_{9}$$

'Look, it always turns out the same.' Seen like that, we have performed an experiment. We have applied the rules of one-and-one and from those you can't tell straight off that they lead to the same result in the three cases.
It's as if we're surprised that the numerals cut adrift from their definitions function so unerringly. Or rather: that the rules for the numerals work so unerringly (when they are not under the supervision of the definitions).

This is connected (oddly enough) with the internal consistency of geometry.

For, you can say the rules for the numerals always presuppose the definitions. But in what sense? What does it mean to say one sign presupposes another that strictly speaking isn't there at all? It presupposes its possibility; its possibility in sign-space (in grammatical space).

It's always a question of whether and how it's possible to represent the most general form of the application of arithmetic. And here the strange thing is that in a certain sense it doesn't seem to be needed. And if in fact it isn't needed then it's also impossible.

The general form of its application seems to be represented by the fact that *nothing* is said about it. (And if that's a possible representation, then it is also *the* right one.)

What is characteristic of a statement of number is that you may replace one number by any other and the proposition must always still be significant; and so the infinite formal series of propositions.

111   The point of the remark that arithmetic is a kind of geometry is simply that arithmetical constructions are autonomous like geometrical ones, and hence so to speak themselves guarantee their applicability.

For it must be possible to say of geometry, too, that it is its own application.

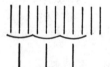 That is an arithmetical construction, and in a *somewhat* extended sense also a geometrical one.

Suppose I wish to use this calculation to solve the following problem: if I have 11 apples and want to share them among some people in such a way that each is given 3 apples, how many people can there be? The calculation supplies me with the answer 3. Now, suppose I were to go through the whole process of sharing and at the end 4 people each had 3 apples in their hands. Would I then say that the computation gave a wrong result? Of course not. And that of course means only that the computation was not an experiment.

It might look as though the mathematical computation entitled us to make a prediction – say, that I could give 3 people their share and there will be two apples left over. But that isn't so. What justifies us in making this prediction is an hypothesis of physics, which lies outside the calculation. The calculation is only a study of logical forms, of structures, and of itself can't yield anything new.

112   Different as strokes and court cases are, you can still use strokes to represent court cases on a calendar. And you can count the former instead of the latter.

This isn't so, if, say, I want to count hat-sizes. It would be unnatural to represent three hat-sizes by three strokes. Just as if I were to represent a measurement, 3 ft, by 3 strokes. You can certainly do so, but then '|||' represents in a different way.

If 3 strokes on paper are the sign for the number 3, then you can say the number 3 is to be applied in the way in which the 3 strokes can be applied.

Of what 3 strokes are a picture, of that they can be used as a picture.

113   The natural numbers are a form given in reality through things, as the rational numbers are through extensions etc. I mean, by actual forms. In the same way, the complex numbers are given by actual manifolds. (The *symbols* are actual.)

What distinguishes a statement of number about the extension of a concept from one about the range of a variable? The first is a proposition, the second not. For the statement of number about a variable can be derived from the variable itself. (It must show itself.)

But can't I specify a variable by saying that its values are to be all objects satisfying a certain material function? In that case the variable is not a form! And then the sense of one proposition depends on whether another is true or false.

A statement of number about a variable consists in a transformation of the variable rendering the number of its values visible.

114 What kind of proposition is 'There is a prime number between 5 and 8'? I would say 'That shows itself'. And that's correct, but can't you draw attention to this internal state of affairs? You could surely say: Search the interval between 10 and 20 for prime numbers. How many are there? Wouldn't that be a straightforward problem? And how would its result be correctly expressed or represented? What does the proposition 'There are 4 primes between 10 and 20' mean?

This proposition seems to draw our attention to a particular aspect of the matter.

If I ask someone, 'How many primes are there between 10 and 20?', he may reply, 'I don't know straight off, but I can work it out any time you like.' For it's as if there were somewhere where it was already written out.

If you want to know what a proposition means, you can always ask 'How do I know that?' Do I know that there are 6 permutations of 3 elements in the same way in which I know there are 6 people in this room? No. Therefore the first proposition is of a different *kind* from the second.

Another equally useful question is 'How would this proposition actually be used in practice?'; and there the proposition from the theory of combinations is of course used as a law of inference in the transition from one proposition to another, each of which describes a reality, not a *possibility*.

You can, I think, say in general that the use of apparent propositions about possibilities – and impossibilities – is always in the passage from one actual proposition to another.

Thus I can, e.g., infer from the proposition 'I label 7 boxes with permutations of *a, b, c*' that at least *one* of the labels is repeated. – And from the proposition 'I distribute 5 spoons among 4 cups' it follows that one cup gets 2 spoons, etc.

If someone disagrees with us about the number of men in this room, saying there are 7, while we can only see 6, we can understand him even though we disagree with him. But if he says that for him there are 5 pure colours, in that case we don't understand him, or must suppose we completely misunderstand one another. This number is demarcated in dictionaries and grammars and not within language.

XI

115 A statement of number doesn't always contain something general or indefinite: 'The interval AB is divided into two (3, 4 etc.) equal parts.'

There doesn't even need to be a certain element of generality in a statement of number. Suppose, e.g., I say 'I see three equal circles equidistant from one another'.

If I give a correct description of a visual field in which three red circles stand on a blue ground, it surely won't take the form of saying '$(\exists x,y,z)$: x is circular and red and y is circular and red, etc. etc.'

You might of course write it like this: there are 3 circles with the property of being red. But at this point the difference emerges between improper objects – colour patches in a visual field, sounds, etc. etc. – and the elements of knowledge, the genuine objects.

It is plain that the proposition about the three circles isn't general or indefinite in the way a proposition of the form $(\exists x,y,z) \cdot \varphi x \cdot \varphi y \cdot \varphi z$ is. That is, in such a case, you may say: Certainly I know that three things have the property φ, but I don't know which; and you can't say this in the case of three circles.

'There are now 3 red circles of such and such a size and in such and such a place in my visual field' determines the facts completely and it would be nonsense to say I don't know which circles they are.

Think of such 'objects' as: a flash of lightning, the simultaneous occurrence of two events, the point at which a line cuts a circle, etc.; the three circles in the visual field are an example for all these cases.

You can of course treat the subject-predicate form (or, what comes to the same thing, the argument-function form) as a norm of representation, and then it is admittedly important and characteristic that whenever we use numbers, the number may be represented as the property of a predicate. Only we must be clear about the fact that now we are not dealing with objects and concepts as the results of an analysis, but with moulds into which we have squeezed the proposition. And of course it's significant that it can be fitted into this mould. But squeezing something into a mould is the opposite of analysis. (If you want to study the natural growth of an apple tree, you don't look at an espalier tree – except to see how *this* tree reacts to *this* pressure.)

That implies the Fregean theory of number would be applicable provided we were not intending to give an analysis of propositions. This theory explains the concept of number for the idioms of everyday speech. Of course, Frege would have said (I remember a conversation we had) that the simultaneous occurrence of an eclipse of the moon and a court case was an object. And what's wrong with that? Only that we in that case use the word 'object' ambiguously, and so throw the results of the analysis into disarray.

If I say, 'There are 4 men in this room', then at any rate a disjunction seems to be involved, since it isn't said *which* men. But this is quite inessential. We could imagine all men to be indistinguishable from one another apart from their location (so that it would be a question of humanity at a particular place), and in that case all indefiniteness would vanish.

116   If I am right, there is no such concept as 'pure colour'; the proposition '*A* has a pure colour' simply means '*A* is red, or yellow, or green, or blue'. 'This hat belongs to either *A* or *B* or *C*' isn't the same proposition as 'This hat belongs to someone in this room', even if as a matter of fact only *A*, *B*, and *C* are in the room, since that needs saying. – 'There are two pure colours on this surface', *means* 'On this surface there is red and yellow, or red and blue, or red and green etc.'

Even if I may not say 'There are four pure colours', still the pure colours and the number 4 are somehow connected, and that must come out in some way or other, e.g. if I say, 'I can see 4 colours on this surface: yellow, blue, red and green.'

The situation must be exactly similar for permutations. The permutations (without repetition) of *AB are AB, BA*. They are not the extension of a concept: they alone are the concept. But in that case you cannot say of these that they are two. And yet apparently we do just that in the theory of combinations. It strikes me as a question of a correlation similar to the one between algebra and inductions in arithmetic. Or is the connection the same as that between geometry and arithmetic? The proposition that there are two permutations of *AB* is in fact completely on all fours with the proposition that a line meets a circle in 2 points. Or, that a quadratic equation has two roots.

If we say that *AB* admits of two permutations, it sounds as though we had made a *general* assertion, analogous with 'There are two men in the room', in which nothing further is said or need be known about the men. But this isn't so in the *AB* case. I cannot give a more general description of *AB, BA*, and so the proposition that two permutations are possible cannot say any less than that the permutations *AB, BA* are possible. To say that 6 permutations of 3 elements are possible cannot say less, i.e. anything more general, than is shown by the schema:

ABC For it's *impossible* to know the number of possible per-
ACB mutations without knowing which they are. And if this
BAC weren't so, the theory of combinations wouldn't be
BCA capable of arriving at its general formulae. The law
CAB which we see in the formulation of the permutations is
CBA represented by the equation $p = n!$ In the same sense, I
   believe, as that in which a circle is given by its equation.

– Of course, I can correlate the number 2 with the permutations *AB, BA*, just as I can 6 with the complete set of permutations of *A, B, C*, but this doesn't give me the theorem of combination theory – What I see in *AB*, *BA* is an internal relation which therefore cannot be described. – That is, *what* cannot be described is that which makes this class of permutations complete. – I can only count what is actually there, not possibilities. But I can, e.g., work out how many rows a man must write if in each row he puts a permutation of 3 elements and goes on until he can't go any further without repetition. And this means he needs 6 rows to write down the permutations *ABC*, *ACB*, etc. since these just are '*the* permutations of A, B, C'. But it makes no sense to say that these are all the permutations of A, B, C.

117 We could imagine a combination computer exactly like the Russian abacus.

It is clear that there is a mathematical question: 'How many permutations of – say – 4 elements are there?', a question of precisely the same kind as 'What is 25×18?'. For in both cases there is a general method of solution.

But still it is only with respect to this method that this question exists.

The proposition that there are 6 permutations of 3 elements is identical with the permutation schema, and thus there isn't here a proposition, 'There are 7 permutations of 3 elements', for no such schema corresponds to it.

You may also say that the proposition 'There are 6 permutations of 3 elements' is related to the proposition 'There are 6 people in this room' in precisely the same way as is '$3 + 3 = 6$', which you could also cast in the form 'There are 6 units in $3 + 3$'. And just as in the one case I can count the rows in the permutation schema, so in the other I can count the strokes in $\substack{||| \\ |||}$.

Just as I can prove that $4 \times 3 = 12$ by means of the schema: o o o

o o o

o o o

o o o

I can also prove $3! = 6$ by means of the permutation schema.

118 What is meant by saying I have as many spoons as *can* be put in 1–1 correspondence with a dozen bowls?

Either this proposition assumes I have 12 spoons, in which case I can't say that they can be correlated with the 12 bowls, since the opposite would be impossible; or else it doesn't assume I have 12 spoons, in which case it says I *can* have 12 spoons, and that's self-evident and once more cannot be said.

You could also ask: does this proposition say any *less* than that I have 12 spoons? Does it say something which only together with another proposition implies that I have 12 spoons? If p follows q alone, then q already says p. An apparent process of thought, making the transition, doesn't come in.

The symbol for a class is a list.

Can I know there are as many apples as pears on this plate, without knowing how many? And what is meant by not knowing how many? And how can I find out how many? Surely by counting. It is obvious that you can discover that there are the same number by correlation, without counting the classes.

In Russell's theory only an *actual* correlation can show the 'similarity' of two classes. Not the *possibility* of correlation, for this consists precisely in the numerical equality. Indeed, the possibility must be an *internal* relation between the extensions of the concepts, but this internal relation is only given through the equality of the 2 numbers.

A cardinal number is an internal property of a list.

119 We divide the evidence for the occurrence of a physical event according to the various kinds of such evidence, into the heard, seen, measured etc., and see that in each of these taken singly there is a formal element of order, which we can call space.

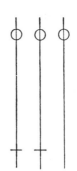

What sort of an *impossibility* is the impossibility, e.g., of a 1–1 correlation between 3 circles and 2 crosses? We could also ask – and it would obviously be a question of the same sort – what sort of an impossibility is the impossibility of making a correlation by drawing parallel lines, if the arrangement is the given one?

That a 1–1 correlation is possible is shown in that a significant proposition – true or false – asserts that it obtains. And that the correlation discussed above is not possible is shown by the fact that we cannot describe it.

We can say that there are 2 circles in this square, even if in reality there are 3, and this proposition is simply false. But I cannot say that this group of circles is comprised of 2 circles, and just as little that it's comprised of 3 circles, since I should then be ascribing an *internal* property.

It is nonsense to say of an extension that it has such and such a number, since the number is an *internal* property of the extension. But you can ascribe a number to the concept that collects the extension (just as you can say that this extension satisfies the concept).

120   It is remarkable that in the case of a tautology or contradiction you actually could speak of sense and reference in Frege's sense.

If we call its property of being a tautology the reference of a tautology, then we may call the way in which the tautology comes about here the sense of the tautology. And so for contradiction.

If, as Ramsey proposed, the sign '=' were explained by saying that $x = x$ is a tautology, and $x = y$ a contradiction, then we may say that the tautology and the contradiction have no 'sense' here.

So, if a tautology shows something through the fact that just *this* sense gives *this* reference, then a tautology à la Ramsey shows nothing, since it is a tautology by definition.

What then is the relation between the sign '$\overset{\text{Def}}{=}$' and the equals sign explained by means of tautology and contradiction?

Is '$p \cdot q = \sim (\sim p \vee \sim q)$' a tautology for the latter? You could say '$p \cdot q = p \cdot q$' is taut., and since according to the definition you may substitute '$\sim (\sim p \vee \sim q)$' for one of the signs '$p \cdot q$', the previous expression is also a tautology.

Hence you should not write the explanation of the equals sign thus:

$$x = x \text{ is taut.}$$
$$x = y \text{ is contra.}$$

but must say: if, and *only* if, 'x' and 'y' have the same reference according to the sign-rules, then '$x = y$' is taut: if 'x' and 'y' do not have the same reference according to the sign-rules, then '$x = y$' is contra. In that case it would be to the point to write the equals sign thus defined differently, to distinguish it from '$x = y$', which represents a rule for signs and says that we may substitute y for x. That is just what I cannot gather from the sign as explained above, but only from the fact that it is a tautology, but I don't know that either unless I already know the rules of substitution.

It seems to me that you may compare mathematical equations only with significant propositions, not with tautologies. For an equation contains precisely this assertoric element – the equals sign – which is not designed for showing something. Since whatever shows itself, shows itself without the equals sign. The equals sign doesn't correspond to the '$. \supset .$' in '$p \cdot (p \supset q). \supset .q$' since the '$. \supset .$' is only *one* element among others which go to make up the tautology. It doesn't drop out of its context, but belongs to the proposition, in the same way that the '$\cdot$' or '$\supset$' do. But the '$=$' is a copula, which alone makes the equation into something propositional. A tautology shows something, an equation shows nothing: rather, it indicates that its sides show something.

121   An equation is a rule of syntax.

Doesn't that explain why we cannot have questions in mathematics that are in principle unanswerable? For if the rules of syntax cannot be grasped, they're of no use at all. And equally, it explains why an infinity that transcends our powers of comprehension cannot enter into these rules. And it also makes intelligible the attempts of the formalists to see mathematics as a game with signs.

You may certainly construe sign-rules, for example definitions, as propositions about signs, but you don't *have to* treat them as propositions at all. They belong to the devices of language. Devices of a different kind from the propositions of language.

Ramsey's theory of identity makes the mistake that would be made by someone who said that you could use a painting as a mirror as well, even if only for a single posture. If we say this, we overlook that what is essential to a mirror is precisely that you can infer from it the posture of a body in front of it, whereas in the case of the painting you have to know that the postures tally before you can construe the picture as a mirror image.

Weyl's [1] 'heterological' paradox:
$$\sim \varphi\,('\varphi') \overset{\text{Def}}{=} '\varphi' \text{ is heterological} \overset{\text{Def}}{=} F\,('\varphi')$$
$$F('F') = \,\sim F('F') = \,\sim [\,\sim(\,\sim\hat{\varphi}('\hat{\varphi}'))\,('\sim\hat{\varphi}('\hat{\varphi}')')]$$

122   We may imagine a mathematical proposition as a creature which itself knows whether it is true or false. (In contrast with genuine propositions.)

A mathematical proposition itself knows that it is true or that it

---

1] Grelling's.

is false. If it is about all the numbers, it must also survey all the numbers.

Its truth or falsity must be contained in it, as is its sense.

It's as though the generality of such a proposition as '$(n) \sim$ Chr n' were only a pointer to the genuine, actual, mathematical generality of a proposition [1]. As though it were only a description of the generality, not the generality itself. As if the proposition formed a sign only in a purely external way and you still needed to give the sign a sense from within.

We feel the generality possessed by the mathematical assertion to be different from the generality of the proposition proved.

1] 'Chromatic number': a fictitious designation of a number that is perhaps not given by any law or calculation. In the manuscript, W. wrote, among other things:

You could ask: What does $(x)2x = x + x$ say? It says that all equations of the form $2x = x + x$ are correct. But does that mean anything? May one say: Yes, I see that all equations of this form are correct, so now I may write '$(x)2x = x + x$'?

Its meaning must derive from its proof. What the proof proves – that is the meaning of the proposition (neither more nor less) . . .

An algebraic proof is the general form of a proof which can be *applied* to any number. If, referring to this proof, I say I have demonstrated that there is no chromatic number, then this proposition obviously says something other than '$\sim (\exists n) \cdot$ Chr n.'

And in that case what does the proposition '*There is* a chromatic number' say? It ought, surely, to say the opposite of what was demonstrated by the proof. But then, it doesn't say '$(\exists n) \cdot$ Chr n.'

If you make the wrong transition from the variable proposition to the general proposition (in the way Russell and Whitehead said was permissible), then the proof looks as if it's only a source for knowledge of the general proposition, instead of an analysis of its actual sense.

How is a mathematical problem related to its solution?

We could say: a mathematical proposition is an allusion to a proof.

A generalization cannot be both empirical and provable.

If a proposition is to have a definite sense (and it's nonsense otherwise), it must comprehend – survey – its sense completely; a generalization only makes sense if it – i.e. all values of its variables – is completely determined.

Then you could also say: perhaps the proposition is correct, even though it can't be proved.

If this proof yields the proposition $Fa \neq fa$, what in this case is its opposite? (Surely – in our sense – not $Fa = fa$).

Indeed, I have here only a form that I have proved possesses certain properties. On the strength of these properties, I can use it now in certain ways, viz. to show in any particular case that the number in question isn't chromatic. I can, of course, negate that form, but that doesn't give me the sense I want, and all I can do now is to deny the proof. But what does that mean? It doesn't of course, mean that It was wrongly – fallaciously – executed, but that it can't be carried out. That then means: the inequality doesn't derive from the forms in question; the forms do not exclude the inequality. But then, what else does? Does the development depend then on something further? That is, can the case arise in which the equation doesn't hold, and the form doesn't exclude it?

XII

123   If, by making a series of tests, I advance along an endless
stretch, why should it be any different in the case of an infinite one?
And in that case of course, I can never get to the end.

But if I only advance along the infinite stretch step by step, then
I can't grasp the infinite stretch at all.

So I grasp it in a different way; and if I have grasped it, then a
proposition about it can only be verified in the way in which the
proposition has taken it.

So now it can't be verified by putative endless striding, since
even such striding wouldn't reach a goal, since of course the
proposition can outstrip our stride just as endlessly as before.
No: it can only be verified by *one* stride, just as we can only grasp
the totality of numbers at *one* stroke.

We may also say: there is no path to infinity, *not even an endless
one*.

The situation would be something like this: We have an infinitely long row of trees, and so as to inspect them, I make a path
beside them. All right, the path must be endless. But if it is endless,
then that means precisely that you can't walk to the end of it. That
is, it does *not* put me in a position to survey the row. (*Ex hypothesi*
not.)

That is to say, the endless path doesn't have an end 'infinitely
far away', it has no end.

124   It isn't just impossible 'for us men' to run through the natural
numbers one by one; it's *impossible*, it means nothing.

Nor can you say, 'A proposition cannot deal with all the numbers one by one, so it has to deal with them by means of the concept of number', as if this were a *pis aller*: 'Because we can't do it *like this*, we have to do it another way.' But it's not like that: of course it's possible to deal with the numbers one by one, but that *doesn't* lead to the totality. For the totality is only given as a concept.

If it's objected that 'if I run through the number series I either eventually come to the number with the required property, or I never do', we need only reply that it makes no sense to say that you *eventually* come to the number and *just as little* that you *never* do. Certainly it's correct to say 101 is or is not the number in question. But you can't talk about *all* numbers, because there's no such thing as *all* numbers.

125   Can you say you couldn't foresee that $6 - 4$ would be precisely 2, but only see it when you get there?

That, in the case of the logical concept $(1, \xi, \xi + 1)$, the existence of its objects is already given with the concept, of itself shows that it determines them.

Besides, it's quite clear that every number has its own irreducible individuality. And if I want to prove that a number has a certain property, in one way or another I must always bring in the number itself.

In this sense you might say that the properties of a particular number cannot be *foreseen*. You can only see them when you've got there.
Someone may say: Can't I prove something about the number 3^{10}, even though I can't write it down? Well, 3^{10} already is the number, only written in a different way.

What is fundamental is simply the repetition of an operation. Each stage of the repetition has its own individuality.
But it isn't as if I use the operation to move from one individual to another so that the operation would be the means for getting from one to the other – like a vehicle stopping at every number

which we can then study: no, applying the operation $+ 1$ three times yields and *is* the number 3.

An 'infinitely complicated law' means no law at all. How are you to know it's infinitely complicated? Only by there being as it were infinitely many approximations to the law. But doesn't that imply that they in fact *approach* a limit? Or could the infinitely many descriptions of intervals of the prime number series be called such approximations to a law? No, since no description of a finite interval takes us any nearer the goal of a complete description.

Then how would an infinitely complicated law in this sense differ from no law at all?

In that case, the law would, at best, run 'Everything is as it is'.

126   Yet it still looks now as if the quantifiers make no sense for numbers. I mean: you can't say '$(n) \cdot \varphi n$', precisely because 'all natural numbers' isn't a bounded concept. But then neither should one say a general proposition follows from a proposition about the nature of number.

But in that case it seems to me that we can't use generality – all, etc. – in mathematics at all. There's no such thing as 'all numbers', simply because there are infinitely many. And because it isn't a question here of the amorphous 'all', such as occurs in 'All the apples are ripe', where the set is given by an external description: it's a question of a collection of structures, which must be given precisely as such.

It's, so to speak, no business of logic how many apples there are when we talk of all the apples. Whereas it's different in the case of the numbers: there, it has an individual responsibility for each one of them.

127   What is the meaning of such a mathematical proposition as '$(\exists n) \cdot 4 + n = 7$'? It might be a disjunction – $4 + 0 = 7 \cdot v \cdot 4 + 1 = 7 \cdot v \cdot 4 + 2 = 7 \cdot v \cdot$ etc. *ad inf.* But what does that mean? I can

understand a proposition with a beginning and an end. But can one also understand a proposition with no end? [1]

I also find it intelligible that one can give an infinite rule by means of which you may form infinitely many finite propositions. But what does an endless proposition mean?

If no finite product makes a proposition true, that means *no* product makes it true. And so it *isn't* a logical product.

128 But then can't I say of an equation 'I know it doesn't hold for some substitution – I've forgotten now which; but whether it doesn't hold in general, I don't know'? Doesn't that make good sense, and isn't it compatible with the generality of the inequality?

Is the reply: 'If you know that the inequality holds for some substitution, that can never mean "for some (arbitrary) member of the infinite number series", but I always know too that this number lies between 1 and 10^7, or within some such limits'?

Can I know that *a* number satisfies the equation without a finite section of the infinite series being marked out as one within which it occurs? No.

'Can God know all the places of the expansion of π?' would have been a good question for the schoolmen to ask. In all such cases the answer runs, 'The question is senseless.'

1] (Later marginal note): Is '$(\exists n)\ 4 + n = 7$' . . . α a disjunction? No, since a disjunction wouldn't have the sign 'etc. *ad inf.*' at the end but a term of the form $4 + x$.

α is neither the same sort of proposition as 'There are men in this house', nor as 'There's a colour that goes well with this', nor as 'There are problems I find too difficult for me', nor as 'There's a time of day when I like to go for a walk'.

'No degrees of brightness below this one hurt my eyes': that means, I have observed that my previous experiences correspond to a formal law.

129 A proposition about all propositions, or all functions, is *a priori* an impossibility: what such a proposition is intended to express would have to be shown by an induction. (For instance, that *all* propositions $\sim^{2n}p$ say the same.) [1]

This induction isn't itself a proposition, and that excludes there being any vicious circle.

What do we want to differentiate propositions from when we form the concept 'proposition'?

Isn't it the case that we can only give an external description of propositions in general?

Equally, if we ask: Is there a general form of law? As opposed to what? Laws must of course fill the whole of logical space, and so I can no longer mark them off.

Generality in arithmetic is indicated by an induction.
An induction is the expression for arithmetical generality.

Suppose one of the rules of a game ran 'Write down a fraction between 0 and 1'. Wouldn't we understand it? Do we need any limits here? And what about the rule 'Write down a number greater than 100'? Both seem thoroughly intelligible.

I have always said you can't speak of *all* numbers, because there's no such thing as 'all numbers'. But that's only the expression of a feeling. Strictly, one should say, . . . 'In arithmetic we never *are* talking about *all* numbers, and if someone nevertheless does speak in that way, then he so to speak invents something – nonsensical

---

1] In the manuscript: 'that *all* propositions, $\sim p$, $\sim \sim \sim p$, $\sim \sim \sim \sim \sim p$, etc. say the same.'

– to supplement the arithmetical facts.' (Anything invented as a supplement to *logic* must of course be nonsense.)

130 It is difficult to extricate yourself completely from the extensional viewpoint: You keep thinking 'Yes, but there must still be an internal relation between $x^3 + y^3$ and z^3, since the extension, if only I knew it, would have to show the result of such a relation.' Or perhaps: 'It must surely be either *essential* to *all n* to have the property or not, even if I can't know it.'

If I write '$(\exists x) \cdot x^2 = 2x$', and don't construe the '$(\exists x)$' extensionally, it can only mean: 'If I apply the rules for solving such an equation, I arrive at a particular number, in contrast with the cases in which I arrive at an identity or a prohibited equation.'

The defect (circle) in Dedekind's explanation of the concept of infinity lies in its application of the concept 'all' in the formal implication that holds independently – if one may put it like this – of the question whether a finite or an infinite number of objects falls under its concepts. The explanation simply says: if the one holds of an object, so does the other. It does not consider the totality of objects at all, it only says something about the object at the moment in front of it, and *its application* is finite or infinite as the case may be.

But how are we to know such a proposition? – How is it verified? What really corresponds to what we mean isn't a proposition at all, it's the *inference* from φx to ψx, if this inference is permitted – but the inference isn't expressed by a proposition.

What does it mean to say a line can be extended indefinitely? Isn't this a case of an 'and so on *ad inf.*' that is quite different from that in mathematical induction? According to what's gone before, the expression for the possibility of extending it further would exist in the sense of a description of the extended line or of the act of extending it. Now at first this doesn't seem to be connected with numbers at all. I can imagine the pencil drawing the line going on moving and keeping on for ever. But is it also conceivable that there should be no possibility of accompanying this process with a countable process? I think not.

131   The generality of a Euclidean proof. We say, the demonstration is carried out for *one* triangle, but the proof holds for all triangles – or for an arbitrary triangle. First, it's strange that what holds for one triangle should therefore hold for every other. It wouldn't be possible for a doctor to examine *one* man and then conclude that what he had found in his case must also be true of every other. And if I now measure the angles of a triangle and add them, I can't in fact conclude that the sum of the angles in every other triangle will be the same. It is clear that the Euclidean proof can say nothing about a totality of triangles. A proof can't go beyond itself.

But once more the construction of the proof is not an experiment, and were it so, its outcome couldn't prove anything for other cases. That is why it isn't even necessary for the construction actually to be carried out with pencil and paper, but a description of the construction must be sufficient to show all that is essential. (The description of an experiment isn't enough to give us the result of the experiment: it must actually be performed.) The construction in a Euclidean proof is precisely analogous to the proof that $2 + 2 = 4$ by means of the Russian abacus.

And isn't this the kind of generality the tautologies of logic have, which are demonstrated for p, q, r, etc.?

The essential point in all these cases is that what is demonstrated can't be expressed by a proposition.

132   If I say 'The world will *eventually* come to an end' then that means nothing at all if the date is left indefinitely open. For it's compatible with this statement that the world should still exist on any day you care to mention. – What is *infinite* is the *possibility* of numbers in propositions of the form 'In *n* days the world will come to an end'.

To understand the sense of a question, consider what an answer to it would look like.

To the question 'Is A my ancestor?' the only answers I can imagine are 'A is to be found in my ancestral gallery' or 'A is not to be found in my ancestral gallery' (Where by my ancestral gallery I understand the sum total of all kinds of information about my predecessors). But in that case the question can't mean anything more than 'Is A to be found in my ancestral gallery?' (An ancestral gallery has an end: that is a proposition of syntax.) If a god were to reveal to me that A was my ancestor, but not at what remove, even this revelation could only mean to me that I shall find A among my ancestors if I search long enough; but since I shall search through N ancestors, the revelation must mean that A is one of those N.

If I ask how many 9s immediately succeed one another after 3.1415 in the development of π, meaning my question to refer to the extension, the answer runs either, that in the development of the extension up to the place last developed (the *N*th) we have gone beyond the series of 9s, or, that 9s succeed one another up to the *N*th place. But in this case the question cannot have a different sense from 'Are the first *N*-5 places of π all 9s or not?' – But of course, that isn't the question which interests us.

133   In philosophy it's always a matter of the application of a series of utterly simple basic principles that any child knows, and the – enormous – difficulty is only one of applying these in the confusion our language creates. It's never a question of the latest

results of experiments with exotic fish or the most recent developments in mathematics. But the difficulty in applying the simple basic principles shakes our confidence in the principles themselves.

134 What sort of proposition is: 'On this strip you may see all shades of grey between black and white'? Here it looks at first glance as if we're talking about infinitely many shades.

Indeed we are apparently confronted here by the paradox that we can, of course, only distinguish a finite number of shades, and naturally the distinction between them isn't infinitely slight, and yet we see a continuous transition.

It is just as impossible to conceive of a particular grey as being one of the infinitely many greys between black and white as it is to conceive of a tangent t as being one of the infinitely many transitional stages in going from t_1 to t_2. If I see a ruler roll from t_1 to t_2, I see – if its motion is continuous – none of the individual intermediate positions in the sense in which I see t when the tangent is at rest; or else I see only a finite number of such positions.

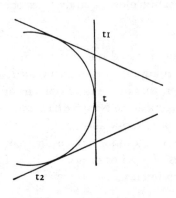

But if in such a case I appear to infer a particular case from a general proposition, then the general proposition is never derived from experience, and the proposition isn't a real proposition.

If, e.g., I say 'I saw the ruler move from t_1 to t_2, *therefore* I must have seen it at t', this doesn't give us a valid logical inference. That is, if what I mean is that the ruler must have *appeared* to me at t – and so, if I'm talking about the position in visual space – then it doesn't in the least follow from the premiss. But if I'm talking about the physical ruler, then of course it's possible for the ruler to have skipped over position t, and yet for the phenomena in visual space to have remained continuous.

135 Ramsey proposed to express the proposition that infinitely many objects satisfied a function by denying all propositions of the form:

$\sim (\exists x) \cdot \varphi x$

$(\exists x) \cdot \varphi x \cdot \sim (\exists x,y) \cdot \varphi x \cdot \varphi y$

$(\exists x,y) \cdot \varphi x \cdot \varphi y \cdot \sim (\exists x,y,z) \cdot \varphi x \cdot \varphi y \cdot \varphi z$, etc.

But let's suppose there are only three objects, i.e., there are only three names with a meaning. Then we can no longer write down the fourth proposition of the series, since it makes no sense to write: $(\exists x,y,z,u) \cdot \varphi x \cdot \varphi y \cdot \varphi z \cdot \varphi u$. So I don't arrive at the infinite by denying all the propositions in this series.

'We only know the infinite by description.' Well then, there's just the description and nothing else.

136 To what extent does a notation for the infinite presuppose infinite space or infinite time?

Of course it doesn't presuppose an infinitely large sheet of paper. But how about the possibility of one?

We can surely imagine a notation which extends through time, not space. Such as speech. Here too we clearly find it possible to imagine a representation of infinity, yet in doing so we certainly don't make any *hypothesis* about time. Time appears to us to be essentially an *infinite* possibility.

Indeed, obviously infinite from what we know of its structure.

Surely it's impossible that mathematics should depend on an hypothesis concerning physical space. And surely in this sense *visual space* isn't infinite.

And if it's a matter, not of the reality, but of the possibility of the hypothesis of infinite space, then this possibility must surely be prefigured somewhere.

Here we run into the problem that also arises for the extension of visual space – that of the smallest visible distinction. The existence of a smallest visible distinction conflicts with continuity, and yet the two must be reconcilable with one another.

137 If I have a series of alternately black and white patches, as shown in the diagram

then by continual bisection, I will soon arrive at a limit where I'm no longer able to distinguish the black and white patches, that is, where I have the impression of a grey strip.

But doesn't that imply that a strip in my visual field cannot be bisected indefinitely often? And yet I don't see a discontinuity and of course I wouldn't, since I could only see a discontinuity if I hadn't yet reached the limit of divisibility.

This seems very paradoxical.

But what about the continuity between the individual rows? Obviously we have a last but one row of distinguishable patches and then a last row of uniform grey; but could you tell from this last row that it was in fact obtained by bisecting the last but one? Obviously not. On the other hand, could you tell from the so-called last but one row that it can no longer be visibly bisected? It seems to me, just as little. In that case, there would be no last visibly bisected row!

If I cannot visibly bisect the strip any further, I can't even *try* to, and so can't see the failure of such an attempt. (This is like the case of the limitlessness of visual space.)

Obviously, the same would hold for distinctions between colours.

Continuity in our visual field consists in our not seeing discontinuity.

138   But if I can always see only a finite number of things, divisions, colours, etc., than there just isn't an infinity at all; in no sense whatever. The feeling here is: if I am always able to see only so few, then there aren't any more. As if it were a case like this: if I can only see 4, then there aren't 100. But infinity doesn't have the role of a number here. It's perfectly true; if I can only see 4, there aren't 100, there aren't even 5. But there is the infinite possibility that isn't exhausted by a small number any more than by a large: and in fact just because it *isn't* itself a quantity.

We all of course know what it means to say there is an infinite possibility and a finite reality, since we say space and time are infinite but we can always only see or live through finite bits of them. But from where, then, do I derive any knowledge of the infinite at all? In some sense or other, I must have two kinds of experience: one which is of the finite, and which cannot transcend the finite (the idea of such a transcendence is nonsense even on its own terms), and one of the infinite. And that's how it is. Experience as experience of the facts gives me the finite; the objects *contain* the infinite. Of course not as something rivalling finite experience, but in intension. Not as though I could see space as practically empty, with just a very small finite experience in it. But, I can see in space the possibility of any finite experience. That is, no experience could be too large for it or exhaust it: not of course because we are acquainted with the dimensions of every experience and know space to be larger, but because we understand this as belonging to the essence of space. – We recognize this essential infinity of space in its smallest part.

Where the nonsense starts is with our habit of thinking of a large number as closer to infinity than a small one.

As I've said, the infinite doesn't rival the finite. The infinite is that whose essence is to exclude nothing finite.

The word 'nothing' occurs in this proposition and, once more, this should not be interpreted as the expression for an infinite disjunction, on the contrary, 'essentially' and 'nothing' belong together. It's no wonder that time and again I can only explain infinity in terms of itself, i.e. *cannot explain* it.

Space has no extension, only spatial objects are extended, but infinity is a property of space.

(This of itself shows it isn't an infinite extent.)

And the same goes for time.

139   How about infinite divisibility? Let's remember that there's a point to saying we can conceive of *any* finite number of parts but not of an infinite number; but that this is precisely what constitutes infinite divisibility.

Now, 'any' doesn't mean here that we can conceive of the *sum total* of *all* divisions (which we can't, for there's no such thing). But that there is the *variable* 'divisibility' (i.e. the concept of divisibility) which *sets no limit* to actual divisibility; and that constitutes its infinity.

But how do we construct an infinite hypothesis, such as that there are infinitely many fixed stars (it's clear that *in the end* only a finite reality can correspond to it)? Once more it can only be given through a law. Let's think of an infinite series of red spheres. – Let's think of an infinite film strip. (It would give the possibility of everything finite that happens on the screen.) This is a typical case of an hypothesis reaching out to infinity. It's clear to us that no experience *corresponds* with it. It only exists in 'the second system', that is, in language; but how is it expressed there? (If a man can *imagine* an infinite strip, then as far as he's concerned there is an infinite reality, and also the 'actual infinite' of mathematics.) It is expressed by a proposition of the form '$(n):(\exists nx).\ \varphi x$'. Everything relating to the infinite possibility (every infinite assertion about the film), is reproduced in the expression in the first bracket, and the reality corresponding to it in the second.

But what then has divisibility to do with actual division, if something can be divisible that *never is* divided?

Indeed, what does divisibility mean at all in the case of that which is given as primary? How can you distinguish between reality and possibility here?

It must be wrong to speak as I do of restricting infinite possibility to what is finite.

For it makes it look as if an infinite reality were conceivable – even if there isn't one – and so once more as though it were a question of a possible infinite extension and an actual finite one: as though infinite possibility were the possibility of an infinite number.

And that again shows we are dealing with two different meanings of the word 'possible' when we say 'The line can be divided into 3 parts' and when we say 'The line can be divided infinitely often'. (This is also indicated by the proposition above, which questions whether there are actual and possible in visual space.)

What does it mean to say a patch in visual space can be divided into three parts? Surely it can mean only that a proposition describing a patch divided in this way makes sense. (Provided it isn't a question of a confusion between the divisibility of physical objects and that of a visual patch.)

Whereas infinite – or better *unlimited* – divisibility doesn't mean there's a proposition describing a line divided into infinitely many parts, since there isn't such a proposition. Therefore this possibility is not brought out by any reality of the signs, but by a possibility of a *different* kind in the signs themselves.

If you say space is infinitely divisible, then strictly speaking that means: space isn't made up of individual things (parts).

In a certain sense, infinite divisibility means that space is indivisible, that *it* is not affected by any division. That it is above such things: *it* doesn't consist of parts. Much as if it were saying to reality: you may do what you like in me (you can be divided as often as you like in me.)

Space gives to reality an infinite opportunity for division.

And that is why there is only *one* letter in the first bracket. Obviously only an opportunity, nothing more.

140   Is primary time infinite? That is, is it an infinite possibility? Even if it is only filled out as far as memory extends, that in no way implies that it is finite. It is infinite in the same sense as the three-dimensional space of sight and movement is infinite, even if in fact I can only see as far as the walls of my room. For what I see presupposes the possibility of seeing further. That is to say, I could correctly represent what I see only by an infinite form.

Is it possible to imagine time with an end, or with two ends?

What can happen *now*, could also have happened earlier, and could always happen in the future if time remains as it is. But *that* doesn't depend on a future experience. Time contains the possibility of all the future *now*.

But all that of itself implies that time isn't infinite in the sense of the primitive conception of an infinite set.

And so for space. If I say that I can imagine a cylinder extended to infinity, that is already contained in its nature. So again, contained in the nature of the homogeneity of the cylinder and of the space in which it is – and the one of course presupposes the other – and this homogeneity is in the finite bit that I see.

The space of human movement is infinite in the same way as time.

141   The rules for a number-system – say, the decimal system –

contain everything that is infinite about the numbers. That, e.g. *these rules* set no limits on the left or right hand to the numerals; *this* is what contains the expression of infinity.

Someone might perhaps say: True, but the numerals are still limited by their use and by writing materials and other factors. That is so, but that isn't expressed in the *rules* for their use, and it is only in these that their real essence is expressed.

Does the relation $m = 2n$ correlate the class of all numbers with one of its subclasses? No. It correlates any arbitrary number with another, and in that way we arrive at infinitely many pairs of classes, of which one is correlated with the other, but which are *never* related as class and subclass. Neither is this infinite process itself in some sense or other such a pair of classes.

In the superstition that $m = 2n$ correlates a class with its subclass, we merely have yet another case of ambiguous grammar.

What's more, it all hangs on the syntax of reality and possibility. $m = 2n$ contains the *possibility of correlating any number* with another, *but doesn't correlate all numbers with others.*

The word 'possibility' is of course misleading, since someone will say, let what is possible now become actual. And in thinking this, we always think of a temporal process and infer from the fact that mathematics has nothing to do with time, that in its case possibility is (already) actuality.

(But in truth the opposite is the case, and what is called possibility in mathematics is precisely the same as it is in the case of time.)

$m = 2n$ points along the number series, and if we add 'to infinity', that simply means that it doesn't point at an object a definite distance away.

142   The infinite number series is itself only such a possibility –
as emerges clearly from the single symbol for it '$(1, x, x + 1)$' [1].
This symbol is itself an arrow with the first '1' as the tail of the
arrow and '$x + 1$' as its tip and what is characteristic is that – just
as length is inessential in an arrow – the variable x shows here that
it is immaterial how far the tip is from the tail.

It is possible to speak of things which lie in the direction of the
arrow but nonsense to speak of all possible positions for things
lying in the direction of the arrow as an equivalent for this direction
itself.

A searchlight sends out light into infinite space and so illuminates
everything in its direction, but you can't say it illuminates infinity.

You could also put it like this: it makes sense to say there can be
infinitely many objects in a direction, but no sense to say there are
infinitely many. And this conflicts with the way the word 'can' is
normally used. For, if it makes sense to say a book can lie on this
table, it also makes sense to say it is lying there. But here we are led
astray by language. The 'infinitely many' is so to speak used
adverbially and is to be understood accordingly.

That is to say, the propositions 'Three things can lie in this
direction' and 'Infinitely many things can lie in this direction'
are only apparently formed in the same way, but are in fact different
in structure: the 'infinitely many' of the second proposition
doesn't play the same role as the 'three' of the first.

It is, again, only the ambiguity of our language that makes it
appear as if numerals and the word 'infinite' are both given as
answers to the same question. Whereas the questions which have
these words as an answer are in reality fundamentally different.

1] In the manuscript he writes ξ instead of x, cf. above, §125.

(The usual conception really amounts to the idea that the absence of a limit is itself a limit. Even if it isn't put as baldly as that.)

If two arrows point in the same direction, isn't it in such a case absurd to call these directions equally long because whatever lies in the direction of the one arrow, also lies in that of the other?

Generality in mathematics is a direction, an arrow pointing along the series generated by an operation. And you can even say that the arrow points to infinity; but does that mean that there is something – infinity – at which it points, as at a thing? Construed in that way, it must of course lead to endless nonsense.

It's as though the arrow designates the possibility of a position in its direction.

143 In what sense is endless time a possibility and not a reality? For someone might object to what I am saying by arguing that time must be just as much a reality as, say, colour.

But isn't colour taken by itself also only a possibility, until it is in a particular time and place? Empty infinite time is only the possibility of facts which alone are the realities.

But isn't the infinite *past* to be thought of as filled out, and doesn't that yield an infinite reality?

And if there is an infinite reality, then there is also contingency in the infinite. And so, for instance, also an infinite decimal that isn't given by a law. Everything in Ramsey's conception stands or falls with that.

That we don't think of time as an infinite reality, but as infinite in intension, is shown in the fact that on the one hand we can't imagine an infinite time interval, and yet see that no day can be the last, and so that time cannot have an end.

We might also say: infinity lies in the nature of time, it isn't the extension it happens to have.

We are of course only familiar with time – as it were – from the bit of time before our eyes. It would be extraordinary if we could grasp its infinite extent in this way (in the sense, that is to say, in which we could grasp it if we ourselves were its contemporaries for an infinite time.)

We are in fact in the same position with time as with space. The actual time we are acquainted with is limited (finite). Infinity is an internal quality of the form of time.

144   The infinite number series is only the infinite possibility of finite series of numbers. It is senseless to speak of the *whole* infinite number series, as if it, too, were an extension.

Infinite possibility is represented by infinite possibility. The signs themselves only contain the possibility and not the reality of their repetition [1].

Doesn't it come to this: the facts are finite, the infinite possibility of facts lies in the objects. That is why it is shown, not described.

Corresponding to this is the fact that numbers – which of course are used to describe the facts – are finite, whereas their possibility, which corresponds with the *possibility* of facts, is infinite. It finds expression, as I've said, in the possibilities of the symbolism.

The feeling is that there can't be possibility and actuality in mathematics. It's all on *one* level. And is, in a certain sense, actual.

1] W. had just written in the manuscript: One is constantly confused by the thought 'but can there be a possibility without a corresponding reality?'

And that is correct. For what mathematics expresses with its signs is all on *one* level; i.e. it doesn't speak sometimes about their possibility, and sometimes about their actuality. No, it can't even try to speak about their possibility. On the other hand, there is a possibility in its signs, i.e. the possibility found in genuine propositions, in which mathematics is applied.

And when (as in set theory) it tries to *express* their possibility, i.e. when it confuses them with their reality, we ought to cut it down to size.

We reflect far too little on the fact that a sign really cannot mean more than it is.

The infinite possibility in the symbol relates – i.e. refers – only to the essence of a finite extension, and this is its way of leaving its size open.

If I were to say, 'If we were acquainted with an infinite extension, then it would be all right to talk of an actual infinite', that would really be like saying, 'If there were a sense of abracadabra then it would be all right to talk about abracadabraic sense-perception'.

We see a continuous colour transition and a continuous movement, but in that case we just see *no* parts, *no* leaps (not infinitely many).

145 What is an infinite decimal not given by a rule? Can you give an infinite sequence of digits by a non-mathematical – and so external – description, instead of a law? (Very strange that there should be two modes of comprehension.)

'The number that is the result when a man endlessly throws a die', appears to be nonsense because no infinite number results from it.

But why is it easier to imagine life without end than an endless series in space? Somehow, it's because we simply take the endless life as never complete, whereas the infinite series in space ought, we feel, already to exist as a whole.

Let's imagine a man whose life goes back for an infinite time and who says to us: 'I'm just writing down the last digit of π, and it's a 2'. Every day of his life he has written down a digit, without ever having begun; he has just finished.

This seems utter nonsense, and a *reductio ad absurdum* of the concept of an infinite *totality*.

Suppose we travel out along a straight line in Euclidean Space and say that at 10 m intervals we encounter an iron sphere of a certain diameter, *ad infinitum*; is this a construction? It seems so. What is strange is that you can construe such an infinite complex of spheres as the endless repetition of the same sphere in accordance with a certain law – and yet the moment you think of these spheres as each having its own individual characteristics, their infinite number seems to become nonsense.

Let's imagine an infinite row of trees, all of different heights between 3 and 4 yards. If there is a law governing the way the heights vary, then the series is defined and can be imagined by means of this law (this is assuming that the trees are indistinguishable save in their height). But what if the heights vary at random? Then – we're forced to say – there's only an infinitely long, an endless description. But surely that's not a description! I can suppose there to be infinitely many descriptions of the infinitely many finite stretches of the infinite row of trees, but in that case I have to know these infinitely many descriptions by means of a law governing their sequence. Or, if there's no such law, I once more require an infinite description of these descriptions. And that would again get me nowhere.

Now I could of course say that I'm aware of the law that each tree must differ in height from all its predecessors. It's true that this is a law, but still not such as to define the series. If I now assume there could be a random series, then that is a series about which, by its very nature, nothing can be known apart from the fact that I can't know it. Or better, that it can't be known. For is this a situation in which 'the human intellect is inadequate, but a higher might succeed'? How then does it come about that human understanding frames this question at all, sets out on this path whose end is out of its reach?

What is infinite about endlessness is only the endlessness itself.

146   What gives the multiplicative axiom its plausibility? Surely that in the case of a finite class of classes we can in fact make a selection [choice]. But what about the case of infinitely many subclasses? It's obvious that in such a case I can only know the law for making a selection.

Now I can make something like a *random* selection from a finite class of classes. But is that *conceivable* in the case of an infinite class of classes? It seems to me to be nonsense.

Let's imagine someone living an endless life and making successive choices of an arbitrary fraction from the fractions between 1 and 2, 2 and 3, etc. *ad. inf.* Does that yield us a selection from all those intervals? No, since he does *not* finish. But can't I say nonetheless that all those intervals must turn up, since I can't cite any which he wouldn't *eventually* arrive at? But from the fact that given *any* interval, he will *eventually* arrive at it, it doesn't follow that he will *eventually* have arrived at them all.

But doesn't this still give the description of a process that generates selections without end, and doesn't that mean precisely that an endless selection is formed? But here the infinity is only in the rule.

Imagine the following hypothesis: there is in space an infinite series of red spheres, each one metre behind its predecessor. What *conceivable* experience could correspond to this hypothesis? I think for instance of my travelling along this series and every day passing a certain number, *n*, of red spheres. In that case, my experience ought to consist in the fact that on *every possible* day in the future I see *n* more spheres. But when shall I have had this experience? Never!

147 You can only answer the objection 'But if nevertheless there were infinitely many things?' by saying 'But there aren't'. And what makes us think that perhaps there are is only our confusing the things of physics with the elements of knowledge [1].

For this reason we also can't suppose an hypothetical infinite visual space in which an infinite series of red patches is visible.

What we imagine in physical space is not that which is primary, which we can know only to a greater or lesser extent; rather, what we can know of physical space shows us how far what is primary reaches and how we have to *interpret* physical space.

But how is a proposition of the form 'The red patch *a* lies somewhere between *b* and *c*' to be analysed? This doesn't mean: 'The

b   c

patch *a* corresponds to one of the infinitely many numbers lying between the numbers of *b* and *c*' (it isn't a question of a disjunction). It's clear that the infinite possibility of positions of *a* between *b* and *c* isn't expressed in the proposition. Just as, in the case of 'I have locked him in the room', the infinitely many possible positions

1] The only reason why you can't say there are infinitely many things is that there aren't. If there were, you could also express the fact! [Manuscript]

of the man shut in the room play no role whatever.

'Each thing has one and only one predecessor; a has no successor; everything except for a has one and only one successor.' These propositions appear to describe an infinite series (and also to say that there are infinitely many things. But this would be a presupposition of the propositions' making sense). They appear to describe a *structure amorphously*. We can sketch out a structure in accordance with these propositions, which they describe unambiguously. But where can we discover this structure in them?

But couldn't we regard this set of propositions simply as propositions belonging to physics, setting out a scientific hypothesis? In that case they would have to be unassailable. But what would it be like if a biologist discovered a species of animal, in which *every* individual appeared to be the offspring of *one* earlier one, and put this forward as an hypothesis?

Are we misled in such a case by the illusion that parcels of matter – i.e. in this case the members of a species of animal – were the simple objects?

That is to say, isn't that which we can imagine multiplied to infinity never the things themselves, but combinations of the things in accordance with their infinite possibilities?

The things themselves are perhaps the four basic colours, space, time and other data of the same sort.

In that case, how about a series of fixed stars, in which *each* has a predecessor (in a particular spacial direction)? And this hypothesis would come out in the same way as that of an endless life. This seems to me to make sense, precisely because it doesn't conflict with the insight that we cannot make any hypothesis concerning the number of objects (elements of facts). Its analysis only presupposes the infinite possibility of space and time and a *finite* number of elements of experience.

XIII

148   We might also ask: What is it that goes on when, while we've as yet no idea how a certain proposition is to be proved, we still ask 'Can it be proved or not?' and proceed to look for a proof? If we 'try to prove it', what do we do? Is this a search which is essentially unsystematic, and therefore strictly speaking *not a search at all*, or can there be some plan involved? How we answer this question is a pointer as to whether the as yet unproved – or as yet unprovable – proposition is senseless or not. For, in a very important sense, every significant proposition must teach us through its sense how we are to convince ourselves whether it is true or false. 'Every proposition says what is the case if it is true.' And with a mathematical proposition this 'what is the case' must refer to the way in which it is to be proved. Whereas – and this is the point – you cannot have a logical plan of search for a *sense* you don't know. The sense would have to be, so to speak, revealed to us: revealed from without – since it can't be obtained from the propositional sign alone – in contrast with its truth, where the proposition itself tells us how to look for its truth and compare the truth with it.

This amounts to asking: Does a mathematical proposition tie something down to a Yes or No answer? (i.e. precisely a sense.)

My explanation mustn't wipe out the existence of mathematical problems. That is to say, it isn't as if it were only certain that a mathematical proposition made sense when it (or its opposite) had been proved. (This would mean that its opposite would never have a sense (Weyl).) On the other hand, it could be that certain apparent problems lose their character as problems – the question as to Yes or No.

149   Is it like this: I need a new insight at each step in a proof? This is connected with the question of the individuality of each

number. Something of the following sort: Supposing there to be a certain general rule (therefore one containing a variable), I must recognize each time afresh that this rule may be applied *here*. No act of foresight can absolve me from this act of *insight* [1]. Since the form to which the rule is applied is in fact different at every step.

A proof of relevance would be a proof which, while yet not proving the proposition [would show the form of a method to be followed in order to test such a proposition] [2]. And just that could make such a proof possible. It wouldn't get to the top of the ladder since *that* requires that you pass every rung; but only show that the ladder leads in this direction. That is, there's no substitute for stepping on every rung, and whatever is equivalent to doing so must in its turn possess the same multiplicity as doing so. (There are no surrogates in logic.) Neither is an arrow a surrogate for going through all the stages towards a particular goal. This is also connected with the impossibility of an hierarchy of proofs.

Wouldn't the idea of an hierarchy mean that merely posing a problem would have to be already preceded by a proof, i.e. a proof that the question makes sense? But then I would say that a proof of sense must be a radically different sort of proof from one of a proposition's truth, or else it would in its turn presuppose yet another and we'd get into an infinite regress.

Does the question of relevance make sense? If it does, it must always be possible to say whether the axioms are relevant to this proposition or not, and in that case this question must always be decidable, and so a question of the *first* type has already been decided. And if it can't be decided, it's completely senseless.

1] (Later marginal note): Act of *decision*, not *insight*.
2] This sentence is incomplete in the manuscript. [ed.]

What, apart from Fermat's alleged proof, drives us to concern ourselves with the formula $x^n + y^n = z^n \ldots (F)$, is the fact that we never happen upon cardinal numbers that satisfy the equation; but that doesn't give the *slightest* support (probability) to the general theorem and so doesn't give us any good reason for concerning ourselves with the formula. Rather, we may look on it simply as a notation for a particular general form and ask ourselves whether syntax is *in any way at all* concerned with this form.

I said: Where you can't look for an answer, you can't ask either, and that means: Where there's no logical method for finding a solution, the question doesn't make sense either.

Only where there's a method of solution is there a problem (of course that doesn't mean 'Only when the solution has been found is there a problem').

That is, where we can only expect the solution from some sort of revelation, there isn't even a problem. A revelation doesn't correspond to any question.

It would be like wanting to ask about experiences belonging to a sense organ we don't yet possess. Our being given a new sense, I would call revelation.

Neither can we *look for* a new sense (sense-perception).

150   We come back to the question: In what sense can we *assert* a mathematical proposition? That is: what *would* mean nothing would be to say that I can only assert it if it's correct. – No, to be able to make an assertion, I must do so with reference to its sense, not its truth. As I've already said, it seems clear to me that I can assert a general proposition as much or as little as the equation $3 \times 3 = 9$ or $3 \times 3 = 11$.

It's almost unbelievable, the way in which a problem gets completely barricaded in by the wrong expressions which generation upon generation throw up for miles around it, so that it's virtually impossible to get at it.

What makes understanding difficult is the misconception of the *general* method of solution as only an – incidental – expedient for deriving numbers satisfying the equation. Whereas it is in itself a clarification of the essence (nature) of the equation. Again, it isn't an incidental device for discovering an extension, it's an end in itself.

What questions can be raised concerning a form, e.g. $fx = gx$? – Is $fx = gx$ or not (x as a general constant)? Do the rules yield a solution of this equation or not (x as unknown)? Do the rules prohibit the form $fx = gx$ or not (x construed as a stop-gap)?

None of these cases admits of being tested empirically, and so extensionally.

Not even the last two, since I see that e.g., '$x^2 = 4$' is permitted no less from $7^2 = 4$ than from $2^2 = 4$, and that $x^2 = -4$ is prohibited isn't shown me by $2^2 \neq -4$ in any different way from that by which $8^2 \neq -4$ shows it me. That is, in the particular case, I again see here only the rule.

The question 'Do any numbers satisfy the equation?' makes no sense, no more than does 'It is satisfied by numbers', or, of course, than 'It is satisfied by all (no) numbers'.

The important point is that, even in the case where I am given that $3^2 + 4^2 = 5^2$, I ought *not* to say '$(\exists x, y, z, n) \cdot x^n + y^n = z^n$', since taken extensionally that's meaningless, and taken intensionally this doesn't provide a proof of it. No, in this case I ought to express only the first equation.

It's clear that I may only write down the general proposition (using general constants), when it is analogous to the proposition $25 \times 25 = 625$, and that will be when I know the rules for calculating with a and b just as I know those for 6, 2 and 5. This illustrates precisely what it means to call a and b constants here – i.e. constant forms [1].

Is it like this: I can't use the word 'yields' while I am unaware of any method of solution, since *yields* refers to a structure that I cannot designate unless I am aware of it. Because the structure must be *represented*.

Every proposition is the signpost for a verification.

If I construe the word 'yields' in an essentially intensional way, then the proposition 'The equation E yields the solution a' means nothing until the word 'yields' stands for a definite method. For it is precisely this which I wish to refer to.

1] In this connection, W. had written in the manuscript:
  'I still haven't stressed sufficiently that $25 \times 25 = 625$ is on *precisely* the same level as and of *precisely the same kind* as $x^2 + y^2 + 2xy = (x + y)^2$. . . . .
  In the case of general propositions, what corresponds to the proposition $25^2 \neq 620$? It would be $\sim (x,y)\,(x + y)^2 = x^2 + y^2$, or in words, it is not a rule that '$(x + y)^2 = x^2 + y^2$', or more precisely, the two sides of this equation – taken in the way the '(x)' indicates – are not equal to one another.'
  But this sign '(x)' says exactly the opposite of what it says in non-mathematical cases . . . i.e. precisely that we should treat the variables in the proposition as constants. You could paraphrase the above proposition by saying 'It isn't correct – if we treat x and y as constants – that $(x + y)^2 = x^2 + y^2$'. . . . . .
  $\left.\begin{array}{l}(a + b)^2 = a^2 + xab + b^2 \text{ yields } x = 2 \\ (x + b)^2 = x^2 + 2xb + b^2 \text{ yields } x = x\end{array}\right\}$ and refer to the same state of affairs which is also affirmed by $(a + b)^2 = a^2 + 2ab + b^2$. (But is that true?)'

  And *after* the remark given in the text: 'But what is meant by knowing the rules for calculating?'

I have here nothing other than the old case that I cannot say two complexes stand in a relation without using a logical mapping of the relation.

'The equation yields a' means: If I transform the equation in accordance with certain rules, I get a, just as the equation $25 \times 25 = 620$ says that I get 620 if I apply the rules for multiplication to 25×25. But these rules must already be given to me before the word 'yields' has a meaning and before the question whether the equation yields a has a sense.

Thus Fermat's proposition makes no *sense* until I can *search* for a solution to the equation in cardinal numbers.

And 'search' must always mean: search systematically. Meandering about in infinite space on the look-out for a gold ring is no kind of search.

You can only *search* within a system: And so there is necessarily something you *can't* search for [1].

151 We may only put a question in mathematics (or make a conjecture), where the answer runs: 'I must work it out'.

But can't I also say this is the case of $1/3 = 0.\dot{3}$, where the result isn't an extension, but the formation of the inductive relationship?

But even so, we must also have a clear idea of this inductive relationship if we are to expect it.

That is: even here we still can't conjecture or expect in a void.

What 'mathematical questions' share with genuine questions is simply that they can be answered.

1] Cf. below p. 178.

If the $\frac{1}{3}$ in $1/3 = 0.\overline{3}$ refers to a definite method, then o.11o as connected with F means nothing, since a method is lacking here [1].

A law I'm unaware of isn't a law.

A mathematical question must be as exact as a mathematical proposition.

The question 'How many solutions are there to this equation?' is the holding in readiness of the general method for solving it. And that, in general, is what a question is in mathematics: the holding in readiness of a general method.

I need hardly say that where the law of the excluded middle doesn't apply, no other law of logic applies either, because in that case we aren't dealing with propositions of mathematics. (Against Weyl and Brouwer.)

Wouldn't all this lead to the paradox that there are no difficult problems in mathematics, since, if anything is difficult, it isn't a problem?

But it isn't like that: The difficult mathematical problems are those for whose solution we don't yet possess a *written* system. The mathematician who is looking for a solution then has a system in some sort of psychic symbolism, in images, 'in his head', and endeavours to get it down on paper. Once that's done, the rest is easy. But if he has *no kind* of system, either in written or unwritten

---

1] By this point in his manuscript Wittgenstein had already written the paragraph in §189: 'I say that the so-called "Fermat's last Theorem"[1] is no kind of *proposition*[1] (not even in the sense of a proposition of arithmetic). It would, rather, correspond to a proof by induction. But if, now, there is a number $F = 0.110000$ etc. and the proof succeeds, then it would surely give us a proof that $F = 0.11$ and surely that's a proposition! Or: it's a proposition in the case of the law F being a number.'

[1] Satz.

symbols, then he can't *search* for a solution either, but at best can only grope around. – Now, of course you may find something even by random groping. But in that case you haven't searched for it, and, from a logical point of view, the process was synthetic; whereas searching is a process of analysis.

Whatever one can tackle is a problem [1].

Only where there can be a problem can something be asserted.

If I know the rules of elementary trigonometry, I can check the proposition $\sin 2x = 2 \sin x \cdot \cos x$, but not the proposition $\sin x = x - \frac{x^3}{3!} + \ldots$. But that means that the sine function of elementary trigonometry and that of higher trigonometry are *different* concepts. If we give them the same name, we admittedly do so with good reason, since the second concept includes within itself the multiplicity of the first; but as far as the system of elementary trigonometry is concerned, the second proposition makes *no sense*, and it is of course senseless in this context to ask whether $\sin x = x$ – etc.

152   Is it a genuine question if we ask whether it's possible to trisect an angle? And of what sort is the proposition and its proof that it's impossible with ruler and compasses alone?

We might say, since it's impossible, people could never even have tried to look for a construction.

Until I can *see* the larger system encompassing them both, I can't try to solve the higher problem.

I can't ask whether an angle can be trisected with ruler and compasses, until I can see the system 'Ruler and Compasses' as embedded in a larger one, where the problem is soluble; or better, where the problem is a problem, where this question has a sense.

1] Manuscript (a bit earlier): 'Whatever one can tackle is a problem. (So mathematics is all right.)' [In English]

This is also shown by the fact that you *must* step outside the Euclidean system for a proof of the impossibility.

A system is, so to speak, a world.

Therefore we can't search for a system: What we *can* search for is the expression for a system that is given me in unwritten symbols.

A schoolboy, equipped with the armoury of elementary trigonometry and asked to test the equation sin $x = x -$ etc., simply wouldn't find what he needs to tackle the problem. If the teacher nevertheless expects a solution from him, he's assuming that the multiplicity of the syntax which such a solution presupposes is in some way or other present in a different form in the schoolboy's head – present in such a way that the schoolboy sees the symbolism of elementary trigonometry as a part of this unwritten symbolism and now translates the rest from an unwritten into a written form.

The system of rules determining a calculus thereby determines the 'meaning' of its signs too. Put more strictly: The form and the rules of syntax are equivalent. So if I change the rules – seemingly supplement them, say – then I change the form, the meaning.

I cannot draw the limits of my world, but I can draw limits within my world. I cannot ask whether the proposition p belongs to the system S, but I can ask whether it belongs to the part s of S. So that I can locate the problem of the trisection of an angle within the larger system, but can't ask, within the Euclidean system, whether it's soluble. In what *language* should I ask this? in the Euclidean? But neither can I ask in Euclidean language about the possibility of bisecting an angle within the Euclidean system. For in this language that would boil down to a question about absolute possibility, and such a question is always nonsense.

But there's nothing to be found here which we could call a hierarchy of types.

In mathematics, we cannot talk of systems in general, but only *within* systems. They are just what we can't talk about. And so, too, what we can't search for.

The schoolboy that lacked the equipment for answering the second question, couldn't merely not answer it, he couldn't even understand it. (It would be like the task the prince set the smith in the folk tale: Fetch me a 'Fiddle-de-dee'.)

Every legitimate mathematical proposition must put a ladder up against the problem it poses, in the way that $12 \times 13 = 137$ does – which I can then climb if I choose.
This holds for propositions of any degree of generality. (N.B. there is no ladder with 'infinitely many' rungs.)

Now suppose I have two systems: I can't enquire after one system encompassing them both, since not only am I unable *now* to search for this system, but even in the event of one turning up that encompasses two systems analogous to the original ones, I see that I could never have looked for it.

153   Proofs proving the same thing may be translated into one another, and to that extent are the same proof. The only proofs for which this doesn't hold are like: 'From two things, I infer that he's at home: first his jacket's in the hall, and also I can hear him whistling'. Here we have two independent ways of knowing. This proof requires grounds that come from outside, whereas a mathematical proof is an analysis of the mathematical proposition.

What is a proof of provability? It's different from the proof of proposition.

And is a proof of provability perhaps the proof that a proposition makes sense? But then, such a proof would have to rest on *entirely different* principles from those on which the proof of the proposition rests. There cannot be an hierarchy of proofs!

On the other hand there can't in any fundamental sense be such a thing as meta-mathematics. Everything must be of one type (or, what comes to the same thing, not of a type).

Now, is it possible to show that the axioms are relevant to a proposition (i.e. prove it or its opposite), without actually bringing them to bear directly on it? That is, do we only know whether they are relevant when we've got there, or is it possible to know this at an earlier stage? And is the possibility of checking $36 \times 47 = 128$ a proof of this? It obviously makes sense to say 'I know how you check that', even before you've done so.

Thus, it isn't enough to say that p is provable, what we must say is: provable according to a particular system.

Further, the proposition doesn't assert that p is provable in the system S, but in *its own* system, the system of p. That p belongs to the system S cannot be asserted, but must show itself.

You can't say p belongs to the system S; you can't ask which system p belongs to; you can't search for the system of p. Understanding p means understanding its system. If p appears to go over from one system into another, then p has, in reality, changed its sense.

Ramsey believed that what I call recognizing the system was nothing more than the application – perhaps unconscious – of a general mathematical proposition. So that if I know that the question of the correctness of $\sin 3a = 5 \cos a$ is decidable, I merely deduce that from the laws for sin $(a + b)$ etc. But this isn't right: on the contrary, I derive it from the fact that there is such a law, not from how it runs.

154   I could gather together numerical equations and equations using variables as follows: Transforming the left-hand side in accordance with certain rules either does or does not yield the right-hand side.

But for this to be so, the two sides of the equation (N.B. of the *general* equation) must, so to speak, be *commensurable*.

The classifications made by philosophers and psychologists are like those that someone would give who tried to classify clouds by their shapes.

What a mathematical proposition says is always what its proof proves. That is to say, it never says more than its proof proves.

If I had a method for distinguishing equations with a solution from those without, then in terms of this method the expression '$(\exists x) \cdot x^2 = 2x$' would make sense.

I can ask 'What is the solution of the equation $x^2 = 2x$?', but not 'Has it a solution?' For what would it look like for it to have none? A proposition has a sense only if I know what is the case if it is false. – But suppose the alternative case were something like the equation '$(\exists x) \cdot x^2 - 2x - x(x - 2) = 0$'? In that case at any rate, the proposition $(\exists x) \cdot x^2 = 2x$ would make sense and it would be proved by the fact that the rules don't allow us to reduce the two sides to one another. In reply to the question 'Is there a solution of the equation $x^n + ax^{n-1} + \ldots + z = 0$?', we may always ask 'As opposed to what?'

$25 \times 25 = 625$. What constitutes the system which shows me the commensurability in this case?
Surely that multiplication of two numbers written in this form always gives me a number of the same form, and a rule for two

numerical signs of this form decides whether they designate the same or different numbers.

We could also characterize this idea as follows: 'It's impossible for us to discover rules of a new type that hold for a form with which we are familiar. If they are rules which are new to us, then it isn't the old form. The edifice of rules must be *complete*, if we are to work with a concept at all – *we cannot make any discoveries in syntax*. – For, only the group of rules *defines* the sense of our signs, and any alteration (e.g. supplementation) of the rules means an alteration of the sense.

Just as we can't alter the marks of a concept without altering the concept itself. (Frege)

A system is a formal series, and it is precisely in the rules of the series that the iterations yielding its successive members are described.

The negation of 'It is necessary that p holds for all numbers' is of course 'It is not necessary that . . .', not 'It is necessary that not . . .'. But now we think: if it isn't *necessary* that p holds for all numbers, it's surely still possible. But this is where the fallacy lies, since we don't see that we've slipped into the extensional way of looking at things: the proposition 'It's possible – though not necessary – that p should hold for all numbers' is nonsense. For in mathematics '*necessary*' and '*all*' go together. (Unless we replace these idioms throughout by ones which are less misleading.)

155 What kind of discovery was it, e.g., that Sheffer made when he showed that we can reduce all the truth-functions to $p|q$? Or the discovery of the method for extracting the cube root? What's going on when we have to resort to a dodge in Mathematics? (As when solving an equation or integrating.) Here it's like unravelling a knot. I can try out one way or another at random and

the knot may get even more tangled or come undone. (Whatever happens, each operation is a permissible one and leads *somewhere*.)

I want to say that finding a system for solving problems which previously could only be solved one by one by separate methods isn't merely discovering a more convenient vehicle, but is something completely new which previously we didn't have at all. The uniform method precisely isn't just the method for constructing an object, which is the same no matter how it was constructed. The method isn't a vehicle taking us to a place which is our real goal no matter how we arrive at it.

That is to say: In my opinion, no *way* can be found in mathematics which isn't also a goal. You can't say: I already had all these results, now all I've done is find an even better way that leads to all of them. No: this way is a new place that we previously lacked. The new way amounts to a new system.

Wouldn't this imply that we can't learn anything new about an object in mathematics, since, if we do, it is a new object?

This boils down to saying: If I hear a proposition of, say, number theory, but don't know how to prove it, then I don't understand the proposition either. This sounds extremely paradoxical. It means, that is to say, that I don't understand the proposition that there are infinitely many primes, unless I know its so-called proof: when I learn the proof, I learn something *completely new*, and not just the way leading to a goal with which I'm already familiar.

But in that case it's unintelligible that I should admit, when I've got the proof, that it's a proof of precisely *this* proposition, or of the induction meant by this proposition.

I want to say, it isn't the prose which is the mathematical proposition, it's the exact expression [1].

There can't be two independent proofs of one mathematical proposition.

156 Unravelling knots in mathematics: Can someone *try* to unravel a knot which is subsequently shown to be impossible to untie? People succeeded in resolving the cubic equation, they *could not* have succeeded in trisecting an angle with ruler and compasses; people had been grappling with both these problems long before they knew how to solve the one and that the other was insoluble.

Let's consider something that appears to be a knot, but is in reality made up of many loops of thread and perhaps also a few threads with loose ends. I now set someone the task of unravelling the knot. If he can see the arrangement of the threads clearly, he'll

---

1] Earlier in the manuscript W. had distinguished 'the real mathematical proposition' (i.e. the proof) from 'the so-called mathematical proposition' (existing without its proof), e.g. in the following context:

'What sort of a proposition is "there is a prime number between 5 and 8"? I would say: "That *shows* itself". And that is correct; but can't we draw attention to this internal state of affairs? . . .

 . . . I can, e.g., write the number 5 in such a way that you can clearly see that it's only divisible by 1 and itself: . . . Perhaps this comes down to the same thing as what I meant earlier when I said that the real mathematical proposition is a proof of a so-called mathematical proposition. The real mathematical proposition is the proof: that is to say, the thing which shows how matters stand.'

say 'That's not a knot and so there's no such thing as unravelling it'. If he can only see a jumble of threads, then he may try to untie it, pulling various ends at random, or actually making a few transformations that are the result of having a clear picture of some parts of the knot, even though he hasn't seen its structure as a whole.

I would say here we may only speak of a genuine attempt at a solution *to the extent* that the structure of the knot is seen clearly. To the extent that it isn't, everything is groping in the dark, since it's certainly possible that something which looks like a knot to me isn't one at all; (the best proof that I in fact had no method for searching for a solution). We can't compare what goes on here with what happens when I make a methodical search of a room for something, and so discover that it isn't there. For in this case I am searching for a possible state of affairs, not an impossible one.

But now I want to say that the analogy with a knot breaks down, since I can have a knot and get to know it better and better, but in the case of mathematics I want to say it isn't possible for me to learn more and more about something which is already given me in my signs, it's always a matter of learning and designating something *new*.

I don't see how the signs, which we ourselves have made for expressing a certain thing, are supposed to create problems for us.

It's more like a situation in which we are gradually shown more and more of a knot or tangle, and we make ourselves a series of pictures of as much of it as we can see. We have no idea what the part of the knot not yet revealed to us is like and can't in any way make conjectures about this (say, by examining the pictures of the part we know already).

157 What did people discover when they found there was an infinity of primes? What did people discover when they realized there was an infinity of cardinals? – Isn't it exactly similar to the recognition – if that is what it is – that Euclidean Space is infinite, long after we have been forming propositions about the objects in this space.

What is meant by an investigation of space? – For every mathematical investigation is a sort of investigation of space [1]. It's clear that we can investigate the *things* in space – but space itself! (Geometry and Grammar always correspond with one another.)

Let's remember that in mathematics, the signs themselves *do* mathematics, they don't describe it. The mathematical signs *are* like the beads of an abacus. And the beads are in space, and an investigation of the abacus is an investigation of space.

What wasn't foreseen, wasn't foreseeable; for people lacked the system within which it could have been foreseen. (And would have been.)

You can't write mathematics [2], you can only do it. (And for that very reason, you can't 'fiddle' the signs in mathematics.)

Suppose I wanted to construct a regular pentagon but didn't know how, and were now to make experiments at random, finally coming upon the right construction by accident: Haven't we here an actual case of a knot which is untied by trial and error? No, since if I don't understand this construction, as far as I'm concerned it doesn't even begin to be the construction of a pentagon.

Of course I can write down the solution of a quadratic equation by accident, but I can't understand it by accident. The way I have

---

1] See above p. 132. [ed.]
2] In the sense in which you write history. [ed.]

arrived at it vanishes in what I understand. I then understand what I understand. That is, the accident can only refer to something purely external, as when I say 'I found that out after drinking strong coffee.' The coffee has no place in what I discovered.

158 The discovery of the connection between two systems wasn't in the *same* space as those two systems, and if it had been in the same space, it wouldn't have been a discovery (but just a piece of homework).

Where a connection is now known to exist which was previously unknown, there wasn't a gap before, something incomplete which has now been filled in! – (At the time, we weren't in a position to say 'I know this much about the matter, from here on it's unknown to me.')

That is why I have said there are no gaps in mathematics. This contradicts the usual view.

In mathematics there is no 'not yet' and no 'until further notice' (except in the trivial sense that we haven't yet multiplied two 1,000-digit numbers together).

An induction has a great deal in common with the multiplicity of a class (a finite class, of course). But all the same it isn't one, and now it is called an infinite class. –

If, e.g., I say, 'If I know one whorl, I know the whole spiral', that strictly means: if I know the law of a spiral, that's in many respects analogous with the case in which I know a totality of whorls. – But naturally a 'finite' totality, since that's the only kind there is. – We can't now say: I agree it's in many ways analogous with a finite totality, but on the other hand it's completely analogous with an infinite one; that an induction isn't *completely* analogous with a totality is simply all we can say.

Mathematics cannot be incomplete; any more than a *sense* can be incomplete. Whatever I can understand, I must completely understand. This ties up with the fact that my language is in order just as it stands, and that logical analysis does not have to add anything to the sense present in my propositions in order to arrive at complete clarity. So that even the most unclear seeming proposition retains its previous content intact after the analysis and all that happens is that its grammar is made clear.

159   But doesn't it still have to count as a question, whether there is a finite number of primes or not? – Once you have acquired this concept at all. For it certainly seems that the moment I'm introduced to the concept of a prime number, I can ask 'How many are there?' Just as I can ask 'How many are there?' straight off when I am given the concept 'man in this room'.

If I am misled by this analogy, it can only be because the concept 'prime number' is given me in a completely different way from a genuine concept. For, what is the strict expression of the proposition '7 is a prime number'? Obviously it is only that dividing 7 by a smaller number always leaves a remainder. There cannot be a different expression for that, since we can't describe mathematics, we can only do it. (And that of itself abolishes every 'set theory'.)

Therefore once I can write down the general form of prime number, i.e. an expression in which anything analogous to 'the number of prime numbers' is contained at all, then there is no longer a question of 'how many' primes there are, and until I can do this, I also can't put the question. For, I can't ask 'Does the series of primes *eventually* come to an end?' nor, 'Does another prime *ever* come after 7?'

For since it was possible for us to have the phrase 'prime number' in ordinary language, even before there was the strict expression which so to speak admitted of having a number assigned to it, it was also possible for people to have wrongly formed the question how many primes there were. This is what creates the impression that previously there was a problem which is now solved. Verbal language seemed to permit this question both before and after, and so created the illusion that there had been a genuine problem which was succeeded by a genuine solution. Whereas in exact language people originally had nothing of which they could ask how many, and later an expression from which one could immediately read off its multiplicity.

Thus I want to say: only in our verbal language (which in this case leads to a misunderstanding of logical form) are there in mathematics 'as yet unsolved problems' or the problem of the finite 'solubility of every mathematical problem'.

160   It seems to me that the idea of the consistency of the axioms of mathematics, by which mathematicians are so haunted these days, rests on a misunderstanding.

This is tied up with the fact that the axioms of mathematics are not seen for what they are, namely, propositions of syntax.

There is no question as to provability, and in *that* sense no proof of provability either. The so-called proof of provability is an induction, to recognize which is to recognize a new system.

A consistency proof can't be essential for the application of the axioms.

A postulate is only the postulation of a form of expression. The 'axioms' are postulates of the form of expression.

161   The comparison between a mathematical expedition and a polar expedition. There is a point in drawing this comparison, and it is a very useful one.

How strange it would be if a geographical expedition were uncertain whether it had a goal, and so whether it had any route whatsoever. We can't imagine such a thing, it's nonsense. But this is precisely what it is like in a mathematical expedition. And so perhaps it's a good idea to drop the comparison altogether.

It would be an expedition, which was uncertain of *the space* it was in!

How can there be conjectures in mathematics? Or better: what sort of thing is it that looks like a conjecture in mathematics? Such as making a conjecture about the distribution of primes.

I might, e.g., imagine that someone is writing the primes in series in front of me without my knowing they are the primes – I might for instance believe he is writing down numbers just as they occur to him – and I now try to detect a law in them. I might now actually form an hypothesis about this number sequence, just as I could about any other sequence yielded by an experiment in physics.

Now in what sense have I, by so doing, made an hypothesis about the distribution of primes?

You might say that an hypothesis in mathematics has the value that it trains your thoughts on a particular object – I mean a particular region – and we might say 'we shall surely discover something interesting about these things'.

The trouble is that our language uses each of the words 'question', 'problem', 'investigation', 'discovery' to refer to such basically different things. It's the same with 'inference', 'proposition', 'proof'.

The question again arises, what kind of verification do I count as valid for my hypothesis? Or, can I – *faute de mieux* – allow an empirical one to hold for the time being, until I have a 'strict proof'? No. Until there is such a proof, there's no connection at all between hypothesis and the 'concept' of a prime number.

The concept of a prime number is the general law by means of which I test whether a number is a prime number or not.

Only the so-called proof establishes any connection between my hypothesis and the primes *as such*. And that is shown by the fact that – as I've said – until then, the hypothesis can be construed as one belonging purely to physics. – On the other hand, when we have supplied a proof, it doesn't prove what was conjectured at all, since I can't conjecture to infinity. I can only conjecture what can be confirmed, but experience can only confirm a finite number of conjectures and you can't conjecture the proof until you've got it – and not then either.

The concept 'prime number' is the general form of investigation of a number for the relevant property; the concept 'composite' the general form of investigation for divisibility etc.

162   What kind of discovery did Sheffer make when he found that $p \vee q$ and $\sim p$ can be expressed by means of $p|q$? People had no method for looking for $p|q$, and if someone were to find one today, it wouldn't make any difference.

What was it we didn't know before the discovery? It wasn't anything that we didn't know, it was something with which we weren't acquainted.

You can see this very clearly if you imagine someone objecting that $p|p$ isn't at all the same as is said by $\sim p$. The reply, of course, is that it's only a question of the system $p|q$ etc. having the necessary multiplicity. Thus Sheffer found a symbolic system with the necessary multiplicity.

Does it count as looking for something, if I am unaware of Sheffer's system and say I would like to construct a system with only *one* logical constant? No!

Systems are certainly not all in *one* space, so that I could say:

there are systems with 3 and with 2 logical constants, and now I am trying to reduce the number of constants *in the same way*. There is no '*same way*' here.

We might also put it like this: the completely analysed mathematical proposition is its own proof.

Or like this: a mathematical proposition is only the immediately visible surface of a whole body of proof and this surface is the boundary facing us.

A mathematical proposition – unlike a genuine proposition – is *essentially* the last link in a demonstration that renders it visibly right or wrong.

We can imagine a notation in which every proposition is represented as the result of performing certain operations – transitions – on particular 'axioms' treated as bases. (Roughly in the same way as chemical compounds are represented by means of such names as 'trimethylamide' etc.)

With a few modifications, such a notation could be constructed out of the instructions with which Russell and Whitehead preface the propositions of *Principia Mathematica*.

A mathematical proposition is related to its proof as the outer surface of a body is to the body itself. We might talk of the body of proof belonging to the proposition.

Only on the assumption that there's a body behind the surface, has the proposition any significance for us.

We also say: a mathematical proposition is the last link in a chain of proof.

XIV

163   $a + (b + c) = (a + b) + c$ ... $A(c)$ can be construed as a basic rule of a system. As such, it can only be laid down, but not *asserted*, or denied (hence no law of the excluded middle). But I can apparently also regard the proposition as the result of a proof. Is this proof the answer to a question and, if so, which? Has it shown an assertion to be true and so its negation to be false?

But now it looks as though I cannot prove the proposition at all in the sense in which it is a basic rule of a system. Rather, I prove something about it.

This is tied up with the question whether you can deny $2 = 2$, as you can $2 \times 35 = 70$, and why you cannot deny a definition.

In school, children admittedly learn that $2 \times 2 = 4$, but not that $2 = 2$.

If we want to see what has been proved, we ought to look at nothing but the proof.

We ought not to confuse the infinite possibility of its application with what is actually proved. The infinite possibility of application is *not* proved!

The most striking thing about a recursive proof is that what it alleges to prove is not what comes out of it.

The proof shows that the form $a + (b + (c + 1)) = (a + b) + (c + 1)$ ... $A(c + 1)$ follows from the form 1) $A(c)$ in accordance with the rule 2) $a + (b + 1) \overset{\text{Def}}{=} (a + b) + 1$ ... $A(1)$. Or, what comes to the same thing, by means of the rules 1) and 2) the form $a + (b + (c + 1))$ can be transformed into $(a + b) + (c + 1)$. This is the sum total of what is actually in the proof. Everything else, and the whole of the usual interpretation, lies in the possibility of its application. And the usual mistake, in confusing the extension of its application with what it genuinely contains.

Of course, a definition is not something that I can deny. So it does not have a sense, either. It is a rule by which I can proceed (or have to proceed).

I cannot negate the basic rules of a system.

In Skolem's proof the '*c*' doesn't have any meaning *during* the proof, it stands for 1 or for what may perhaps come out of the proof, and *after* the proof we are justified in regarding it as some number or other. But it must surely have already meant something in the proof. If 1, why then don't we write '1' instead of '*c*'? And if something else, what? [1]

1] This remark refers to the first section of Th. Skolem's *Begründung der Elementaren Arithmetik durch die Rekurrierende Denkweise ohne Anwendung Scheinbarer Veränderlichen mit Unendlichem Ausdehnungsbereich* (Videnskap-sselskapets Skrifter. 1 Math.-Naturv. Klasse 1923, No. 6.). [Translated in van Heijenhoort: *From Frege to Gödel,* Harvard University Press, 1967, pp. 302–333.]
The text runs:

§ 1
Addition

I will introduce a descriptive function of two variables a and b, which I will designate by means of $a + b$ and call the sum of a and b, in that, for $b = 1$, it is to mean simply the successor of a, $a + 1$. And so this function is to be regarded as already defined for $b = 1$ and arbitrary a. In order to define it in general, I in that case only need to define it for $b + 1$ and arbitrary a, on the assumption that it is already defined for b and arbitrary a. This is done by means of the following definition:

Def. 1. $a + (b + 1) = (a + b) + 1$

In this manner, the sum of a and $b + 1$ is equated with the successor of $a + b$. And so if addition is already defined for arbitrary values of a for a certain number b, then by Def. 1 addition is explained for $b + 1$ for arbitrary a, and

If we now suppose that I wish to apply the theorem to 5, 6, 7, then the proof tells me I am certainly entitled to do so. That is to say, if I write these numbers in the form $((1 + 1) + 1)$ etc., then I can recognize that the proposition is a member of the series of propositions that the final proposition of Skolem's chain presents me with. Once more, this recognition is not provable, but intuitive.

---

thereby is defined in general. This is a typical example of a recursive definition.

Theorem 1. The associative law: $a + (b + c) = (a + b) + c$.

Proof: The theorem holds for $c = 1$ in virtue of Def. 1. Assume that it is valid for a certain c for arbitrary a and b.

Then we must have, for arbitrary values of a and b

$$(\alpha) \qquad a + (b + (c + 1)) = a + ((b + c) + 1)$$

since, that is to say, by Def. 1 $b + (c + 1) = (b + c) + 1$. But also by Def. 1

$$(\beta) \qquad a + ((b + c) + 1) = (a + (b+c)) + 1.$$

Now, by hypothesis, $a + (b + c) = (a + b) + c$, whence

$$(\gamma) \qquad (a + (b + c)) + 1 = ((a + b) + c) + 1.$$

Finally, by Def. 1 we also have

$$(\delta) \qquad ((a + b) + c) + 1 = (a + b) + (c + 1).$$

From (α), (β), (γ), and (δ) there follows

$$a + (b + (c + 1)) = (a + b) + (c + 1),$$

whence the theorem is proved for $c + 1$ with a and b left undetermined. Thus the theorem holds generally. This is a typical example of a recursive proof (proof by complete induction).

In the margin of his copy, Wittgenstein drew arrows pointing to 'Theorem 1' and to (α) and wrote: 'the c is a different kind of variable in these two cases'. He puts a question mark against the equals sign in (γ); and another question mark and 'Transition?' against the words 'whence the theorem is proved for $c + 1$ with a and b left undetermined'. Cf. above footnote on p. 144: 'If one makes the wrong transition from a variable proposition to a general proposition. . . .'

'Every symbol is what it is and not another symbol.'

Can there be no proof which merely shows that every multiplication in the decimal system in accordance with the rules must yield a number of the decimal system? (So that recognizing the same system would thus after all depend on recognizing the truth of a mathematical proposition.)

It would have to be analogous to a proof that by addition of forms $((1 + 1) + 1)$ etc. numbers of this form would always result. Now, can that be proved? The proof obviously lies in the rule for addition of such expressions, i.e. in the definition and in nothing else.

Indeed, we might also reply to the question for which this proof is to provide the answer: Well, what *else* do you expect the addition to yield?

164 A recursive proof is only a general guide to an arbitrary special proof. A signpost that shows every proposition of a particular form a particular way home. It says to the proposition $2 + (3 + 4) = (2 + 3) + 4$: 'Go in *this* direction (run through this spiral), and you will arrive home.'

To what extent, now, can we call such a guide to proofs the proof of a general proposition? (Isn't that like wanting to ask: 'To what extent can we call a signpost a route?')

Yet it surely does justify the application of $A(c)$ to numbers. And so mustn't there, after all, be a legitimate transition from the proof schema to this expression?

I know a proof with endless possibility, which, e.g., begins with '$A(1)$' and continues through '$A(2)$' etc. etc. The recursive proof is the general form of continuing along this series. But it itself must still prove something since it in fact spares me the trouble of proving each proposition of the form '$A(7)$'. But how can it prove this proposition? It obviously points along the series of proofs

$$a + (b + (\xi + d)) = (a + (b + \xi)) + d = ((a + b) + \xi) + d = (a + b) + (\xi + d)$$

$$a + (b + ((\xi + d))) = (a + (b + (\xi + d))) + d = ((a + b) + (\xi + d)) + d = (a + b) + ((\xi + d) + d)$$

That is a stretch of the spiral taken out of the middle.

ξ is a stop-gap for what only emerges in the course of the development.

If I look at this series, it may strike me that it is akin to the definition $A(1)$; that if I substitute '1' for 'c' and '1' for 'd', the two systems are the same.

In the proof, at any rate, what is to be proved is not the end of the *chain of equations*.

The proof shows the spiral form of the law.

But not in such a way that it comes out as the conclusion of the chain of inferences.

It is also very easy to imagine a popular introduction of the proof using 1, perhaps followed by dots to indicate what we are to look out for. It wouldn't in essence be any less strict. (For the peculiarity of the proof stands out even more clearly in this case.)

Let's imagine it like this. *How* does it then justify the proposition $A(c)$?

If one regards the proof as being of the same sort as the derivation of $(x + y)^2 = x^2 + 2xy + y^2$, then it proves the proposition '$A(c + 1)$' (on the hypothesis '$A(c)$', and so of the proposition I really want to prove). And justifies – on this assumption – special cases such as $3 + (5 + (4 + 1)) = (3 + 5) + (4 + 1)$. It also has a generality, but not the one we desire. This generality does not lie in the letters, but just as much in the particular numbers and consists in the fact that we can repeat the proof.

But how can I use the sign '$f(a)$' to indicate what I see in the passage from $f(1)$ to $f(2)$? (i.e. the possibility of repetition.)

Neither can I prove that $a + (b + 1) = (a + b) + 1$
is a special case of $a + (b + c) = (a + b) + c$:
I must see it.
(No rule can help me here either, since I would still have to know what would be a special case of this general rule.)

This is the unbridgeable gulf between rule and application, or law and special case.

$A(c)$ [1] is a definition, a rule for algebraic calculation. It is *chosen* in such a way that this calculation agrees with arithmetical calculation. It permits the same transition in algebraic calculation that holds for cardinal numbers, as may be seen in the recursive proof. Thus $A(c)$ is not the result of a proof, it so to speak runs parallel with it.

What we gather from the proof, we cannot represent in a proposition at all and of course for the same reason we can't deny it either.

But what about a definition like $A(1)$ [2]? This is not meant as a rule for algebraic calculation, but as a device for explaining arithmetical expressions. It represents an *operation*, which I *can* apply to an arbitrary pair of numbers.

165   The correct expression for the associative law is not a proposition, but precisely its 'proof', which admittedly doesn't state the law, but shows it. And at this point it becomes clear that we cannot

---

1] $a + (b + c) = (a + b) + c.$
2] $a + (b + 1) \overset{\text{Def}}{=} (a + b) + 1.$

deny the law, since it doesn't figure in the form of a proposition at all. We could of course deny the individual equations of the law, but would not thereby deny the law: that *eludes* affirmation and denial.

To know that you can prove something is to have proved it.

$7 + (8 + 9) = (7 + 8) + 9$. How do I know that this is so, without having to give a particular proof of it? And do I know *just as well* as if I had given a complete derivation of it? Yes! – Then that means it really is proved. What's more, in that case it cannot have a still *better* proof; say, by my carrying out the derivation as far as this proposition itself. So it must be possible for me to say after running through one turn of the spiral 'Stop! I don't need any more, I can already see how it goes on', and then every higher step must be purely superfluous and doesn't make the matter clearer. If I draw all the whorls of the spiral as far as my point, I cannot see that the spiral leads to it any better than if I draw only *one*. It is only that each shows the same thing in a different form. I can so to speak blindly follow the spiral that has been completely drawn in and arrive at my point, whereas the *one* whorl which has been drawn has to be interpreted in a particular way for me to perceive that, if continued, it leads to the point A.

That is to say: from the proof for $6 + (7 + 8) = (6 + 7) + 8$ which has been completely worked out, I can extract the same as from the one which only describes one 'whorl', but in a different way. And at any rate the *one* whorl *in conjunction with the numerical forms* of the given equation is a complete proof of this equation. It's as though I were to say: 'You want to get to the point A? Well, you can get *there* along *this* spiral.'

When we teach someone how to take his first step, we thereby enable him to go any distance.

166   As the immediate datum is to a proposition which it verifies, so is the arithmetical relation we see in the structure to the equation which it verifies.

It is the real thing, not an expression for something else for which another expression could also be substituted. That is, it is not a symptom of something else, but the thing itself.

For that is how it is usually construed (i.e. in the wrong way). One says an induction is a sign that such and such holds for all numbers. But the induction isn't a sign for anything but itself. If there were yet something besides the induction, for which *it* was a sign, this something would have to have its specific expression which would be nothing but the complete expression for this something.

And this conception is then developed into the idea that the algebraic equation tells us what we see in the arithmetical induction. For that, it would have to have the same multiplicity as what it describes.

How a proposition is verified is what it says. Compare the generality of genuine propositions with generality in arithmetic. It is differently verified and so is of a different kind.

The verification is not *one* token of the truth, it is *the* sense of the proposition. (Einstein: How a magnitude is measured is what it is.)

Indeed Russell has really already shown by his theory of descriptions, that you can't get a knowledge of things by sneaking up on them from behind and it can only *look* as if we knew more about things than they have shown us openly and honestly. But he has obscured everything again by using the phrase 'indirect knowledge'.

167   An algebraic schema derives its sense from the way in which it is applied. So this must always be behind it. But then so must the inductive proof, since that justifies the application.

An algebraic proposition is just as much an equation as $2 \times 2 = 4$, it is only applied differently. Its relation to arithmetic is different. It deals with the substitutability of other parts of speech.

That is to say, an algebraic equation as an equation between real numbers is, *to be sure*, an arithmetical equation, since something arithmetical lies behind it. Only it lies behind the *algebraic* equation in a different way from the way it lies behind $1 + 1 = 2$.

An induction doesn't prove the algebraic proposition, since only an equation can prove an equation. But it justifies the setting up of algebraic equations from the standpoint of their application to arithmetic.

That is, it is only through the induction that they gain their sense, not their truth.

For this reason, what can no longer be reduced to other equations, and can only be justified by induction, is a *stipulation*.

Which is connected with the fact that in the application of this algebraic proposition I cannot appeal to it, but once again only to the induction.

Hence these last equations can't be denied – i.e. there is no arithmetical content corresponding to their negation.

Through them alone the algebraic system becomes applicable to numbers.

And so in a particular sense they are certainly the expression of something arithmetical, but as it were the expression of an arithmetical *existence*.

They alone make algebra into clothing for arithmetic – and are therefore arbitrary to the extent that no one compels us to use algebra in this way. They fit algebra on to arithmetic.
And while it is wearing these clothes, it can move about in them.

They are not the expression of something computable and to that extent are stipulations.

Can someone who sees these stipulations learn something from them, in arithmetic? And, if so, what? – Can I learn an arithmetical state of affairs, and, if so, which?
A stipulation is more like a name than like a proposition.

You can only prove those propositions whose truth you can enquire into. 'Is it so or not?' 'I will prove to you it *is so*.'

An induction is related to an algebraic proposition not as a proof is to what is proved, but as what is designated to a sign.

The system of algebraic propositions corresponds to a *system* of inductions.

168   A proof by induction, if it were a proof, would be a proof of generality, not a proof of a certain property of all numbers.

We can only ask from a standpoint from which a question is possible. From which a doubt is possible.
If one wanted to ask about $A(c)$, it wouldn't strictly speaking be the induction that answered us, but the humiliating feeling that we

could only arrive at the thought of this equation by way of the induction.

If we ask 'Does $a + (b + c) = (a + b) + c$?', what could we be after? Taken purely algebraically, the question means nothing, since the answer would be: 'Just as you like, as you decide.' Neither can the question mean 'Does this hold for all numbers?', it can only ask what the induction says: it, however, says nothing at all to us.

We cannot ask about that which alone makes questions possible at all.

Not about what first gives the system a foundation.

That some such thing must be present is clear.

And it is also clear that in algebra this first thing must present itself as a rule of calculation, which we can then use to test the other propositions.

An algebraic proposition always gains only arithmetical significance if you replace the letters in it by numerals, and then always only *particular* arithmetical significance.

Its generality doesn't lie in itself, but in the possibility of its correct application. And for that it has to keep on having recourse to the induction.

That is, it does not assert its generality, it does not express it; the generality is, rather, shown in the formal relation to the substitution, which proves to be a term of the inductive series.

$(\exists 24x) \cdot \varphi x \cdot (\exists 18x) \cdot \psi x \cdot \text{Ind}: \supset :(\exists 24 + 18x) \cdot \varphi x \vee \psi x$. How do I know that this is so, unless I have introduced the concept of addition for the context of this application? I can only arrive at this proposition by induction. That is to say, corresponding to the general proposition – or rather, the tautology – $(\exists nx) \cdot \varphi x \cdot (\exists mx) \cdot \psi x \cdot \text{Ind}: \supset :(\exists n + mx) \cdot \varphi x \vee \psi x$, there is an induction, and this induction is the proof of the above proposition '$(\exists 24x) \cdot$ etc.', even before we have actually worked out $24 + 18$ and have tested whether it is a tautology.

To *believe* Goldbach's Conjecture, means to believe you have a proof of it, since I can't, as it were, believe it *in extenso*, because that doesn't mean anything, and you cannot imagine an induction corresponding to it until you have one.

If the proof that every equation has a root is a recursive proof, then that means the Fundamental Theorem of Algebra isn't a genuine mathematical *proposition* [1].

169 If I want to know what '$1/3 = 0.\dot{3}$' means, it's a relevant question to ask 'How can I know that?' For the proof comes as a reply to this 'how?', and more than is shown by this proof I certainly do not know.

It is clear that every multiplication in the decimal system has a solution and therefore that one can prove any arithmetical equation of the form $a \times b = c$ or prove its opposite. What would a proof of this provability look like? It is obviously nothing further than a clarification of the symbolism and an exhibition of an induction from which it can be seen what sort of propositions the ladder leads to.

I cannot deny the *generality* of a general arithmetical proposition.

Isn't it only this generality that I cannot reflect in the algebraic proposition?

An equation can only be proved by reducing it to equations.
The last equations in this process are definitions.
If an equation can't be reduced to other equations, then it is a definition.
An induction cannot justify an equation.
Therefore, e.g. the introduction of the notation $\dot{3}$ cannot refer to the induction whose sign it appears to be. The relation must be similar to that of '$A(c)$' to its proof by induction.

1] Fundamental Theorem = Hauptsatz, proposition = Satz. [trans.]

Or better, it certainly refers to the bare facts of the induction, but not to the generality, which is its true sense.

XV

170 The theory of aggregates attempts to grasp the infinite at a more general level than a theory of rules. It says that you can't grasp the actual infinite by means of arithmetical symbolism at all and that therefore it can only be described and not represented. The description would encompass it in something like the way in which you carry a number of things that you can't hold in your hands by packing them in a box. They are then invisible but we still know we are carrying them (so to speak, indirectly). The theory of aggregates buys a pig in a poke. Let the infinite accommodate itself in this box as best it can.

With this there goes too the idea that we can use language to describe logical forms. In a description of this sort the structures and e.g. correlations etc., are presented in a package, and so it does indeed look as if one could talk about a structure without reproducing it in the proposition itself. Concepts which are packed up like this and so whose structures are not recognisable may, to be sure, be used, but they always derive their meaning from definitions which package the concepts in this way; and if we trace our way back through these definitions the concepts are then unpacked again and so are present in their structure.

This is what Russell does with R^*; he wraps the concept up in such a way that its form disappears.

The point of this method is to make everything amorphous and treat it accordingly.

If in logic a question can be answered (1) generally and (2) in particular, the particular answer must always show itself to be a special case of the general answer; put differently: the general case must always include the particular as a possibility.

A case of this is the calculation of a limit with δ and ν, which must include the number system of the particular computation.

There must be a determinate way for translating the general form and the particular form into one another.

171 Any proof of the continuity of a function must relate to a numerical scale – a number system.

For if I say, 'Given any ν there is a δ for which the function is less than ν', I am *ipso facto* referring to a general arithmetical criterion that indicates when $\varphi(\delta)$ is less than ν.

It is impossible that what in the nature of this case comes to light when calculating the function – namely, the numerical scale – should be allowed to disappear in the general treatment.

If the numerical system belongs to the essence of number, then the general treatment cannot do away with it.

And if, therefore, the notation of the numerical system reflects the essence of number, then this essential element must also find its way into the general notation. In this way the general notation acquires the structure of the numbers.

If, in the nature of the case, I cannot write down a number independently of a number system, that must also be reflected in the general treatment of number.

A number system is not something inferior – like a Russian abacus – that is only of interest to elementary schools, while the higher, general discussion can afford to disregard it.

The Cretan liar paradox could also be set up with someone writing the proposition: 'This proposition is false'. The demonstrative takes over the role of the 'I' in 'I'm lying'. The basic mistake consists, as in the previous philosophy of logic, in assuming that a word can make a sort of allusion to its object (point at it from a distance) without necessarily going proxy for it.

So the question would really be: Can the continuum be described? As Cantor and others tried to do.

A form cannot be described: it can only be presented.

Dedekind's definition of an infinite set is another example of an attempt to describe the infinite, without *presenting* it.

It would be like describing an illness by the external symptoms we know always accompany it. Only in this case there is a connection which isn't formal in nature.

172 'The highest point of a curve' doesn't mean 'the highest point among all the points of the curve' – after all, we don't see these – it is a specific point yielded by the curve. In the same way the maximum of a function isn't the largest value among all its values (that's nonsense, save in the case of finitely many, discrete points), it's a point yielded by a law and a condition; which, to be sure, is higher than any other point taken at random (*possibility*, not reality). And so also the point of intersection of two lines isn't the common member of two classes of points, it's the meeting of two laws. As indeed is perfectly clear in analytic geometry.

The maximum of a function is susceptible of an intensional explanation. The highest point of a curve is admittedly higher than any other point taken at random, but I don't find it by sifting through the points of the curve one by one, looking for a yet higher one.

Here again it is grammar which, as always in the sphere of the infinite, is playing tricks on us.

We say 'the highest point of the curve'. But that can't mean 'the highest point of all the points in the curve' in the sense in which we talk of the largest of these three apples, since we don't have all the points of the curve before us – in fact that's a nonsense expression.

It's the same defect in our syntax which presents the proposition 'The apple may be divided into two parts' as of the same form as 'a length may be divided without limit', with the result that we can apparently say in both cases, 'Let's suppose the possible division to have been carried out'.

But in truth the expressions 'divisible into two parts' and 'divisible without limit' have completely different forms.

This is, of course, the same case as the one in which someone operates with the word 'infinite' as if it were a number word; because, in everyday speech, both are given as answers to the question 'How many?'

The curve exists, independently of its individual points. This also finds expression in the fact that I *construct* its highest point: that is, derive it from a law and not by examining individual points.

We don't say 'among *all* its points, there is only one at which it intersects the straight line'; no, we only talk about *one* point.

So to speak, about one that runs along the straight line, but not about one among all the points of the line.

The straight line isn't *composed* of points.

173   But then what would a correct, as opposed to an amorphous explanation of R* be like? Here I do need '$(n)\ldots$'. In this case, this expression seems to be admissible.

But, to be sure, '$(\exists x)\cdot \varphi x$' also says 'There is a number of x satisfying φx', and yet the expression '$(\exists x)\cdot \varphi x$' can't be taken to presuppose the totality of all numbers.

Ramsey's explanation of infinity also is nonsense for the same reason, since '$(n):(\exists nx)\cdot \varphi x$' would presuppose that we were given the actual infinite and not merely the unlimited possibility of going on [1].

But is it inconceivable that I should know someone to be my ancestor without having *any* idea at what remove, so that *no* limits would be set to the number of people in between [2].

But how would we put the proposition: 'φ is satisfied by the same number of objects as ψ'? One would suppose: '$(\exists n):(\exists n x)\cdot \varphi x\cdot(\exists n x)\cdot \psi x$'.

Brouwer is right when he says that the properties of his pendulum number are incompatible with the law of the excluded middle. But, saying this doesn't reveal a peculiarity of propositions about infinite aggregates. Rather, it is based on the fact that logic presupposes that it cannot be *a priori* – i.e. logically – impossible to tell whether a proposition is true or false. For, if the question of the truth or falsity of a proposition is *a priori* undecidable, the consequence is that the proposition loses its sense and the consequence of this is precisely that the propositions of logic lose their validity for it.

Just as in general the whole approach that if a proposition is valid for one region of mathematics it need not necessarily be valid for a second region as well, is quite out of place in mathematics, completely contrary to its essence. Although these authors hold

---

1] In the notebook W. then wrote: 'Strangely enough the general concept of the ancestral relation also seems to me to be nonsense now. It seems to me that the variable *n* must always be confined as lying within two limits.'
2] 'If it were admissible to write '$(\exists n x)\cdot \varphi x$' instead of '$(\exists x)\cdot \varphi x$', then it would be admissible to write '$(n x)\cdot \varphi x$' instead of '$\sim(\exists x)\sim\cdot \varphi x$' – and so of '$(x)\cdot \varphi x$' – and that presupposes that there are infinitely many objects.

And so the $(\exists n x)\ldots$, if it has any justification at all, here may not mean 'there is one among all the numbers . . .' [Manuscript]

just this approach to be particularly subtle, and to combat prejudice.

Mathematics is ridden through and through with the pernicious idioms of set theory. *One* example of this is the way people speak of a line as composed of points. A line is a law and isn't composed of anything at all. A line as a coloured length in visual space can be composed of shorter coloured lengths (but, of course, not of points). And then we are surprised to find, e.g., that 'between the everywhere dense rational points' there is still room for the irrationals! What does a construction like that for $\sqrt{2}$ show? Does it show how there is yet room for this point in between all the rational points? It merely shows that the point *yielded* by the construction is *not rational*.

And what corresponds to this construction and to this point in arithmetic? A sort of number which manages *after all* to squeeze in between the rational numbers? A law that is not a law of the nature of a rational number.

The Dedekind cut proceeds as if it were clear what was meant when one says: There are only three cases: either R has a last member and L a first, or, etc. In truth none of these cases can be conceived (or imagined).

174 Set theory is wrong because it apparently presupposes a symbolism which doesn't exist instead of one that does exist (is alone possible). It builds on a fictitious symbolism, therefore on nonsense.

There is no such thing as an hypothesis in logic.

When people say 'The set of all transcendental numbers is greater that that of algebraic numbers', that's nonsense. The set is of a different kind. It isn't 'no longer' denumerable, it's simply not denumerable!

The distribution of primes would then for once provide us with something in logic that a god could know and we couldn't. That is to say, there would be something in logic that could be known, but not by us.

That there is a process of solution is something that cannot be asserted. For, were there none, the equation, as a general proposition, would be nonsensical.
We can assert anything which can be checked in practice.

It's a question of the possibility of checking.

If someone says (as Brouwer does) that for $(x) \cdot f_1 x = f_2 x$, there is, as well as yes and no, also the case of undecidability, this implies that '$(x) \ldots$' is meant extensionally and we may talk of the case in which all x happen to have a property. In truth, however, it's impossible to talk of such a case at all and the '$(x) \ldots$' in arithmetic cannot be taken extensionally.

We might say, 'A mathematical proposition is a pointer to an insight'. The assumption that no insight corresponded to it would reduce it to utter nonsense.
We cannot *understand* the equation unless we recognize the connection between its two sides.

Undecidability presupposes that there is, so to speak, a subterranean connection between the two sides; that the bridge *cannot* be made with symbols.

A connection between symbols which exists but cannot be represented by symbolic transformations is a thought that cannot be thought. If the connection is there, then it must be possible to see it.

For it *exists* in the same way as the connection between parts of visual space. It isn't a *causal* connection. The transition isn't produced by means of some dark speculation different in kind from what it connects. (Like a dark passage between two sunlit places.)

Of course, if mathematics were the natural science of infinite extensions of which we can never have exhaustive knowledge, then a question that was in principle undecidable would certainly be conceivable.

175   Is there a sense in saying: 'I have as many shoes as the value of a root of the equation $x^3 + 2x - 3 = 0$'? Even if solving it were to yield a positive integer?

For, on my view, we would have here a notation in which we cannot immediately tell sense from nonsense.

If one regards the expression 'the root of the equation $\varphi x = 0$' as a Russellian description, then a proposition about the root of the equation $x + 2 = 6$ must have a different sense from one saying the same about 4.

I cannot use a proposition before knowing whether it makes sense, whether it is a proposition. And this I don't know in the above case of an unsolved equation, since I don't know whether cardinal numbers correspond to the roots in the prescribed manner. It is clear that the proposition in the given case becomes nonsense and not false (not even a contradiction), since 'I have n shoes and $n^2 = 2$' is obviously tantamount to 'I have $\sqrt{2}$ shoes'.

But I can establish this – or at any rate it can be established – if we only look at the signs. But I mustn't chance my luck and incorporate the equation in the proposition, I may only incorporate it if I know that it determines a cardinal number, for in that case it is simply a different notation for the cardinal number. Otherwise, it's just like throwing the signs down like so many dice and leaving it to chance whether they yield a sense or not.

$(x + y)^2 = x^2 + y^2 + 2xy$ is correct in the same sense as $2 \times 2 = 4$.

And $2 + n = 1$ (where n is a cardinal number) is just as wrong as $2 + 3 = 1$ and $2 + n \neq 1$ as correct as the above.

176   What makes one dubious about a purely internal generality is the fact that it can be refuted by the occurrence of a single case (and so by something extensional).

But what sort of collision is there here between the general and the particular proposition? The particular case refutes the general proposition from within, not in an external way.

It attacks the internal proof of the proposition and refutes it thus – not in the way that the existence of a one-eyed man refutes the proposition 'Every man has two eyes'.

'$(x) \cdot x^2 = x + x$' seems to be false because working out the equation gives $x = \{ {0 \atop 2} \}$ and not that the two sides cancel out. Trying the substitution $x = 3$, say, also yields the general result – $(\exists x) . x^2 \neq 2x$ – and so must, to the extent that its result tallies with that of the general solution, itself tally with the general method.

If the equation $x^2 + 2x + 2 = 0$ yields, by applying the algebraic rules, $x = -1 \pm \sqrt{-1}$, that is quite in order so long as we don't require the rules for x to accord with the rules for real numbers. In that case the outcome of the algebraic calculation means that the equation has no solution.

My difficulty is: When I solve equations in the real, rational or whole number domain by the appropriate rules, in certain cases I arrive at apparent nonsense. Now, when that happens: am I to say this proves that the original equation was nonsense? Which would mean I could only see whether it was sense or nonsense after I had finished applying the rules?! Isn't what we have to say, rather: The result of the apparently nonsensical equation does after all show something about the general form, and does indeed establish a connection between the forbidden equation and equations which have a normal solution. After all, the solution always does show the distance of the abnormal solution from a normal one. If, e.g., $\sqrt{-1}$ is the result, I at least know that $\sqrt{-1+1}$ would be a normal root. The continuity, the connection with the normal solution, has not been disrupted. Would this imply that in the concept of the real numbers as we represent it in our symbolism and its rules, the concept of the imaginary numbers is already prefigured?

That would amount to roughly the same thing as saying of a straight line g that it is a distance a away from cutting the circle, instead of simply saying it doesn't cut it.

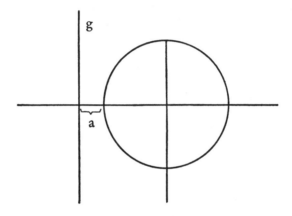

One might say 'It fails to intersect it by a certain amount' and this would represent the continuity with normal intersection. 'It misses it by a certain amount.'

The difference between the two equations $x^2 = x \cdot x$ and $x^2 = 2x$ *isn't* one consisting in the extensions of their validity.

I can, it is true, define $m > n$ as $(\exists x) \cdot n + x = m$, but I only know whether $x = m - n$ yields a number if I know the rule for subtraction, and in this context this does duty for the rule for determining greater and less. Thus formulated, this rule runs: m is greater than n, if, according to the rule for subtraction, $m - n$ yields a number.

XVI

177 What makes it apparent that space is not a collection of points, but the realization of a law?

It seems as though we should have first to erect the entire structure of space without using propositions; and then one may form all the correct propositions within it.

In order to represent space we need – so it appears to me – something like an expansible sign.
A sign that makes allowance for an interpolation, similar to the decimal system.
The sign must have the multiplicity and properties of space.

The axioms of a geometry are not to include any truths.

We can be sure of getting the correct multiplicity for the designations if we use analytic geometry.
That a point in the plane is represented by a number-pair, and in three-dimensional space by a number-triple, is enough to show that the object represented isn't the point at all but the point-network.

178 The geometry of visual space is the syntax of the propositions about objects in visual space.

The axioms – e.g. – of Euclidean geometry are the disguised rules of a syntax. This becomes very clear if you look at what corresponds to them in analytic geometry.

You could imagine the constructions of Euclidean geometry actually being carried out, say by using the edges of bodies as straight lines and the surfaces as planes. The axiom – for instance – that a straight line can be drawn through any two points has here the clear sense that, although no straight line *is* drawn between any 2 arbitrary points, it is *possible* to draw one, and that only means that the proposition 'A straight line passes through these points' makes *sense*. That is to say, Euclidean geometry is the syntax of assertions about objects in Euclidean space. And these objects are not lines, planes and points, but *bodies*.

How are the equations of analysis connected with the results of spatial measurements? I believe, in such a way that they (the equations) fix what is to count as an accurate measurement and what as an error.

One could almost speak of an external and an internal geometry. Whatever is arranged in visual space stands in this *sort* of order *a priori*, i.e. in virtue of its logical nature, and geometry here is simply grammar. What the physicist sets into relation with one another in the geometry of physical space are instrument readings, which do not differ in their *internal* nature whether we live in a linear space or a spherical one. That is to say, it isn't an investigation of the logical properties of these readings that leads the physicist to make an assumption about the nature of physical space, but the facts that are derived from them.

The geometry of physics in this sense doesn't have to do with possibility, but with the facts. It is corroborated by facts: in the sense, that is, in which a *part* of an hypothesis is corroborated.

Comparison between working with an adding machine and measuring geometrical structures: In such measurement, do we perform an experiment, or is the situation here the same as in the case of the adding machine, where we only establish internal relations and the physical result of our operations proves nothing?

In visual space, of course, there is no such thing as a geometrical experiment.

I believe this is where the main source of misunderstanding about the *a priori* and the *a posteriori* in geometry lies.

The question is, in what sense can the results of measurement tell us something concerning *that* which we also see.

What about the proposition 'The sum of the angles of a triangle is 180°'? At any rate, it doesn't give the appearance of a proposition of syntax.

The proposition 'Vertically opposite angles are equal' means that if they turn out to be different when they are measured, I shall declare the measurement to be in error; and 'The sum of the angles of a triangle is 180°' means that, if the sum doesn't turn out to be 180° when measured, I shall assume an error in the measurement. In this way, the proposition is a postulation concerning the way to describe the facts: and so a proposition of syntax.

There is obviously a method for constructing a straight ruler. This method involves an ideal: I mean, an approximation procedure with unlimited *possibility*, for it is simply this procedure which *is* the ideal.

Or better: Only if it is a procedure with unlimited possibility, can (not must) the geometry of this procedure be Euclidean.

Euclidean geometry doesn't presuppose *any method for measuring* angles and lengths, it no more says when two angles are to be counted as equal, than probability theory says when two cases are to be counted as equally likely. If a particular method of measurement is now adopted – say one with metal rulers – the question then arises whether the results of measurements carried out in this way yield Euclidean results.

179 Imagine we are throwing a two-sided die, such as a coin. I now want to determine a point of the interval A B by continually tossing the coin, and always bisecting the side prescribed by the

throw: say: heads means I bisect the right-hand interval, tails the left-hand one

Now, does it describe the position of a point of the interval if I say 'It is *the* point which is approached indefinitely by bisection as prescribed by the endless tossing of the coin'?

In this way I can approach without limit every point of the interval by continual bisection, and with infinitely fine eyesight and instruments *every* stage of the bisection would be determined. (The infinitely fine eyesight doesn't introduce a vicious circle.)

Now, could we call an infinite series of digits which was thus determined an infinite decimal? That is, does this geometrical process define a *number*?

The geometrical process does not involve a vicious circle, since only an infinite possibility is presupposed by it, not an infinite reality. (Lines and points being given by the boundaries of coloured surfaces.)

To what extent can you say that I have in this way really divided the rationals into two classes? In fact, of course, this division is never accomplished. But I have a *process* by means of which I approach such a division indefinitely? I have an unlimited process, whose results as such don't lead me to the goal, but whose unlimited possibility is itself the goal. But what does this limitlessness consist in – don't we here have once more merely an operation and the *ad infinitum*? Certainly. But the operation is not an arithmetical one.

(And the point which I call to my aid in my endless construction can't be given arithmetically at all.)

At this point many people would say: it doesn't matter that the method was geometrical, it is only the resulting *extension* itself that is our goal. But, then, do I have this?

What is the analogue in arithmetic to the geometrical process of bisection? It must be the converse process: that of determining a point by a law. (Instead of the law by a point.)

It would in fact correspond to the endless process of choosing between 0 and 1 in an infinite binary expansion $0 . \genfrac{}{}{0pt}{}{00000}{11111} \ldots$ *ad inf.* The law here would run 'You must put a 1 or a 0 in succession *ad inf.*, each yields a law, each a different one.'

But that doesn't imply that a law would be given *in that* I say 'In every case throw either heads or tails.' Of course, in this way I would necessarily obtain a special case of the general law mentioned, but wouldn't know from the outset which. No law of succession is described by the instruction to toss a coin.

What is arithmetical about the process of tossing the coin isn't the actual result, it is its infinite indefiniteness. But that simply does not *define* a number [1].

If I adumbrate a law thus: '0.001001001 . . . *ad inf.*', what I want to show is not the finite series as a specimen of a section of an infinite series, but rather the kind of regularity to be perceived in it. But in $0 . \genfrac{}{}{0pt}{}{000}{111} \ldots$ I don't perceive *any* law – on the contrary, precisely that a law is absent. Save, say, the law that the results of the specific laws are written with '0' and '1' and no other signs.

The rules of combination for 0 and 1 yield the totality of *all* finite

---

1] (Later gloss): This isn't true! The process of measuring! Nothing determines what the outcome of the process of bisection is going to be.

fractions. This would be an infinite extension, in which the infinite extension of fractions 0.1, 0.101, 0.10101 etc. *ad inf.* would also have to occur and, generally, all the irrational numbers.

What is it like if someone so to speak checks the various laws by means of the set of finite combinations?

The results of a law run through the finite combinations, and hence the laws are complete as far as their extensions are concerned, once *all* the finite combinations have been gone through.

Neither may we say: Two laws are identical in the case where they yield the same result at every stage. No, they are identical if it is of their essence to yield the same result, i.e. if they are identical.

180 If an amorphous theory of infinite aggregates is possible, it can describe and represent only what is amorphous about these aggregates.

It would then really have to construe the laws as merely inessential devices for representing an aggregate. And abstract from this inessential feature and attend only to what is essential. But to what?

Is it possible within the law to abstract from the law and see the extension presented as what is essential?

This much at least is clear: that there isn't a dualism: the law and the infinite series obeying it; that is to say, there isn't something in logic like description and reality.

Suppose I cut at a place where there is no rational number. Then there *must* surely be approximations to this cut. But what does 'closer to' mean here? *Closer* to what? For the time being I have nothing in the domain of number which I can approach. But I do in the case of a geometrical stretch. Here it is clear I can come arbitrarily close to any non-rational cut. And it is also clear that this is a process without an end and I am shown unambiguously how to go on by the spatial fact.

Once more it is only infinite possibility, but now the law is given in a different way.

But can I be in doubt whether all the points of a line can actually be represented by arithmetical rules [1]. Can I then ever find a point for which I can show that this is not the case? If it is given by means of a construction, then I can translate this into an arithmetical rule, and if it is given by chance, then there is, no matter how far I continue the approximation, an arithmetically defined decimal expansion which is concomitant with it.

It is clear that a point corresponds to a rule.

What is the situation with regard to types [2] of rules, and does it make sense to talk of all rules, and so, of all points?

In some sense or other there can't be irrational numbers of different types.

My feeling here is the following: no matter how the rule is formulated, in every case I still arrive at nothing else but an endless series of rational numbers. We may also put it like this: no matter how the rule is formulated, when I translate it into geometrical notation, everything is of the same type.

In the case of approximation by repeated bisection, we approach *every* point via *rational* numbers. There is no point which we could only approach with irrational numbers of a specific type.

It is of course possible that in determining a maximum I may stumble upon a new rule, but this has nothing essential to do with determining the maximum; it doesn't refer explicitly to a totality of real numbers.

1] In this, and the following paragraphs: rule = Vorschrift (prescription). [trans.]
2] In Russell's sense of type. [trans.]

XVII

181   The question would be: what criterion is there for the irrational numbers being *complete*?

Let us look at an irrational number: it runs through a series of rational approximations. When does it leave this series behind? Never. But then, the series also never comes to an end.

Suppose we had the totality of all irrational numbers with one single exception. How would we feel the lack of this one? And – if it were to be added – how would it fill the gap? – Suppose that it's π. If an irrational number is given through the totality of its approximations, then up to *any* point taken at random there is a series coinciding with that of π. Admittedly, for each such series there is a point where they diverge. But this point can lie arbitrarily far 'out'. So that for any series agreeing with π, I can find one agreeing with it still further. And so if I have the totality of all irrational numbers except π, and now insert π, I cannot cite a point at which π is now really needed. At *every* point it has a companion agreeing with it from the beginning on.

This shows clearly that an irrational number isn't the extension of an infinite decimal fraction, that it's a law.

Somehow it seems to follow from this – and this is something I find very compelling – that infinitely long isn't a measure of distance.

Our answer to the question above must be 'If π were an extension, we would never feel the lack of it', i.e. it would be impossible for us to observe a gap. If someone were to ask us, 'But have you then an infinite decimal expansion with m in the r-th place and n in the s-th place, etc. ?', we could always oblige him.

Now let's assume we have been given all the irrational numbers that can be represented by laws, but that there are yet other irrationals, and I am given a cut representing a number not belonging to the first class: How am I to tell that this is so? This is impossible, since no matter how far I go with my approximations, there will always also be a corresponding fraction.

And so we cannot say that the decimal fractions developed in accordance with a law still need supplementing by an infinite set of irregular infinite decimal fractions that would be 'brushed under the carpet' if we were to *restrict* ourselves to those *generated by a law*. Where is there such an infinite decimal that is generated by no law? And how would we notice that it was missing? Where is the gap it is needed to fill?

If from the very outset only laws reach to infinity, the question whether the totality of laws exhausts the totality of infinite decimal fractions can make no sense at all.

The usual conception is something like this: it is true that the real numbers have a different multiplicity from the rationals, but you can still write the two series down alongside one another to begin with, and sooner or later the series of real numbers leaves the other behind and goes infinitely further on.

But my conception is: you can only put finite series alongside one another and in that way compare them; there's no point in putting dots after these finite stretches (as signs that the series goes on to infinity). Furthermore, you can compare a law with a law, but not a law with *no* law.

182    $\sqrt[5 \to 3]{2}$ [1]: I'm tempted to say, the individual digits are always only the results, the bark of the fully grown tree. What

---

1] This sign is to express the prescription: write out the digits of $\sqrt{2}$: but whenever a 5 occurs in $\sqrt{2}$, substitute a 3 for it. Wittgenstein also writes this prescription in the form '$\sqrt{2}$. $\sqrt[4]{2}$ means: $\sqrt{2}$ expanded to 4 places in a given counts, or what something new can still grow from, is the inside of the trunk, where the tree's vital energy is. Altering the surface doesn't change the tree at all. To change it, you have to penetrate the trunk which is still living.

Thus it's as though the digits were dead excretions of the living essence of the root. Just as when in the course of its vital processes a snail discharges chalk, so building on to its shell.

There must first be the rules for the digits, and then – e.g. – a root is expressed in them. But this expression in a sequence of digits only has significance through being the expression for a real number. If someone subsequently alters it, he has only succeeded in distorting the expression, but not in obtaining a new number.

The rules for the digits belong at the beginning, as a preparation for the expression.
For the construction of the system in which the law lives out its life.

183   And so I would say: If $'\sqrt{2}$ is anything at all, then it is the same as $\sqrt{2}$, only another expression for it; the expression in another system.

In that case we might also put this quite naïvely as follows: I understand what $'\sqrt[4]{2}$ means, but not $'\sqrt{2}$, since $\sqrt{2}$ has no places at all, and I can't substitute others for none.

How about $\frac{1}{7}$ $(5 \rightarrow 3)$? Of course $0.\dot{1}4283\dot{7}$ isn't an infinite extension but once again an infinite rule, with which an extension

---

system – say the decimal system. Sometimes he also writes $^{7\rightarrow3}_{}\pi$, or π', and that means: write out the decimal expansion of π, but whenever a 7 occurs, substitute a 3 for it. "π_4" would mean: π expanded to 4 places (e.g. in the decimal system). Thus π_1 would be 3, π_2, 3.1 in the decimal system.

can be formed. But it is such a rule as can so to speak digest the $(5 \rightarrow 3)$.

The suffix $(1 \rightarrow 5)$ so to speak strikes at the heart of the law $0.1010010001 \ldots$ The law talks of a 1 and a 5 is to be substituted for this 1.

Could we perhaps put it by saying $'\sqrt{2}$ isn't a measure until it is in a system?

It's as if a *man* were needed before the rule $'\sqrt{2}$ could be carried out. Almost: if it's to be of any concern to arithmetic, the rule itself must understand *itself*. The rule $'\sqrt{2}$ doesn't do this, it is made up out of two heterogeneous parts. The man applying it puts these parts together [1].

Does this mean that the rule $'\sqrt{2}$ lacks something, viz. the connection between the system of the root and the system of the sequence of digits?

You would no more say of $'\sqrt{2}$ that it is a limit towards which the values of a series were tending, than you would of the instruction to throw dice.

How far does $\sqrt[4]{2}$ have to be expanded for us to have some acquaintance with it? This of course means nothing. So we are already acquainted with it without its having been expanded at all. But in that case $'\sqrt{2}$ doesn't mean a thing.

1] Cf. for example what A. Fränkel says about Cantor's "diagonal number": ". . . for whilst in general, for every k, δ_k is to be set equal to 1, this rule is subject to an exception solely for those values of k for which the digit 1 is already in the relevant diagonal place of Φ, i.e. at the position of the kth digit of the kth decimal fraction; for such, and only for such, values of k, δ_k is to be set equal to 2." *Einleitung in die Mengenlehre*, 3rd ed. 1928, p. 47. [ed.]

The idea behind $\sqrt{2}$ is this: we look for a rational number which, multiplied by itself, yields 2. There isn't one. But there are those which in this way come close to 2 and there are always some which approach 2 more closely still. There is a procedure permitting me to approach 2 indefinitely closely. This procedure is itself something. And I call it a real number.

It finds expression in the fact that it yields places of a decimal fraction lying ever further to the right.

Only what can be foreseen about a sequence of digits is essential to the real number.

184   That we can apply the law, holds also for the law to throw the digits like dice.

And what distinguishes π' from this can only be its arithmetical definiteness. But doesn't that consist in our knowing that there must be a law governing the occurrences of the digit 7 in π; even if we don't yet know what this law is?

And so we could also say: π' alludes to a law which is as yet unknown (unlike $\frac{1}{7}'$).

But mightn't we now say: π contains the description of a law – 'the law in accordance with which 7 occurs in the expansion of π'? Or would this allusion only make sense if we knew how to derive this law? (Solution of a mathematical problem.)

In that case I confessedly cannot simply read this law off from the prescription, and so the law in it is contained in a language I can't read. And so in this sense too I don't understand π'.

But then how about the solubility of the problem of finding this law? Isn't it only a problem in so far as we *know* the method for solving it?

And if it is known, precisely *that* gives π' its sense, and if unknown, we can't speak about the law which we don't yet know, and π' is bereft of all sense. For if no law presents itself, π' becomes analogous to the instruction to follow the throws of dice.

185   A real number lives in the substratum of the operations out of which it is born.

We could also say: "$\sqrt{2}$" means the method whereby x^2 approximates to 2.

Only a path approaches a goal, positions do not. And only a law approaches a value.

x^2 approaching 2, we call x approaching $\sqrt{2}$.

186   The letter π stands for a law. The sign π' (or: $\frac{7\to3}{\pi}$) means nothing, if there isn't any talk of a 7 in the law for π, which we could then replace by a 3. Similarly for $\frac{3\to5}{\sqrt{2}}$. (Whereas $\frac{2\to5}{\sqrt{2}}$ might mean $\sqrt{5}$).

A real number *yields* extensions, it is not an extension.
A real number is: an arithmetical law which endlessly yields the places of a decimal fraction.
This law has its position in arithmetical space. Or you might also say: in algebraic space.
Whereas π' doesn't use the idioms of arithmetic and so doesn't assign the law a place in this space.
It's as though what is lacking is the arithmetical creature which produces these excretions.
The impossibility of comparing the sizes of π and π' ties in with this homelessness of π'.

You cannot say: two real numbers are identical, if all their places coincide. You cannot say: they are different, if they disagree in one of the places of their expansion. No more can you say the one is greater than the other if the first place at which they disagree is greater for the first than the second.

Suppose someone were to invent a new arithmetical operation, which was normal multiplication, but modified so that every 7 in the product was replaced by a 3. Then the operation $\times$ ' would have something about it we didn't understand so long as we lacked a law through which we could understand the occurrence of 7 in the product in general.

We would then have here the extraordinary fact that my symbolism would express something I don't understand. (But that is absurd.)

It is clear that were I able to apply $\times$ ' all doubts about its legitimacy would be dispelled. For the possibility of application is the real criterion for arithmetical reality.

Even if I wasn't already familiar with the rule for forming $\sqrt{2}$, and I took $\overset{7\to3}{\sqrt{2}}$ to be the original prescription, I would still ask: what's the idea of this peculiar ceremony of replacing 7 by 3? Is it perhaps that 7 is tabu, so that we are forbidden to write it down? For substituting 3 for 7 surely adds absolutely nothing to the law, and in this system it isn't an arithmetical operation at all.

Put geometrically: it's not enough that someone should – supposedly – determine a point ever more closely by narrowing down its whereabouts; we must be able to construct *it*.

To be sure, continual throwing of a die indefinitely restricts the possible whereabouts of a point, but it doesn't determine a point.

After *every* throw the point is still infinitely indeterminate.

Admittedly, even in the course of extracting a root in the usual way, we constantly have to apply the rules of multiplication appropriate at that point, and their application has also not been anticipated. But neither is there any mention of them and their application in the principle of $\sqrt{2}$.

A number must measure. And this doesn't mean merely: values in its expansion must measure. For we can't talk of *all* values, and that rational numbers (which I have formed in accordance with some rule) measure goes without saying.

What I mean might be put like this: for a real number, a construction and not merely a process of approximation must be conceivable. – The construction corresponds to the unity of the law.

187 $\frac{10:3}{10} = 0.3$. That we come full circle is what I actually see and express by means of $\dot{3}$. $\dot{3}$ doesn't mean 'nothing but 3s come', but 'a 3 must recur again and again'.

Understanding the rule and how to carry it out in practice always only helps us over finite stretches. To determine a real number it must be completely intelligible *in itself*. That is to say, it must not be essentially undecided whether a part of it could be dispensed with.

For in that case it simply isn't clearly given, for there is no extension which would be equivalent to it, and in itself it is indeterminate. π' in that case sets out to seek its fortune in infinite space.

Of course, if a and b do not agree for the first time at the fourth place, we can say that therefore they are unequal. This fourth place clearly does belong to both numbers; but not the indefinite nth place in the infinite progression.

Thus we can certainly tell that π and e are different from the difference in their *first* place. But we can't say that they would be equal, if all their places were equal.

If the extensions of two laws coincide as far as we've gone, and I cannot compare the laws as such, the numbers defined, if I have any right to talk of such numbers, cannot be compared, and the question which is greater or whether they are equal is nonsense. Indeed, an equation between them must be nonsense. And that gives one pause for thought. And it's true: we cannot mean anything by equating them, if there is no inner connection between them; if they belong to different systems. (And the extension is of no use to us.)

But then, are what can't be compared with one another really *numbers*?
Doesn't that contradict the simple image of the number line?

188   There is no number outside a system.

The expansion of π is simultaneously an expression of the nature of π *and of the nature of the decimal system.*

Arithmetical operations only use the decimal system as a means to an end; that is, the rules for the operations are of such a kind that they can be translated into the language of any other number system, and do not have any of them as their *subject matter.*

The expansion of π is admittedly an expression both of the nature of π and of the decimal notation, but our interest is usually restricted exclusively to what is essential to π, and we don't bother about the latter. That is a servant which we regard merely as a tool and not as an individual in its own right. But if we now regard it as a member of society, then that alters society.

A general rule of operation gets its generality from the generality of the alteration it effects in the numbers. That is why $^{7 \to 3}_{\times}$ won't do as a general rule of operation, since the result of $a \, ^{7 \to 3}_{\times} \, b$ doesn't depend solely on the nature of the numbers *a* and *b*; the decimal system also comes in. Now, that wouldn't matter, of course, if this system underlay the operation as a further constant $(\Sigma \frac{1}{100}^n)$, and we can certainly find an operation that corresponds to ×′: which then has not only *a* and *b* but also the decimal system as its *subject-matter*. This operation will be written in a number system which withdraws itself as a servant into the background, and *of which* there is no mention in the operation.

In just this way $\overset{7 \to 3}{\pi}$ makes the decimal system into its subject matter (or would have to do so, if it were genuine), and for that reason it is no longer sufficient that we can use the rule to form the extension. For this application has now ceased to be the criterion for the rule's being in order, since it is not the expression of the arithmetical law at all, but only makes a superficial alteration to the language.

And so, if the decimal system is to stop being a servant, it must join the others at table, observing all the required forms, and leave off serving, since it can't do both at once.

This is how it is: the number π is expressed in the decimal system. You can't achieve a modification of this law by fixing on the specific expression in the decimal system. What you thereby influence isn't the law, it's its accidental expression. The influence does not penetrate as far as the law at all. Indeed it stands separated from it on the other side. It's like trying to influence a creature by working on a secretion that has already been discharged.

189   What about a law $\overset{p=p}{\underset{p=1}{\Sigma}} \frac{1}{10^p}$ (where p runs through the series of primes)? Or where *p* runs through the series of whole numbers except for those for which the equation of Fermat's Last Theorem doesn't hold. – Do these laws define real numbers?

I say: the so-called 'Fermat's Last Theorem' isn't a proposition [1]. (Not even in the sense of a proposition of arithmetic.) Rather, it

---

1] Theorem, proposition = Satz. [trans.]

corresponds to a proof by induction. Now, if there is a number $F = 0.110000$ etc., and that proof succeeds, that would surely prove that $F = 0.11$ – and isn't that a proposition?! Or: it is a proposition, if the law F is a number.

A proof proves what it proves and no more.

The number F wants to use the spiral $\sum_{n=1}^{n=n} \frac{1}{10^n}$ and choose sections of this spiral according to a principle. But this principle doesn't belong to the spiral.

If I imagine the windings of the spiral

$$\frac{1}{10^0}, \frac{1}{10^0} + \frac{1}{10^1}, \frac{1}{10^0} + \frac{1}{10^1} + \frac{1}{10^2}, \text{ etc.}$$

to have been written out, then the number F makes a comment on each winding, it puts a tick or a cross against each one; and, what's more, making its choices *according to a law we don't know*.

And this is how we arrive at the paradox that it's nonsense to ask whether $F = 0.11$. For, accepting F depends upon accepting the assumption of a law, an infinite law, which governs the behaviour of the numbers in the Fermat formula. – But what indicates to us the infinity of the law? Only the induction. And where is that to be found here? In the infinite possibility of the exponent n in $x^n + y^n = z^n$, and so in the infinite possibility of making tests. But that doesn't have any different value for us from that of the infinite possibility of throwing dice, since we don't know a law to which the *results* of such tests would conform.

There is admittedly a law there (and so also an arithmetical interest), but it doesn't refer directly to the number. The number is a sort of lawless by-product of the law. As though someone went along the street at a regulation pace, throwing a die at every pace, and constantly either putting a peg in the ground or not, as directed by the fall of the die; in this case these pegs wouldn't be spaced out in accordance with a law.

Or rather, the law spacing them would only be that governing the strides and no other.

Does it then make no sense to say, even after Fermat's Last Theorem has been proved, that $F = 0.110$? (If, say, I were to read about it in the papers.)

The true nature of real numbers must be the induction. What I must look at in the real number, its sign, is the induction. – The '*So*' of which we may say 'and so on'. If the law, the winding of the spiral, is a number, then it must be comparable with all the others through its position (on the number scale).

I certainly do not define that position by means of anything but the law.

Only what I see, is a law; not what I *describe*.

I believe that is the only thing standing in the way of my expressing more by my signs than I can understand.

XVIII

190 In this context we keep coming up against something that could be called an 'arithmetical experiment'. Admittedly the data determine the result, but I can't see *in what way* they determine it. (cf. e.g. the occurrences of 7 in π.) The primes likewise come out from the method for looking for them, as the results of an experiment. To be sure, I can convince myself that 7 is a prime, but I can't see the connection between it and the condition it satisfies. – I have only found the number, not generated it.

I look for it, but I don't generate it. I can certainly see a law in the rule which tells me how to find the primes, but not in the numbers that result. And so it is unlike the case $+ \frac{1}{1!}, - \frac{1}{3!}, + \frac{1}{5!},$ etc., where I can see a law *in the numbers*.

I must be able to write down a part of the series, in such a way that you can *recognize* the law.

That is to say, no *description* is to occur in what is written down, everything must be represented.

The approximations must themselves form what is *manifestly* a series.

That is, the approximations themselves must obey a law.

Can we say that unless I knew the geometrical representation of π and $\sqrt{2}$, I would only have an approximate knowledge of these numbers? Surely not.

191 A number must measure in and of itself.

It seems to me as though that's its job.

If it doesn't do that but leaves it to the rationals, we have no need of it.

It seems to be a good rule that what I will call a number is that which can be compared with any rational number taken at random. That is to say, that for which it can be established whether it is greater than, less than, or equal to a rational number.

That is to say, it makes sense to call a structure a number by analogy, if it is related to the rationals in ways which are analogous to (of the same multiplicity as) greater, less and equal to.

A real number is what can be compared with the rationals.

When I say I call irrational numbers only what can be compared with the rationals, I am not seeking to place too much weight on the mere stipulation of a name. I want to say that this is precisely what has been meant or looked for under the name 'irrational number'.

Indeed, the way the irrationals are introduced in text books always makes it sound as if what is being said is: Look, that isn't a rational number, but still there is a number there. But why then do we still call what *is* there 'a number'? And the answer must be: because there is a definite way for comparing it with the rational numbers.

'The process would only define a number when it has come to an end, but since it goes on to infinity and is never complete, it *doesn't* define a number.'
The process must have infinite foresight, or else it won't define a number. There must be no 'I don't as yet know', since there's no '*as yet*' in the infinite.

Every rational number must stand in a visible relation to the law which is a number.

The true expansion is just the method of comparison with the rationals.

The true expansion of a number is the one which permits a direct comparison with the rationals.

If we bring a rational number into the neighbourhood of the law, the law must give a definite reaction to it.

It must reply to the question 'Is it *this* one?'

I should like to say: The true expansion is that which evokes from the law a comparison with a rational number.

Narrowing down the interval of course contributes to the comparison through the fact that every number thereby comes to lie to the left or right of it.

This only holds when comparing the law with a given rational number forces the law to declare itself in comparison with this number.

192   A real number can be compared with the fiction of an infinite spiral, whereas structures like $F, P[1]$, or π' only with finite sections of a spiral.

For my inability to establish on which side it passes by a point, simply means that it is absurd to compare it with a complete (whole) spiral, for with that I would see how it goes past the point.

You see, at the back of our minds here, we always have the idea that while I don't know the spiral as a whole, and so don't know what its path is at this point, what I don't know is still in fact thus or so.

193   If I say $(\sqrt{2})^2_n$ approaches 2 and so eventually reaches the numbers 1.9, 1.99, 1.999, that is nonsense unless I can state within how many stages these values will be reached, for '*eventually*' means nothing.

To compare rational numbers with $\sqrt{2}$, I have to square them. – They then assume the form $\sqrt{a}$, where $\sqrt{a}$ is now an arithmetical operation.

Written out in this system, they can be compared with $\sqrt{2}$, and it is for me as if the spiral of the irrational number had shrunk to a point.

1] Cf. The opening sentence of §189 (p. 232 above), and below p. 240.

We don't understand why there is a 4 at the third decimal place of $\sqrt{2}$, but then we don't *need* to understand it. – For this lack of understanding is swallowed up in the wider (consistent) use of the decimal system.

In fact, in the end the decimal system as a whole withdraws into the background, and then only what is essential to $\sqrt{2}$ remains in the calculation.

194   Is an arithmetical experiment still possible when a recursive definition has been set up? I believe, obviously not; because via the recursion each stage becomes arithmetically comprehensible.

And in recursion we do not start from another generality, but from a particular arithmetical case.

A recursive definition conveys understanding by building on one particular case that presupposes no generality.

To be sure, I can give a recursive explanation of the rule for investigating numbers in the cases)([1], F, and P, but not of the outcome of such investigation. I cannot construct the result.

. Let → 4 mean: 'The fourth prime number'. Can → 4 be construed as an arithmetical operation applied to the basis 4? So that → 4 = 5 is an equation of arithmetic, like $4^2 = 16$?

Or is it that → 4 can 'only be sought, but not constructed'?

195   Is it possible to prove a greater than b, without being able to prove at which place the difference will come to light? I think not.

1] (Manuscript): What about an operation such as x)(y; we form the product of x and y; if it is greater than 100, the result is the greater of the two numbers, otherwise it is 0?

12)(10 = 12. The operation isn't arithmetically comprehensible.

How many noughts can occur in succession in e? If the nth decimal place is followed by a 0, and if it is fixed after $n + r$ stages of the summation [1] then the 0 must be fixed at the same time as the nth place, for another number can only give way to an 0, if the place preceding it also still changes. Thus the number of noughts is limited.

We can and must show the decimal places to be fixed after a *definite* number of stages.

If I don't know how many 9s may follow after 3.1415, it follows that I can't specify an interval smaller than the difference between π and 3.1416; and that implies, in my opinion, that π doesn't correspond to a point on the number line, since, if it does correspond to a point, it must be possible to cite an interval which is smaller than the interval from this point to 3.1416.

If the rational number with which I want to compare my real number is given in decimal notation, then if I am to carry out the comparison I must be given a relation between the law of the real number and the decimal notation.

1.4 – Is that the square root of 2? No, it's the root of 1.96. That is, I can immediately write it in the form of an approximation to $\sqrt{2}$; and of course, see whether it is an approximation above or below [2].

What is an approximation? (Surely all rational numbers lie either above or below the irrational number.) An approximation is a rational number written in such a form that it can be compared with the irrational number.

In that case, decimal expansion is a method of comparison with

---

1] The words 'of the summation' have been added in the translation to make clearer Wittgenstein's meaning in this highly compressed paragraph: we take the 'stages' referred to in the original as referring to the stages in some method of computing e, and for what Wittgenstein says here to be true, he must have in mind a method such as the summing of the usual series for e, which produces a monotone increasing series of approximations. [trans.]

2] Similar to the above: 'Is 3.14 the circumference of a unit circle? No, it's the perimeter of a ——-gon.' [Manuscript]

the rationals, if it is determined in advance how many places I must expand to in order to settle the issue.

196 A number as the result of an arithmetical experiment, and so the experiment as the *description* of a number, is an absurdity.

The experiment would be the description, not the *representation* of a number.

I *cannot* compare F with $\frac{11}{100}$, and so it isn't a number.

If the real number is a rational number *a*, comparison of its law with *a* must show this. That means the law must be so formed as to 'click into' the rational number when it comes to the appropriate place (this number).

It wouldn't do, e.g., if we couldn't be sure whether $\sqrt{25}$ really breaks off at 5.

We might also put it like this: the law must be such that any rational number can be inserted and tried out.

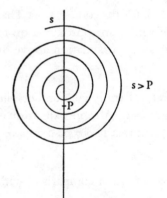

But in that case what about a number like $P = 0.11101010001$ etc.? Suppose someone claimed it was a recurring decimal, and also at some stage or other it looked as if it were, then I would have to be able to try out the supposed number in the law, just as I can see directly by multiplication whether 1.414 is $\sqrt{2}$. But that isn't possible.

The mark of an arithmetical experiment is that there is something opaque about it.

197   A *subsequent* proof of convergence cannot justify construing a series as a number.

Where a convergence *reveals* itself, that is where the number must be sought.

A proof showing something has the properties necessary to a number, must *indicate* the number. That is, the proof is simply what points the number out.

Isn't F also an unlimited contraction of an interval? [1]

How can I know that or whether the spiral will not focus on this point? In the case of $\sqrt{2}$ I do know.

Now, can I also call such a spiral a number? A spiral which can, for all I know, come to a stop at a rational point.

But that isn't possible either: there is a lack of a *method* for comparing with the rationals.

For developing the extension isn't such a method, since I can never know if or when it will lead to a decision.

Expanding indefinitely isn't a method, even when it leads to a

---

1] (Manuscript): I once asked: 'How can I call a law which represents the endless nesting of intervals anything but a number?' – But why do I term such a nesting a number? – Because we can significantly say that every number lies to the left or right of this nesting.

result of the comparison.

Whereas squaring *a* and seeing whether the result is greater or less than 2 is a method.

Could we say: what is a real number is the *general method* of comparison with the rationals?

It must make sense to ask: 'Can this number be π?'

198　*F* is not the interval $0. - 0.1$; for I can also make a certain decision within this interval, but it isn't a number inside this interval, since we can't force the issues that would be necessary for that.

Might we then say: *F* is certainly an arithmetical structure, only not a number (nor an interval)?

That is, I can compare *F* neither with a point nor with an interval. Is there a geometrical structure to which that corresponds?

The law, i.e. the method of comparison, only says that it will yield either the answers 'greater, less or equal' – or – 'greater' (but not equal). As though I go into a dark room and say: I can only find out whether it is lower than I am or the same height – or – higher. And here we might say: and so you can't find out a height; and so what is it you can find out? The comparison only goes lame because I can surely establish the height if I bump my head, whereas, in the case of *F*, I cannot, in principle, ask: 'Is it this point?'

I don't know a method for determining whether it is this point, and so it isn't a point.

If the question how *F* compares with a rational number has no sense, since all expansion still hasn't given us an answer, then this question also had no sense before we tried to settle the question at random by means of an extension.

If it makes no sense now to ask 'Does $F = 0.11$?', then it had no sense even before people examined 100 places of the extension, and so even before they had examined only one.

But then it would make no sense at all to ask in this case whether the number is equal to *any* rational number whatsoever. As long, that is, as we don't possess a method which necessarily settles the question.

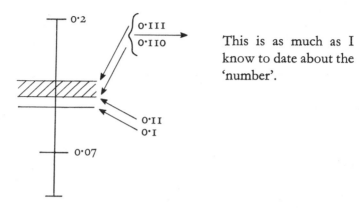

This is as much as I know to date about the 'number'.

The rational number given is either equal to, less than or greater than the interval that has so far been worked out. In the first case the point forms the lower end point of the interval, in the second it lies below, in the third, above the interval. In none of these cases are we talking about comparing the positions of two points.

199   0.3̇ is not a result of 1/3 in the same sense as, say, 0.25 is of 1/4; it points to a different arithmetical fact.

Suppose the division continually yielded the same digit, 3, but without our seeing in it the necessity for this, would it then make sense to form the conjecture that the result will be 0.3̇ ?

That is, doesn't 0.3̇ simply designate an induction we have seen and not – an extension?

We must always be able to determine the order of magnitude. Suppose (in my notation) nothing speaks against 100 threes following in succession in *e* at a particular point, then something speaks against 10^{100} threes doing so. (A great deal must be left open in the decimal system, that is definite in the binary system.)

It isn't only necessary to be able to say whether a given rational number is the real number: we must also be able to say how close it can possibly come to it. That is, it isn't enough to be able to say that the spiral doesn't go through this point but beneath it: we must also know limits within which the distance from the point lies. We must know an order of magnitude for the distance apart.

Decimal expansion doesn't give me this, since I cannot know, e.g. how many 9s will follow a place that has been reached in the expansion.

The question 'Is e 2.7$\frac{1}{3}$?' is meaningless, since it doesn't ask about an extension, but about a law, i.e. an induction of which we have, however, no conception here. We can put this question in the case of division only because we know the form of the induction we call $\frac{1}{3}$.

The question 'Are the decimal places of e eventually fixed?' and the answer 'They are eventually fixed', are both nonsense. The question runs: After how many stages do the places have to remain fixed?

May we say: 'e isn't this number' means nothing – we have to say 'It is at least this interval away from it'?
I believe that's how it is. But that implies it couldn't be answered at all unless we were simultaneously given a concept of the distance apart.

A proof for all real numbers is not analogous to a proof for all rational numbers in such a way that you could say: What we have proved for all rational numbers – i.e. by induction – we can prove for all real numbers in *the same way* by an extension of the method of proof. You can only speak about a real number when you've got it.

Let us assume e.g., I have proved the formula $a^m \cdot a^n = a^{m+n}$ for rational values of m and n (by induction), and would now like to prove it for real number values. What do I do in this case? Obviously it's no longer possible to carry through the proof by induction.

Therefore such a formula doesn't mean: for all real numbers such and such holds, but: given a real number, I interpret the formula so as to mean: such and such holds for the limit and I prove this by the rules of calculation laid down for the real numbers. I prove the formula for rational numbers by induction, and then show it carries over to the real numbers, in fact simply by means of the rules of calculation I have laid down for the real numbers. But I don't prove the formula holds for 'all real' numbers, precisely because the rules of calculation for real numbers do not have the form of an induction.

This, then, is how things are: I treat as given a *particular* real number and keep this constant throughout the proof. That's something totally different from what happens with the rationals; for there it was precisely a question of whether the formula remained correct when the rational numbers were varied, and *that is why* the proof had the form of an induction. But here the question simply doesn't arise whether the formula holds for 'all real' numbers – just because we don't allow the real number to vary at all.

We don't let the variable real number run through all values –

i.e. all laws. We simply rely on the rules of calculation and nothing else.

You might now think: strictly the proposition ought to be proved for all real numbers, and what we give is no more than a pointer. That's wrong. A formula that is proved for real numbers doesn't say: For all real numbers . . . holds; what it says is: Given a real number, then . . . holds. And in fact not on the basis of a proof, but of an interpretation.

XIX

200   Our interest in negation in arithmetic appears to be limited in a peculiar way. In fact it appears to me as if a certain generality is needed to make the negation interesting.

But you can represent *in*divisibility *perspicuously* (e.g. in Eratothenes' sieve). You can *see* how all the composite numbers lie above or below the number under consideration.

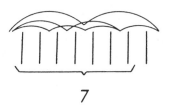

7

Here, arithmetical negation is represented by spatial negation, the 'somewhere else'.

What do I *know*, if I know a mathematical inequality? Is it possible to know just an inequality, without knowing something *positive*?

It seems clear that negation means something different in arithmetic from what it means in the rest of language. If I say 7 is not divisible by 3, then I can't even make a picture of this, I can't imagine how it would be if 7 were divisible by 3. All this follows naturally from the fact that mathematical equations aren't a kind of proposition.

It is very odd that for a presentation of mathematics we should be obliged to use false equations as well. For that is what all this is about. If negation or disjunction is necessary in arithmetic, then false equations are an essential element in its presentation.

What does '$\sim(5 \times 5 = 30)$' mean? It seems to me as if you oughtn't to write it *like that*, but '$5 \times 5 \neq 30$'; the reason being that I am not negating anything, but want to establish a relation, even if an indefinite one, between 5×5 and 30 (and so, something positive). – Admittedly you could say: 'True, but this relation is at any rate incompatible with $5 \times 5 = 30$'. – And so is the relation of indivisibility with the relation of divisibility! It's quite clear that when I exclude divisibility, in this logical system this is equivalent to establishing indivisibility. – And isn't this the same case as that of a number which is less than 5, if it is *not* greater than or equal to it?

201 Now, there is something recalcitrant to the application of the law of the excluded middle in mathematics.

(Of course even the name of this law is misleading: it always sounds as though this were the same sort of case as 'A frog is either green or brown, there isn't a third type'.)

You can show by induction that when you successively subtract 3 from a number until it won't go any further, the remainder can only be either 0 or 1 or 2. You call the cases of the first class those in which the division goes out.

Looking for a law for the distribution of primes is simply an attempt to replace the negative criterion for a prime number by a positive one. Or more correctly, the indefinite one by a definite one.

I believe that negation here is not what it is in logic but an indefiniteness. For how do I recognize – verify – a negative? By something indefinite or positive.

An inequality, like an equation, must be either the result of a calculation or a stipulation.

Just as equations can be construed, not as propositions, but as rules for signs, so it must be possible to treat inequalities in the same way.

How, then, can you use an inequality? That leads to the thought that in logic there is also the internal relation of not following, and it can be important to recognize that one proposition does *not* follow from another.

The denial of an equation is as like and as unlike the denial of a proposition as the affirmation of an equation is like and unlike the affirmation of a proposition.

202   It is quite clear that negation in arithmetic is completely different from the genuine negation of a proposition.

And it is of course clear that where it essentially – on logical grounds – corresponds to a disjunction or to the exclusion of one part of a logical series in favour of another, it must have a completely different meaning.

It must in fact be one and the same as those logical forms and therefore be only apparently a negation.

If 'not equal to' means greater or less than, then that cannot be, as it were, an accident which befalls the 'not'.

A mathematical *proposition* can only be either a stipulation, or a result worked out from stipulations in accordance with a definite method. And this must hold for '9 is divisible by 3' or '9 is not divisible by 3'.

How do you work out $2 \times 2 \neq 5$? Differently from $2 \times 2 = 4$? If at all, then by $2 \times 2 = 4$ and $4 \neq 5$.

And how do you work out '9 is divisible by 3'? You could treat it as a disjunction and first work out $9 \div 3 = 3$, and then, instead of this definite proposition, use a rule of inference to derive the disjunction.

Aren't we helped here by the remark that negation in arithmetic is important only in the context of generality? But the generality is expressed by an induction.

And that is what makes it possible for negation or disjunction, which appear as superfluously indefinite in the particular case, yet to be essential to arithmetic in the general 'proposition', i.e. in the induction.

203   It is clear to me that arithmetic doesn't need false equations for its construction, but it seems to me that you may well say 'There is a prime number between 11 and 17', without *ipso facto* referring to false equations.

Isn't an inequality a perfectly intelligible rule for signs, just as an equation is? The one permits a substitution, the other forbids a substitution.

$$\sqrt{} =\, ^2\sqrt{}\,, \ \sqrt{} \neq\, ^3\sqrt{}$$

Perhaps all that's essential is that you should see that what is expressed by inequalities is *essentially* different from what is expressed by equations. And so you certainly can't immediately compare a law yielding places of a decimal expansion which works with inequalities, with one that works with equations. Here we have before us completely different methods and consequently different kinds of arithmetical structure.

In other words, in arithmetic you cannot just put equations and something else (such as inequalities) on *one* level, as though they were different species of animals. On the contrary, the two methods will be categorically different, and determine (define) structures not comparable with one another.

Negation in arithmetic cannot be the same as the negation of a proposition, since otherwise, in $2 \times 2 \neq 5$, I should have to make myself a picture of how it would be for 2×2 to be 5.

204   You could call '= 5', 'divisible by 5', 'not divisible by 5', 'prime', arithmetical predicates and say: arithmetical predicates always correspond to the application of a definite, generally defined, method. You might also define a predicate in this way: $(\xi \times 3 = 25) \overset{\text{Def}}{=} F(\xi)$.

Arithmetical predicates, which in the particular case are unimportant – because the definite form makes the indefinite superfluous – become significant in the general *law*, i.e. in induction. Since here they are not – so to speak – superseded by a definite form. Or better: In the general law, they are in no way indefinite.

Could the results of an engineer's computations be such that, let us say, it is essential for certain machine parts to have lengths corresponding to the prime number series? No.

Can you use the prime numbers to construct an irrational number? The answer is always: as far as you can foresee the primes and no further.

If you can foresee that a prime number must occur in *this* interval then this interval is what can be foreseen and constructed, and so, I believe, it can play a role in the construction of an irrational number.

XX

205   Can we say a patch is simpler than a larger one?

Let's suppose they are uniformly coloured circles: what is supposed to constitute the greater simplicity of the smaller circle?

Someone might reply that the larger one can be made up out of the smaller one and a further part, but not vice versa. But why shouldn't I represent the smaller one as the difference between the larger one and the ring?

And so it seems to me that the smaller patch is not simpler than the larger one.

It seems as if it is impossible to see a uniformly coloured patch as composite, unless you imagine it as *not* uniformly coloured. The image of a dissecting line gives the patch more than one colour, since the dissecting line must have a different colour from the rest of the patch.

May we say: If we see a figure in our visual field – a red triangle say – we cannot then describe it by e.g. describing one half of the triangle in one proposition, and the other half in another. That is, we may say that there is a sense in which there is no such thing as a half of *this* triangle. We can only speak of the triangle at all if its boundary lines are the boundaries between two colours.

This is how it is with the composition of spatial structures out of their smaller spatial components: the larger *geometrical* structure isn't composed of smaller *geometrical* structures, any more than you can say that 5 is composed of 3 and 2, or for that matter 2 of 5 and − 3. For here the larger determines the smaller quite as much as the smaller the larger. The rectangle ▭ isn't composed of the rectangles ☐ ☐; instead the first geometrical figure determines the other two and conversely. Here, then, Nicod would be right when he says [1] that the larger figure doesn't contain the smaller ones as components. But it is different in actual space: the figure ☐■ is actually composed of the components ☐ ■, even though the purely geometrical figure of the large rectangle is *not* composed of the figures of the two squares.

These 'purely geometrical figures' are of course only logical possibilities. – Now, you can in fact see an actual chess board as a unity – not as composed of its squares – by seeing it as a large rectangle and disregarding its squares. – But if you don't disregard the squares, then it is a complex and the squares are its component parts – they are, in Nicod's phrase, what constitute it.

(Incidentally, I am unable to understand what is supposed to be meant by saying that something is 'determined' by certain objects but not 'constituted' by them. If these two expressions make sense at all, it's the same sense.)

An intellect which takes in the component parts and their relations, but not the whole, is a nonsense notion.

206 Whether it makes sense to say 'This part of a red patch (which isn't demarcated by any visible boundary) is red' depends on whether there is absolute position. For if we can speak of an absolute location in visual space, I can then also ascribe a colour to this absolute location even if its surroundings are the same colour.

I see, say, a uniformly yellow visual field and say: 'The centre of my visual field is yellow.' But then can I describe a *shape* in this way?

An apparent remedy would appear to be to say that red and circular are (external) properties of two objects, which one might call patches and that in addition these patches are spatially related to each other in a certain way; but this is nonsense.

It's obviously possible to establish the identity of a position in the visual field, since we would otherwise be unable to distinguish

---

1] Nicod, *The Foundations of Geometry and Induction.*

whether a patch always stays in the same place or whether it changes its place. Let's imagine a patch which vanishes and then reappears, we can surely say whether it reappears in the same place or at another.

So we can really speak of certain positions in the visual field, and in fact with the same justification as in speaking of different positions on the retina.

Would it be appropriate to compare such a space with a surface that has a different curvature at each of its points, so that each point is marked out as distinct?

If every point in visual space is marked out as distinct, then there is certainly a sense in speaking of *here* and *there* in visual space, and that now seems to me to simplify the presentation of visual states of affairs. But is this property of having points marked out as distinct really essential to visual space; I mean, couldn't we imagine a visual space in which we would only perceive certain spatial relations but no absolute position? That is, could we picture an experience so? In something like the sense in which we can imagine the experiences of a one-eyed man? – I don't believe we could. For instance, one wouldn't be able to perceive the whole visual field turning, or rather this would be inconceivable. How would the hand of a clock look, say, when it moved around the edge of the dial? (I am imagining the sort of dial you find on many large clocks, that only has points on it, and not digits.) We would then indeed be able to perceive the movement from one point to another – if it didn't just jump from one position to the other – but once the hand had arrived at a point, we wouldn't be able to distinguish its position from the one it was in at the last point. I believe it speaks for itself that we can't visualise this.

In visual space there is absolute position and hence also absolute motion. Think of the image of two stars in a pitch-black night, in which I can see nothing but these stars and they orbit around one another.

We can also say visual space is an oriented space, a space in which there is an above and below and a right and left. And *this* above and below, right and left have nothing to do with gravity or right and left hands. It would, e.g., still retain its sense even if we spent our whole lives gazing at the stars through a telescope.

Suppose we are looking at the night sky through a telescope, then our visual field would be completely dark with a brighter circle and there would be points of light in this circle. Let us suppose further that we have never seen our bodies, always only this image, so that we couldn't compare the position of a star with that of our head or our feet. What would then show me that my space has an above and below etc., or simply that it is oriented? I can at any rate perceive that the whole constellation *turns* in the bright circle and that implies I can perceive different orientations of the constellation. If I hold a book the wrong way, I can't read the print at all, or only with difficulty.

It's no sort of *explanation* of this situation to say: it's just that the retina has an above and below etc., and this makes it easy to understand that there should exist the analogue in the visual field. Rather, that is just a *representation* of the situation by the roundabout route of the relations on the retina.

We might also say, the situation in our visual field is always such as would arise if we could see, along with everything else, a co-ordinate frame of reference, in accordance with which we can establish any direction. – But even that isn't an accurate represent-ation, since if we really saw such a set of axes of co-ordinates (say, with arrows), we would in fact be in a position, not only to establish the orientations of objects relative to these axes, but also the position of the cross itself in the space, as though in relation to an unseen co-ordinate system contained in the essence of this space.

What would our visual field have to be like, if this were not so? Then of course I could see relative positions and motions, but not absolute ones. But that would mean, e.g., that there would be no sense in speaking of a rotation of the whole visual field. Thus far it is perhaps comprehensible. But now let's assume that, say, we saw with our telescope only one star at a certain distance from the black edge: that this star vanishes and reappears at the same distance from the edge. In that case we couldn't know whether it reappears at the same place or in another. Or if two stars were to come and go at the same distance from the edge, we couldn't say whether – or that – they were the same or different stars.

Not only: 'we couldn't know whether', but: there would be *no sense* in speaking in this context of the same or different places. And since in reality it has a sense, this isn't the structure of our visual field. The genuine criterion for the structure is precisely which propositions make sense for it – not, which are true. To look for these is the method of philosophy.

We might also put it like this: let's suppose that a set of coordinate axes once flared up in our visual field for a few moments and disappeared again, provided our memory were good enough, we could then establish the orientation of every subsequent image by reference to our memory of the axes. If there were no absolute direction, this would be logically impossible.

But that means we have the possibility of describing a possible location – and so a position – in the visual field, without referring to anything that happens to be there at the time. Thus we can for instance say that something can be at the top on the right, etc.

(The analogy with a curved surface would be to say something like: a patch on an egg can be located near the broad end.)

I can obviously see the sign V at one time as a v, at another as an A, as a 'greater than' or 'less than' sign, even if I were to see it through a telescope and cannot compare its position with the position of my body.

Perhaps someone might reply that I feel the position of my body without seeing it. But position in feeling space (as I'd like to put it for once) has nothing to do with position in visual space, the two are independent of each other, and unless there were absolute direction in visual space, you couldn't correlate direction in feeling space with it at all.

207   Now, can I say something like: The top half of my visual field is red? And what does that mean? Can I say that an object (the top half) has the property of being red?

In this connection, it should be remembered that every part of visual space *must* have a colour, and that every colour *must* occupy a part of visual space. The forms *colour* and *visual space* permeate one another.

It is clear that there isn't a relation of 'being situated' which would hold between a colour and a position, in which it 'was situated'. There is no intermediary between colour and space.

Colour and space saturate one another.

And the way in which they permeate one another makes up the visual field.

208   It seems to me that the concept of distance is given immediately in the structure of visual space. Were it not so, and the concept of distance only associated with visual space by means of a correlation between a visual space without distance and another structure that contained distance, then the case would be conceivable in which, through an alteration in this association, the length *a*, for example, will appear greater than the length *b*, even though we still observe the point B as always between A and C.

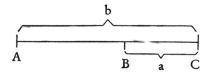

How about when we measure an object in visual space with a yardstick *for a time*? Is it also measured when the yardstick isn't there?

Yes, if any sense can be made at all of establishing the identity between what was measured and what is not.

If I can say: 'I *have* measured *this* length and it was three times as long as *that*', then it makes sense and it is correct to say that the lengths are still in the same relationship to one another now.

A B C C B A
I I I I I I

'CC between AA' follows from 'CC between BB', but only if the partition is really given, through colour boundaries.

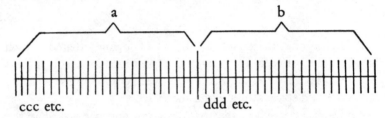

It is obviously possible for the intervals *a* and *b* to appear to me to be the same in length and for the segments *c* and the segments *d* also to appear to me to be the same in length but for there still to be 25 *c*s and 24 *d*s when I count them. And the question arises: how can that be possible? Is it correct to say here: but it is so, and all we see is that visual space does not obey the rules of – say – Euclidean space? This would imply that the question 'How can that be possible?' was nonsense and so unjustified. And so there wouldn't be anything paradoxical in this at all, we would simply have to accept it. But is it *conceivable* that *a* should appear equal to *b* and the *c*s to the *d*s, and a *visibly* different number of *c*s and *d*s be present?

Or should I now say that even in visual space something can after all *appear* different from what it *is*? Certainly not! Or that *n* times an interval and *n* + 1 times the same interval can yield precisely the same result in visual space? That is just as unacceptable. Except if there is no sense at all in saying of intervals in visual space that they *are* equal. If, that is, in visual space it only made sense to talk of a 'seeming' and this expression weren't only appropriate for the relationship between two independent experiences. And so if there were an *absolute* seeming.

And so perhaps also an *absolute* vagueness or an *absolute* unclarity. (Whereas on my view, something can only be vague or unclear with reference to something we have posited as the standard of clarity: therefore relatively.)

Can't I then – in the first case – if I can't take in the number at a glance, make a mistake in determining this number? Or: are *a* and *b* composed of a number of parts at all – in the ordinary sense – if I can't *see* this number in *a* and *b*? For it certainly seems I've no right at all to *conclude* that the same number of *c*s and of *d*s must be present. And this still holds, even if counting really does yield the same number! I mean: even if counting were never to yield different results where *a* and *b* are equal etc.

(This shows, incidentally, how difficult it is to describe what it is that we really see.)

But suppose we have the right to talk of a number of parts – N.B. remaining throughout at the purely visual level – even when we don't see the number immediately; then the question would arise: can I in that case be sure that what I count is really the number I see or rather whose visual result I see? Could I be sure that the number of parts doesn't instantaneously change from 24 to 25 without my noticing it?

If I see $a = b$ and $c = d$ and someone else counts the parts and finds the numbers equal, I shall at least feel that that doesn't contradict what I see. But I am also aware that I can see the same when there are 25 *c*s in *a* and 24 *d*s in *b*. From this I can conclude that I don't notice when there's one part more or one less, and therefore also cannot notice if the number of parts in *b* changes between 24 and 25.

209   But if you can't say that there is a definite number of parts in *a* and *b*, how am I in that case to describe the visual image? Here it emerges – I believe – that the visual image is much more complicated than it seems to be at first glance. What makes it so much more complicated is e.g. the factor introduced by eye movements.

If – say – I were to describe what is seen at a glance by painting a picture instead of using the language of words, then I ought not really to paint all the parts *c* and *d*. In many places I should have to paint something 'blurred' instead, i.e. a grey section.

'Blurred' [1] and 'unclear' are relative expressions. If this often doesn't seem to be so, that results from the fact that we still know too little of the real nature of the given phenomena, that we imagine them as more primitive than they are. Thus it is, e.g., possible that no coloured picture of any kind whatever is able to represent the impression of 'blurredness' correctly. But it doesn't follow from that that the visual image is blurred in itself and so can't be represented by any kind of definite picture whatever. No, this would only indicate that a factor plays a part in the visual image – say through eye movements – which admittedly can't be reproduced by a painted picture, but which is in itself as 'definite' as any other. You might in that case say, what is really given is still always indefinite or blurred relative to the painted picture, but merely because we have in that case made the painted picture arbitrarily into a standard for the given, when this has a greater multiplicity than that of a painted representation.

It we were really to *see* 24 and 25 parts in *a* and *b*, we couldn't then see *a* and *b* as equal.

If this is wrong, the following must be possible: it ought to be possible to distinguish immediately between the cases where *a*

1] Throughout this section we have translated 'verschwommen' by either 'vague' or 'blurred' for purely stylistic reasons. [trans.]

and b both equal 24 and the case where a is 24 and b 25, but it would only be possible to distinguish between the number of parts, and not between the lengths of a and b that result.

We might also put this more simply thus: it would then have to be possible to see immediately that one interval is made up of 24 parts, the other of 25, without it being possible to distinguish the resulting lengths. -- I believe that the word 'equal' has a meaning even for visual space which stamps this as a contradiction.

Do I tell that two intervals of visual space are equal by not telling that they are unequal? This is a question with far-reaching implications.

Couldn't I have two impressions in succession: in one, an interval visibly divided into 5 parts, in the other one visibly divided in the same way into 6 parts, while I yet couldn't say that I had seen the parts or the entire intervals as having different lengths?

Asked 'Were the intervals different in length or the same?' I couldn't answer 'I saw them as different in length', since no difference in length has so to speak 'struck' me. And yet I couldn't – I believe – say that I saw them as equal in length. On the other hand, I couldn't say either: 'I don't know whether they were the same or different in length' (unless my memory had deserted me), for that means nothing so long as I go on talking only of the immediately given.

210   The question is, how to explain certain contradictions that arise when we apply the methods of inference used in Euclidean space to visual space.

I mean: it is possible to carry through a construction (i.e. a chain of inference) in visual space in which we appreciate every step (transition), but whose result contradicts our geometrical concepts.

Now I believe this happens because we can only see the construction piecemeal and not as one whole. The explanation would then consist in saying that there isn't a visual construction at all that is composed of these individual visual pieces. This would be something like what happens when I show someone a small section of a large spherical surface and ask him whether he accepts the great circle which is visible on it as a straight line; and if he did so, I would then rotate the sphere and show him that it came back to the same place on the circle. But I surely haven't proved to him in this way that a straight line in visual space returns to meet itself.

This explanation would be: these are visual *pieces* which do not, however, add up to a visual whole, or at any rate not to the whole the final result of which I believe I can see at the end.

The simplest construction of this sort would, indeed, be the one above of the two equally long intervals into one of which a piece will go n times and into the other $n + 1$ times. The steps of the construction would lie in proceeding from one component part to another and discovering the equality of these parts.

Here you could explain that, in making this progression, I am not really investigating the original visual image of the equally long intervals. But that something else obtrudes into the investigation, which then leads to the startling result.

But there's an objection to this explanation. Someone might say: we didn't hide any part of the construction from you while you were examining the individual parts, did we? So you ought to have been able to see whether anything about the rest changed, shifted in the meantime. If that didn't happen, then you really ought to be able to see, oughtn't you, that everything was above board?

To speak of divisibility in visual space has a sense, since in a description it must be possible to substitute a divided stretch for an undivided one. And then it is clear what, in the light of what I elaborated earlier, the infinite divisibility of this space means.

211   The moment we try to apply exact concepts of measurement to immediate experience, we come up against a peculiar vagueness in this experience. But that only means a vagueness relative to these concepts of measurement. And, now, it seems to me that this vagueness isn't something provisional, to be eliminated later on by more precise knowledge, but that this is a characteristic logical peculiarity. If, e.g., I say: 'I can now see a red circle on a blue ground and remember seeing one a few minutes ago that was the same size or perhaps a little smaller and a little lighter,' then *this* experience cannot be described more precisely.

Admittedly the words 'rough', 'approximate' etc. have only a relative sense, but they are still *needed* and they characterise the nature of our experience; not as rough or vague in itself, but still as rough and vague in relation to our techniques of representation.

This is all connected with the problem 'How many grains of sand make a heap?'

You might say: any group with more than a hundred grains is a heap and less than ten grains do not make a heap: but this has to be taken in such a way that ten and a hundred are not regarded as limits which could be essential to the concept 'heap'.

And this is the same problem as the one specifying which of the vertical strokes we first notice to have a different length from the first.

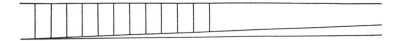

What corresponds in Euclidean geometry to the visual circle isn't a circle, but a class of figures, including the circle, but also, e.g., the hundred-sided regular polygon. The defining characteristic of this class could be something like their all being figures contained in a band which arises through the vibration of a circle. – But even that is wrong: for why should I take precisely the band which arises from vibrating a circle and not that produced by vibrating the hundred-sided polygon?

And here I come up against the cardinal difficulty, since it seems as though an exact *demarcation* of the inexactitude is impossible. For the demarcation is arbitrary, since how is what corresponds to the vibrating circle distinguished from what corresponds to the vibrating hundred-sided polygon?

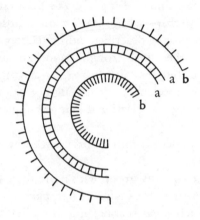

There is something attractive about the following explanation: everything that is within *a a* appears as the visual circle C, every-thing that is outside *b b* does not appear as C. We would then have the case of the word 'heap'. There would be an indeterminate zone left open, and the boundaries *a* and *b* are not essential to the con-cept defined. – The boundaries *a* and *b* are still only like the walls of the *forecourts*. They are drawn arbitrarily at a point where we can still draw something firm. – Just as if we were to border off a swamp with a wall, where the wall is not *the* boundary of the swamp, it only stands around it on firm ground. It is a sign which shows there is a swamp inside it, but not, that the swamp is exactly the same size as that of the surface bounded by it.

212   Now isn't the correlation between visual space and Euclidean space as follows: no matter what Euclidean figure I show to the observer, he must be able to distinguish whether or not it is the visual circle C. That is to say, by constantly reducing the interval between the figures shown I shall be able to reduce the indeterminate interval indefinitely, be able 'to approach indefinitely close to a limit between what I see as C and what I see as not C'.

But on the other hand, I shall never be able to draw such a limit as a curve in Euclidean space, for if I could, it would itself then have to belong to one of the two classes and be the last member of this class, in which case I would have to be able to see a Euclidean curve after all.

If someone says e.g. that we never see a real circle but always only approximations to one, this has a sound, unobjectionable sense, if it means that, given a body which looks circular, we can still always discover inaccuracies by precise measurement or by looking through a magnifying glass. But we lose this sense the moment we substitute the immediately given, the patch or whatever we choose to call it, for the circular body.

If a circle is at all the sort of thing that we see – see in the same sense as that in which we see a blue patch – then we must be able to see it and not merely something like it.

If I cannot see an exact circle then in this sense neither can I see approximations to one. – But then the Euclidean circle – and the Euclidean approximation to one – is in this sense not an object of my perception at all, but, say, only a different logical construction which could be obtained from the objects of a quite different space from the space of immediate vision.

But even this way of talking is misleading, and we must rather say that we see the Euclidean circle in a different sense.

And so that a different sort of projection exists between the

Euclidean circle and the circle perceived than one would naïvely suppose.

If I say you can't distinguish between a chiliagon and a circle, then the chiliagon must here be given through its construction, its origin. For how else would I know that it is 'in fact' a chiliagon and *not* a circle?

In visual space there is no measurement.

We could, e.g., perfectly well give the following definitions for visual space: 'A straight line is one that isn't curved' and 'A circle is a curve with constant curvature'.

213   We need new concepts and we continually resort to those of the language of physical objects. The word 'precision' is one of these dubious expressions. In ordinary language it refers to a *comparison* and then it is quite intelligible. Where a certain degree of imprecision is present, perfect precision is also possible. But what is it supposed to mean when I say I can never see a precise circle, and am now using this word not relatively, but absolutely?

The words 'I see' in 'I see a patch' and 'I see a line' therefore have different meanings.

Suppose I have to say 'I never see a perfectly sharp line'. I have then to ask 'Is a sharp line conceivable?' If it is right to say 'I do not see a sharp line', than a sharp line *is* conceivable. If it makes sense to say 'I never see an exact circle', then this implies: an exact circle is conceivable in visual space.

If an exact circle in a visual field is inconceivable, the proposition 'I never see an exact circle in my visual field' must be the same sort of proposition as 'I never see a high C in my visual field'.

If I say 'The upper interval is as long as the lower' and mean by this what is usually said by the proposition 'the upper interval appears to me as long as the lower', then the word 'equal' [1] means something quite different in this proposition from what it means in the proposition expressed in the same words but which is verified by comparing lengths with dividers. For this reason I can, e.g., speak in the latter case of improving the techniques of comparison, but not in the former. The use of the same word 'equal' with quite different meanings is very confusing. This is the typical case of words and phrases which originally referred to the 'things' of the idioms for talking about physical objects, the 'bodies in space', being applied to the elements of our visual field; in the course of this they inevitably change their meanings utterly and statements which previously had had a sense now lose it and others which had had no sense in the first way of speaking now acquire one. Even though a certain analogy does persist – just the one which tricks us into using the same expression.

It is, e.g., important that the word 'close' means something different in the proposition 'There is a red patch close to the boundary of the visual field' and in such a proposition as 'The red patch in the visual field is close to the brown one'. Furthermore the word 'boundary' in the first proposition also has a different meaning – and is a different sort of word – from 'boundary' in the proposition: 'the boundary between red and blue in the visual field is a circle'.

What sense does it make to say: our visual field is less clear at the edges than towards the middle? That is, if we aren't here talking about the fact that we see physical objects more clearly in the middle of the visual field?

One of the clearest examples of the confusion between physical and phenomenological language is the picture Mach [2] made of his visual field, in which the so-called blurredness of the figures near the edge of the visual field was reproduced by a blurredness (in a quite different sense) in the drawing. No, you can't make a visual picture of our visual image.

1] As Wittgenstein has written these two propositions, the word 'equal' doesn't occur; but this hardly matters.
2] In the first chapter of *Analysis of Sensations*, p. 19.

Can I therefore say that colour patches near the edge of the visual field no longer have sharp contours: are contours then *conceivable* there? I believe it is clear that this lack of clarity is an internal property of visual space. Has, e.g., the word 'colour' a different meaning when it refers to figures near to the edge?

Without this 'blurredness' the limitlessness of visual space isn't conceivable.

214 The question arises what distinctions are there in visual space. Can we learn anything about this from the co-ordination, e.g., of tactile space with visual space? Say, by specifying which changes in one space do not correspond to a change in the other?

The fact that you see a physical hundred-sided polygon as a circle – cannot distinguish it from a physical circle – implies nothing here as to the *possibility* of seeing a hundred-sided polygon.

That it proves impossible for me to find physical bodies which give the visual image of a hundred-sided visual polygon is of no significance for logic. The question is: is there a *sense* in speaking of a hundred-sided polygon? Or: Does it make sense to talk of thirty strokes in a row *taken in at one look*? I believe there is none.

The process isn't at all one of seeing first a triangle, then a square, pentagon etc. up to e.g. a fifty-sided polygon and then the circle coming; no we see a triangle, a square etc., up to, maybe, an octagon, then we see only polygons with sides of varying length. The sides get shorter, then a fluctuation towards the circle begins, and then comes the circle.

Neither does the fact that a physical straight line drawn as a tangent to a circle gives the visual image of a straight line which for a stretch merges with the curve prove that our visual space isn't Euclidean, for a different physical configuration could perfectly well produce the image corresponding to the Euclidean tangent. But in fact such an image is inconceivable.

215   What is meant by the proposition 'We never see a precise circle'? What is the criterion of precision? Couldn't I also perfectly well say: 'Perhaps I see a precise circle, but can never know it'? All this only makes sense, once it has been established in what cases one calls one measurement more precise than another. Now the concept of a circle presupposes – I believe – a concept of 'greater precision', which contains an infinite possibility of being increased. And we may say the concept of a circle *is* the concept of the infinite possibility of greater precision. This infinite possibility of increase would be a postulate of this idiom. Of course, it must then be clear in every case what I would regard as an increase in precision.

It obviously means nothing to say the circle is only an ideal to which reality can only approximate. This is a misleading metaphor. For you can only approximate to something that is there, and if the circle is given us in any form that makes it possible for us to approximate, then precisely that form would be the important thing for us, and approximation to another form in itself of secondary importance. But it may also be that we call an infinite possibility itself, a circle. So that the circle would then be in the same position as an irrational number.

It seems essential to the application of Euclidean geometry that we talk of an *imprecise* circle, an *imprecise* sphere etc. And also that this imprecision must be logically susceptible of an unlimited reduction. And so, if someone is to understand the application of Euclidean geometry, he has to know what the word *'imprecise'* means. For nothing is given us over and above the result of our measuring and the concept of imprecision. These two together must correspond to Euclidean geometry.

Now, is the imprecision of measurement the same concept as the imprecision of visual images? I believe: Certainly not.

If the assertion that we never *see* a precise circle is supposed to mean, e.g., that we never see a straight line touch a circle at one point (i.e. that nothing in our visual space has the multiplicity of a

line touching a circle), then for *this* imprecision, an indefinitely
high degree of precision is not conceivable.

The word 'equality' has a different meaning when applied to
intervals in visual space and when applied in physical space.
Equality in visual space has a different multiplicity from equality
in physical space, so that in visual space g_1 and g_2 can be straight

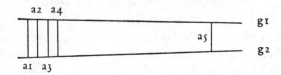

lines (visually straight) and the lengths $a_1 = a_2$, $a_2 = a_3$ etc., but
not $a_1 = a_5$. Equally, a circle and a straight line in visual space have
a different multiplicity from a circle and a straight line in physical
space, for a short stretch of a seen circle can be straight; 'circle'
and 'straight line' simply used in the sense of visual geometry.

Here ordinary language resorts to the words 'seems' or 'appears'.
It says a_1 seems to be equal to a_2, whereas this appearance has
ceased to exist in the case of a_1 and a_5. But it uses the word 'seems'
ambiguously. For its meaning depends on what is opposed to this
appearance as reality. In one case it is the result of measurement,
in another a further appearance. And so the meaning of the word
'seem' is different in these two cases.

216   The time has now come to subject the phrase 'sense-datum'
to criticism. A sense-datum is the appearance of this tree, whether
'there really is a tree standing there' or a dummy, a mirror image,
an hallucination, etc. A sense-datum is the appearance of the tree,
and what we want to say is that its representation in language is
only *one* description, but not *the* essential one. Just as you can say
of the expression '*my* visual image' that it is only one form of
description, but by no means the only possible and correct one.
For the form of words 'the appearance of this tree' incorporates

the idea of a necessary connection between what we are calling the appearance and 'the existence of a tree', in fact whether it be veridical perception or a mistake. That is to say, if we talk about 'the appearance of a tree', we are either taking for a tree something which is one, or something which is not one. But this connection isn't there.

Idealists would like to reproach language with presenting what is secondary as primary and what is primary as secondary. But that is only the case with these inessential valuations which are independent of cognition ('only' an appearance). Apart from that, ordinary language makes no decision as to what is primary or secondary. We have no reason to accept that the expression 'the appearance of a tree' represents something which is secondary in relation to the expression 'tree'. The expression 'only an image' goes back to the idea that we can't eat the image of an apple.

217 We might think that the right model for visual space would be a Euclidean drawing-board with its ideally fine constructions which we make vibrate so that all the constructions are to a certain extent blurred (further, the surface vibrates equally in all the directions lying in it). We could in fact say: it is to be vibrated precisely as far as it can without its yet being noticeable, and then its physical geometry will be a picture of our phenomenological geometry.

But the big question is: Can you translate the 'blurredness' of phenomena into an imprecision in the drawing? It seems to me that you can't.

It is, for instance, impossible to represent the imprecision of what is immediately seen by thick strokes and dots in the drawing.

Just as we cannot represent the memory of a picture by this picture painted in faint colours. The faintness of memory is something quite other than the faintness of a hue we see; and the unclarity of vision different *in kind* from the blurredness of an imprecise drawing. (Indeed, an imprecise drawing is seen with precisely the unclarity we are trying to represent by its imprecision.)

(In films, when a memory or dream is to be represented, the pictures are given a bluish tint. But memory images have no bluish tint, and so the bluish projections are not visually accurate pictures of the dream, but pictures in a sense which is not immediately visual.)

A line in the visual field need not be either straight or curved. Of course the third possibility should not be called 'doubtful' (that is nonsense); we ought to use another word for it, or rather replace the whole way of speaking by a different one.

That visual space isn't Euclidean is already shown by the occurrence of two different kinds of lines and points: we see the fixed stars as points: that is, we can't see the contours of a fixed star, and in a different sense two colour boundaries also intersect in a point; similarly for lines. I can see a luminous line without thickness, since otherwise I should be able to see a cross-section of it as a rectangle or at least the four points of intersection of its contours.

A visual circle and a visual straight line can have a stretch in common.

If I look at a drawn circle with a tangent, it wouldn't be remarkable that I never see a perfect circle and a perfect straight line touch one another, it only becomes interesting when I see this happen, and the straight line and the circle then coincide for a stretch.

For only that would imply that the visual circle and the visual line are essentially different from the circle and line of Euclidean geometry; but the first case, that we have never seen a perfect circle and a perfect line touch one another, would not.

XXI

218   There appear to be simple colours. Simple as psychological phenomena. What I need is a psychological or rather phenomenological colour theory, not a physical and equally not a physiological one.

Furthermore, it must be a theory in *pure* phenomenology in which mention is only made of what is actually perceptible and in which no hypothetical objects – waves, rods, cones and all that – occur.

Now, we can recognize colours as mixtures of red, green, blue, yellow, white and black *immediately*. Where this is still always the colour itself, and not pigment, light, process on or in the retina, etc.

We can also see that one colour is redder than another or whiter, etc. But can I find a metric for colours? Is there a sense in saying, for instance, that with respect to the amount of red in it one colour is *halfway* between two other colours?

At least there seems to be a sense in saying that one colour is closer in this respect to a second than it is to a third.

219   You might say, violet and orange partially obliterate one another when mixed, but not red and yellow.

At any rate orange is a mixture of red and yellow in a sense in which yellow isn't a mixture of red and green, although yellow comes between red and green in the colour circle.

And if that happens to be manifest nonsense, the question arises, at what point does it begin to make sense; that is, if I now move on the circle from red and from green towards yellow and call yellow a mixture of the two colours I have now reached.

That is, in yellow I recognize an affinity with red and with green, viz. the possibility of reddish yellow – and yet I still don't recognize green and red as component parts of yellow in the sense in which I recognize red and yellow as component parts of orange.

I want to say that red is between violet and orange only in the sense in which white is between pink and greenish-white. But, in this sense, isn't any colour between any two other colours, or at least between any two which may be reached from the first by independent routes?

Can one say that in this sense a colour only lies between two others with reference to a specified continuous transition? And so, say, blue between red and black?

Is this then how it is: to say the colour of a patch is a mixture of orange and violet is to ascribe to it a different colour from that ascribed by saying that the patch has the colour common to violet and orange? – But that won't work either; for, in the sense in which orange is a mixture of red and yellow, there isn't a mixture of orange and violet at all. If I imagine mixing a blue-green with a yellow-green, I see straightaway that it can't happen, that, on the contrary, a component part would first have to be 'killed' before the union could occur. This isn't the case with red and yellow. And in this I don't have an image of a continuous transition (via green), only the discrete hues play a part here.

220 I must know what in general is meant by the expression 'mixture of colours A and B', since its application isn't limited to a finite number of pairs. Thus if, e.g., someone shows me any shade of orange and a white and says the colour of a patch is a mixture of these two, then I must understand this, and I can understand it.

If someone says to me that the colour of a patch lies between violet and red, I understand this and can imagine a redder violet than the one given. If, now, someone says to me the colour lies between this violet and an orange – where I don't have a specific continuous transition before me in the shape of a painted colour circle – then I can at best think that here, too, a redder violet is meant, but a redder orange might also be what is meant, since, leaving on one side a given colour circle, there is no colour lying *halfway* between the two colours, and for just this reason neither can I say at what point the orange forming one limit is already too close to the yellow for it still to be mixed with the violet; the point is that I can't tell which orange lies at a distance of 90° from violet on the colour circle. The way in which the mixed colour lies between the others is no different here from the way red comes between blue and yellow.

If I say in the ordinary sense that red and yellow make orange, I am not talking here about a *quantity* of the components. And so, given an orange, I can't say that yet *more* red would have made it a redder orange (I'm not of course speaking about pigments), even though there is of course a sense in speaking of a redder orange. But there is, e.g., no sense in saying this orange and this violet contain the same amount of red. And how much red would *red* contain?

The comparison we are seduced into making is one between the colour series and a system of two weights on the beam of a balance, where I can move the centre of gravity of the system just as I choose, by increasing or moving the weights.

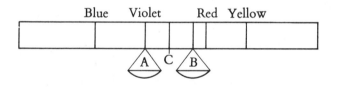

Now it's nonsense to believe that if I held the scale A at violet and moved the scale B into the red-yellow region, C will then move towards red.

And what about the weights I put on the scales: Does it mean anything to say, '*more* of *this* red'? when I'm not talking about pigments. That can only mean something if I understand by pure red a number of units, where the number is stipulated at the outset. But then the complete number of units means nothing but that the scale is standing at red. And so the relative numbers again only specify a point on the balance, and not a point and a weight.

Now so long as I keep my two end colours in say, the blue-red region, and move the redder colour, I can say that the resultant also moves towards red. But if I move one end-colour beyond red, and move it towards yellow, the resultant doesn't now become redder! Mixing a yellowish red with a violet doesn't make the violet redder than mixing pure red with the violet. That the one red has now become yellower even takes away something of the red and doesn't add red.

We could also describe this as follows: if I have a paint pot of violet pigment and another of orange, and now increase the amount of orange added to the mixture, the colour of the mixture will gradually move away from violet towards orange, but not via pure red.

I can say of two different shades of orange that I have no grounds for saying of either that it is closer to red than yellow. – There simply isn't a 'midpoint' here. – On the other hand, I can't see two different reds and be in doubt whether one of them, and if so which, is pure red. That is because pure red is a point, but the midway between red and yellow isn't.

221 Admittedly it's true that we can say of an orange that it's almost yellow, and so that it is 'closer to yellow than to red' and analogously for an almost red orange. But it doesn't follow from this that there must also be a midpoint between red and yellow. Here the position is just as it is with the geometry of visual space as compared with Euclidean geometry. There are here quantities of a different sort from that represented by our rational numbers. The concepts 'closer to' and 'further from' are simply of no use at all or are misleading when we apply these phrases.

Or again: to say of a colour that it lies between red and blue doesn't define it sharply (unambiguously). But the pure colours must be defined *unambiguously* when it is stated that they lie between certain mixed colours. And so the phrase 'lie between' means something *different* from what it meant in the first case. That is to say, if the expression 'lie between' on one occasion designates a mixture of two simple colours, and on another a simple component common to two mixed colours, the multiplicity of its application is different in the two cases. And this is *not* a difference in degree, it's an expression of the fact that we are dealing with two entirely different categories.

We say a colour can't be between green-yellow and blue-red in the same sense as between red and yellow, but we can only say this because in the latter case we can distinguish the angle of 90°; because we see yellow and red as *points*. But there simply is no such distinguishing in the other case – where the mixed colours are regarded as primary. And so in this case we can, so to speak, never be certain whether the mixture is still possible or not. To be sure, I could choose mixed colours at random and stipulate that they include an angle of 90°; but this would be completely arbitrary, whereas it isn't arbitrary when we say that in the first sense there is no mixture of blue-red and green-yellow.

So in the one case grammar yields the 'angle of 90°', and now we are misled into thinking: we only need to bisect it and the adjacent segment too, to arrive at another 90° segment. But here the *metaphor* of an angle collapses.

Of course you can also arrange all the shades in a straight line, say with black and white as endpoints, as has been done, but then you have to introduce rules to exclude certain transitions, and in the end the representation on the line must be given the same kind of topological structure as the octahedron has. In this, it's completely analogous to the relation of ordinary language to a 'logically purified' mode of expression. The two are completely equivalent;

it's just that one of them already wears the rules of grammar on its face.

To what extent can you say that grey is a mixture of black and white *in the same sense* as orange is a mixture of red and yellow? And doesn't lie between black and white in the sense in which red lies between blue-red and orange?

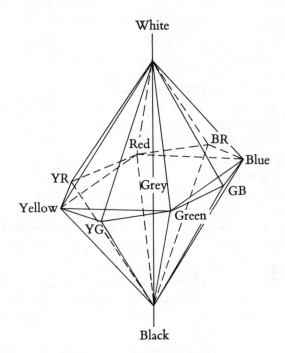

If we represent the colours by means of a double-cone, instead of an octahedron, there is only one *between* on the colour circle, and red appears on it between blue-red and orange in the same sense as that in which blue-red lies between blue and red. And if in fact that is all there is to be said, then a representation by means of a double-cone is adequate, or at least one using a double eight-sided pyramid is.

222 Now strangely enough, it seems clear from the outset that we can't say red has an orange tinge in the same sense as orange

has a reddish tinge. That is to say, it seems to be clear that the phrases 'x is composed of (is a mixture of) y and z' and 'x is the common component of y and z' are not interchangeable here: Were they so, the relation *between* would be all we needed for a representation.

In general, the phrases 'common component of' and 'mixture of' have different meanings only if one can be used in a context where the other can't.

Now, it's irrelevant to our investigation that when I mix blue and green pigments I get a blue-green, but when I mix blue-green and blue-red the result isn't a blue.

If I am right in my way of thinking, then 'Red is a pure colour' isn't a proposition, and what it is meant to show is not susceptible to experimental testing. So that it is inconceivable that at one time red and at another blue-red should appear to us to be pure.

223   Besides the transition from colour to colour on the colour-circle, there seems to be another specific transition that we have before us when we see dots of one colour intermingled with dots of another. Of course I mean here a *seen* transition.

And this sort of transition gives a new meaning to the word 'mixture', which doesn't coincide with the relation 'between' on the colour-circle.

You might describe it like this: I can imagine an orange-coloured patch as having arisen from intermingling red and yellow dots, whereas I can't imagine a red patch as having arisen from intermingling violet and orange dots. – In this sense, grey is a mixture of black and white, but white isn't a mixture of pink and a whitish green.

But I don't mean that it is established by experimental mixing that certain colours arise in this way from others. I could, say, perform the experiment with a rotating coloured disc. Then it might work or might not, but that will only show whether or not the visual process in question can be produced by these physical means – it doesn't show whether the process is possible. Just as physical dissection of a surface can neither prove nor refute visual divisibility. For suppose I can no longer see a physical dissection as a visual dissection, but when drunk see the undivided surface as divided, then wasn't the visual surface divisible?

If I am given two shades of red, say, which are close to one another, it's impossible to be in doubt whether both lie between red and blue, or both between red and yellow, or one between red and blue and the other between red and yellow. And in deciding this, we have also decided whether both will mix with blue or with yellow, or one with blue and one with yellow, and this holds no matter how close the shades are brought together so long as we are still capable of distinguishing the pigments by colour at all.

If we ask whether the musical scale carries with it an infinite possibility of being continued, then it's no answer to say that we can no longer perceive vibrations of the air that exceed a certain rate of vibration as notes, since it might be possible to bring about sensations of higher notes in another way. Rather, the finitude of the musical scale can only derive from its internal properties. For instance, from our being able to tell from a note *itself* that it is the final one, and so that this last note, or the last notes, exhibit inner properties which the notes in between don't have.

Just as thin lines in our visual field exhibit internal properties not possessed by the thicker ones, so that there is a line in our visual field, which isn't a colour boundary but is itself coloured, and yet in a specific sense has no breadth, so that when it inter- sects another such line we do not see four points A, B, C, D.

224 Nowadays the danger that lies in trying to see things as simpler than they really are is often greatly exaggerated. But this danger does actually exist to the highest degree in the phenomenological investigation of sense impressions. These are always taken to be *much* simpler than they are.

If I see that a figure possesses an organization which previously I hadn't noticed, I now see a different figure. Thus I can see |||||| as a special case of || || || or of ||| ||| or of | |||| | etc. This merely shows that that which we see isn't as simple as it appears.

Understanding a Gregorian mode doesn't mean getting used to the sequence of notes in the sense in which I can get used to a smell and after a while cease to find it unpleasant. No, it means hearing something new, which I haven't heard before, much in the same way – in fact it's a complete analogy – as it would be if I were suddenly able to see 10 strokes ||||||||||, which I had hitherto only been able to see as twice five strokes, as a characteristic whole. Or suddenly seeing the picture of a cube as 3-dimensional when I had previously only been able to see it as a flat pattern.

The limitlessness of visual space stands out most clearly, when we can see nothing, in pitch-darkness.

XXII

225 A proposition, an hypothesis, is coupled with reality – with varying degrees of freedom. In the limit case there's no longer any connection, reality can do anything it likes without coming into conflict with the proposition: in which case the proposition (hypothesis) is senseless!

All that matters is that the signs, in no matter how complicated a way, still in the end refer to immediate experience and not to an intermediary (a thing in itself).

All that's required for our propositions (about reality) to have a sense, is that our experience *in some sense or other* either tends to agree with them or tends not to agree with them. That is, immediate experience need confirm only something about them, *some* facet of them. And in fact this image is taken straight from reality, since we say 'There's a chair here', when we only see *one* side of it.

According to my principle, two assumptions must be identical in sense if every possible experience that confirms the one confirms the other too. Thus, if no empirical way of deciding between them is conceivable.

A proposition construed in such a way that it can be uncheckably true or false is completely detached from reality and no longer functions as a proposition.

The views of modern physicists (Eddington) tally with mine completely, when they say that the signs in their equations no longer have 'meanings', and that physics cannot attain to such meanings but must stay put at the signs. But they don't see that these signs have meaning in as much as – and only in as much as – immediately observable phenomena (such as points of light) do or do not correspond to them.

A phenomenon isn't a symptom of something else: it is the reality.

A phenomenon isn't a symptom of something else which alone makes the proposition true or false: it itself is what verifies the proposition.

226   An hypothesis is a logical structure. That is, a symbol for which certain rules of representation hold.

The point of talking of sense-data and immediate experience is that we're after a description that has nothing hypothetical in it. If an hypothesis can't be definitively verified, it can't be verified at all, and there's no truth or falsity for it [1].

My experience speaks in favour of the idea that *this* hypothesis will be able to represent it and future experience *simply*. If it turns out that another hypothesis represents the material of experience more simply, then I choose the simpler method. The choice of representation is a process based on so-called induction (not mathematical induction).

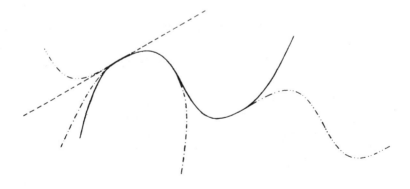

1] Cf. below, p. 285. [ed.]

This is how someone might try to represent the course of an experience which presents itself as the development of a curve by means of various curves, each of which is based on how much of the actual course is known to us.

The curve —— is the actual course, so far as it is to be observed at all. The curves –––, –·–·–·–, –··–··–, show different attempts to represent it that are based on a greater or lesser part of the whole material of observation.

227   We only give up an hypothesis for an even higher gain.

Induction is a process based on a principle of economy.

Any hypothesis has a connection with reality which is, as it were, looser than that of verification.

The question, how simple a representation is yielded by assuming a particular hypothesis, is directly connected, I believe, with the question of probability.

You could obviously explain an hypothesis by means of pictures. I mean, you could, e.g., explain the hypothesis, 'There is a book lying here', with pictures showing the book in plan, elevation and various cross-sections.

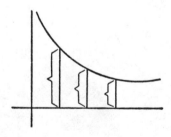

Such a representation gives a *law*. Just as the equation of a curve gives a law, by means of which you may discover the ordinates, if you cut at different abscissae.

In which case the verifications of particular cases correspond to cuts that have actually been made.

If our experiences yield points lying on a straight line, the proposition that these experiences are various views of a straight line is an hypothesis.

The hypothesis is a way of representing this reality, for a new experience may tally with it or not, or possibly make it necessary to modify the hypothesis.

228   What is essential to an hypothesis is, I believe, that it arouses an expectation by admitting of future confirmation. That is, it is of the essence of an hypothesis that its confirmation is never completed.

When I say an hypothesis isn't definitively verifiable, that doesn't mean that there is a verification of it which we may approach ever more nearly, without ever reaching it. That is nonsense – of a kind into which we frequently lapse. No, an hypothesis simply has a different formal relation to reality from that of verification. (Hence, of course, the words 'true' and 'false' are also inapplicable here, or else have a different meaning.)

The nature of the belief in the uniformity of events is perhaps clearest in a case where we are afraid of what we expect to happen. Nothing could persuade me to put my hand in the fire, even though it's *only in the past* that I've burnt myself.

If physics describes a body of a particular shape in physical space, it must assume, even if tacitly, the possibility of verification. The points at which the hypothesis is connected with immediate experience must be anticipated.

An hypothesis is a law for forming propositions.

You could also say: An hypothesis is a law for forming expectations.

A proposition is, so to speak, a particular cross-section of an hypothesis.

229 The probability of an hypothesis has its measure in how much evidence is needed to make it profitable to throw it out.

It's only in this sense that we can say that repeated uniform experience in the past renders the continuation of this uniformity in the future probable.

If, in this sense, I now say: I assume the sun will rise again tomorrow, because the opposite is so unlikely, I here mean by 'likely' and 'unlikely' something completely different from what I mean by these words in the proposition 'It's equally likely that I'll throw heads or tails'. The two meanings of the word 'likely' are, to be sure, connected in certain ways, but they aren't identical.

What's essential is that I must be able to compare my expectation not only with what is to be regarded as its definitive answer (its verification or falsification), but also with how things stand at present. This alone makes the expectation into a picture.

That is to say: it must make sense *now*.

If I say I can see, e.g., a sphere, that means nothing other than that I am seeing a view such as a sphere affords, but this only means I can construct views in accordance with a certain law – that of the sphere – and that this is such a view.

230 Describing phenomena by means of the hypothesis of a world of material objects is unavoidable in view of its simplicity when compared with the unmanageably complicated phenomenological description. If I can see different discrete parts of a circle, it's perhaps impossible to give precise direct description of them, but the statement that they're parts of a circle, which, for reasons which haven't been gone into any further, I don't see as a whole – is simple.

Description of this kind always introduces some sort of parameter, which for our purposes we don't need to investigate.

What is the difference between the logical multiplicity of an explanation of appearances by the natural sciences and the logical multiplicity of a description?

If e.g. a regular ticking sound were to be represented in physics, the multiplicity of the picture |—|—|—|—|—|→ would suffice, but here it's not a question of the logical multiplicity of the sound, but of that of the regularity of the phenomenon observed. And just so, the theory of Relativity doesn't represent the logical multiplicity of the phenomena themselves, but that of the regularities observed.

If, for instance, we use a system of co-ordinates and the equation for a sphere to express the proposition that a sphere is located at a certain distance from our eyes, this description has a greater multiplicity than that of a verification by eye. The first multiplicity corresponds not to *one* verification, but to a *law* obeyed by verifications.

As long as someone imagines the soul as a thing, a body in our heads, there's *no* harm in the hypothesis. The harm doesn't lie in the imperfection and crudity of our models, but in their lack of clarity (vagueness).

The trouble starts when we notice that the old model is inadequate, but then, instead of altering it, only as it were sublimate it. While I say thoughts are in my head, everything's all right; it becomes harmful when we say thoughts aren't in my head, they're in my mind.

Whatever someone *can* mean by a proposition, he also *may* mean by it. When people say, by the proposition 'There's a chair here', I don't merely mean what is shown me by immediate experience, but something over and above that, you can only reply: whatever you can mean must connect with some sort of experience, and whatever you *can* mean is unassailable.

231 We may compare a part of an hypothesis with the movement of a part of a gear, a movement that can be stipulated without prejudicing the intended motion. But then of course you have to make appropriate adjustments to the rest of the gear if it is to produce the desired motion. I'm thinking of a differential gear. – Once I've decided that there is to be no deviation from a certain part of my hypothesis no matter what the experience to be described may be, I have stipulated a mode of representation and this part of my hypothesis is now a postulate. A postulate must be such that no

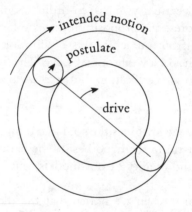

conceivable experience can refute it, even though it may be extremely inconvenient to cling to the postulate. To the extent to which we can talk here of greater or slighter convenience, there is a greater or slighter probability of the postulate.

It's senseless to talk of a measure for this probability at this juncture. The situation here is like that in the case of two kinds of numbers where we can with a certain justice say that the one is more like the other (is closer to it) than a third, but there isn't any numerical measure of the similarity. Of course you could imagine a measure being constructed in such cases, too, say by counting the postulates or axioms common to the two systems, etc., etc.

232   We may apply our old principle to propositions expressing a probability and say, we shall discover their sense by considering what verifies them.

If I say 'That will probably occur', is this proposition verified by the occurrence or falsified by its non-occurrence? In my opinion, obviously not. In that case it doesn't say anything about either. For if a dispute were to arise as to whether it is probable or not, it would always only be arguments from the past that would be adduced. And this would be so even when what actually happened was already known.

If you look at ideas about probability and its application, it's always as though *a priori* and *a posteriori* were jumbled together, as if the same state of affairs could be discovered or corroborated by experience, whose existence was evident *a priori*. This of course shows that something's amiss in our ideas, and in fact we always seem to confuse the natural law we are assuming with what we experience.

That is, it always looks as if our experience (say in the case of card shuffling) agreed with the probability calculated *a priori*. But that is nonsense. If the experience agrees with the computation, that means my computation is justified by the experience, and of course it isn't its *a priori* element which is justified, but its bases, which are *a posteriori*. But those must be certain natural laws which I take as the basis for my calculation, and it is *these* that are confirmed, not the calculation of the probability.

The calculation of the probability can only cast the natural law in a different form. It transforms the natural law. It is the medium through which we view and apply the natural law.

If for instance I throw a die, I can apparently predict *a priori* that the 1 will occur on average once every 6 throws, and that can then be confirmed empirically. But it isn't the calculation I confirm by the experiment, but the natural law which the probability calculation can present to me in different forms. Through the medium of the probability calculation I check the natural law lying behind the calculation.

In our case the natural law takes the form that it is equally likely for any of the six sides to be the side uppermost. It's this law that we test.

233   Of course this is only a natural law if it can be confirmed by a particular experiment, and also refuted by a particular experiment. This isn't the case on the usual view, for if *any* event can be justified throughout an arbitrary interval of time, then *any* experience *whatever* can be reconciled with the law. But that means the law is idling; it's senseless.

Certain possible events must contradict the law if it is to be one at all; and should these occur, they must be explained by a different law.

When we wager on a possibility, it's always on the assumption of the uniformity of nature.

If we say the molecules of a gas move in accordance with the laws of probability, it creates the impression that they move in accordance with some *a priori* laws or other. Naturally, that's nonsense. The laws of probability, i.e. those on which the calculation is *based*, are hypothetical assumptions, which are then rehashed by the calculation and then in another form empirically confirmed – or refuted.

If you look at what is called the *a priori* probability and then at its confirmation by the relative frequency of events, the chief thing that strikes you is that the *a priori* probability, which is, as it were, something smooth, is supposed to govern the relative frequency, which is something irregular. If both bundles of hay are the same size and the same distance away, that would explain why the donkey stands still between them, but it's no explanation of its eating roughly as often from the one as from the other. *That* requires *different* laws of nature to explain it. – The facts that the die is homogeneous and that each side is exactly the same, and that the natural laws with which I'm familiar tell me nothing about the result of a throw, don't give me adequate grounds for inferring that the numbers 1 to 6 will be distributed roughly equally among the numbers thrown. Rather, the prediction that such a distribution will be the case contains an assumption about those natural laws that I don't know precisely: the assumption that *they* will produce such a distribution.

234   Isn't the following fact inconsistent with my conception of probability: it's obviously conceivable that a man throwing dice every day for a week – let's say – throws nothing but ones, and not because of any defect in the die, but simply because the movement of his hand, the position of the die in the box, the friction of the table top always conspire to produce the same result. The man has inspected the die, and also found that when others throw it the normal results are produced. Has he grounds, now, for thinking that there's a natural law at work here which makes him throw nothing but ones? Has he grounds for believing that it's sure now to go on like this, or has he grounds for believing that this regularity can't last much longer? That is, has he grounds for abandoning the game since it has become clear that he can only

throw ones, or for playing on since it is in these circumstances all the more probable that he will now throw a higher number? In actual fact, he will refuse to accept it as a natural law that he can throw nothing but ones. At least, it will have to go on for a long time before he will entertain this possibility. But why? I believe, because so much of his previous experience in life speaks against there being a law of nature of such a sort, and we have – so to speak – to surmount all that experience, before embracing a totally new way of looking at things.

If we infer from the relative frequency of an event its relative frequency in the future, we can of course only do that from the frequency which has in fact been so far observed. And not from one we have derived from observation by some process or other for calculating probabilities. For the probability we calculate is compatible with *any* frequency whatever that we actually observe, since it leaves the time open.

When a gambler or insurance company is guided by probability, they aren't guided by the probability calculus, since one can't be guided by this on its own, because *anything* that happens can be reconciled with it: no, the insurance company is guided by a frequency actually observed. And that, of course, is an absolute frequency.

235   We can represent the equation of this curve:

A   B

as the equation of a straight line with a variable parameter, whose course expresses the deviations from a straight line. It isn't essential that these deviations should be 'slight'. They can be so large that the curve doesn't look like a straight line at all. 'Straight line with deviations' is *only one form* of description. It makes it possible for me to neglect a particular component of the description – if I so wish. (The form: 'rule with exceptions'.)

A Galtonian photograph is the picture of a probability [1].

A probability law is the natural law you see when you screw up your eyes.

To say that the points yielded by this experiment distribute themselves around this curve – e.g. a straight line – means something like: seen from a certain distance, they appear to lie on a straight line.

If I state 'That's the rule', that only has a sense as long as I have determined the maximum number of exceptions I'll allow before knocking down the rule.

236 I can say of a curve ⎯⎯⎯⎯⎯⎯⎯⎯⎯⎯
that the general impression is one of a straight line, but not of the

curve

even though it might be possible to see this stretch in the course of a long stretch of curve in which its divergence from a straight line would be swallowed up.

I mean: it only makes sense to say of the stretch you actually see (and not of an hypothetical one you assume) that it gives the general impression of a straight line.

What is meant in a statistical experiment by 'in the long run'? An experiment must have a beginning and an end.

An experiment with dice lasts a certain time, and our expectations for the future can only be based on tendencies we observe in what happens during this experiment. That is to say, the experiment can only give grounds for expecting that things will go on *in the way* shown by the experiment; but we can't expect that the experiment,

---

1] Francis Galton, *Inquiries into Human Faculty*, London, 1883, Ch. 1 and Appendix A on 'Composite portraiture'.

if continued, will now yield results that tally better with a preconceived idea of its course than did those of the experiment we have actually performed.

So if, for instance, I toss a coin and find no tendency in the results of the experiment itself for the numbers of heads and of tails to approximate to each other more closely, then the experiment gives me no reason to suppose that if it were continued such an approximation would emerge. Indeed, the expectation of such an approximation must *itself* refer to a definite point in time, since I can't expect something to happen *eventually*, without setting any finite limit whatever to the time when.

I can't say: 'The curve looks straight, since it could be part of a line which taken as a whole gives me the impression of a straight line.'

237   Any 'reasonable' expectation is an expectation that a rule we have observed up to now will continue to hold.

But the rule must have been observed and can't, for its part too, be merely expected.

Probability Theory is only concerned with the state of expectation in the sense in which logic is with thinking.

Rather, probability is concerned with the form and a standard of expectation.

It's a question of expecting that future experience will obey a law which has been obeyed by previous experience.

'It's likely that an event will occur' means: *something speaks in favour* of its occurring.

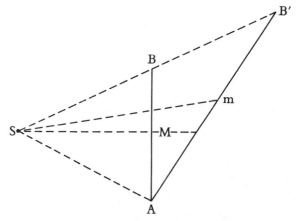

A ray is emitted from the light source S striking the surface AB to form a point of light there, and then striking the surface AB′ to form one there. We have no reason to suppose that the point on AB lies to the left or to the right of M, and equally none for supposing that the point on AB′ lies to the right or to the left of m; this yields apparently incompatible probabilities.

But suppose I have made an assumption about the probability of the point on AB lying in AM, how is this assumption verified? Surely by a frequency experiment. Supposing this confirms the one view, then that is recognized as the right one and so shows itself to be an hypothesis belonging to *physics*. The geometrical construction merely shows that the fact that AM = MB was *no* ground for assuming equal likelihood.

I give someone the following piece of information, and no more: at such and such a time you will see a point of light appear in the interval AB.

Does the question now make sense, 'Is it more likely that this point will appear in the interval AC than in CB?'? I believe, obviously not. – I can of course decide that the probability of the event's happening in CB is to be in the ratio CB/AC to the probability of its happening in AC; however, that's a decision I can have empirical grounds for making, but about which there is nothing to be said *a priori*. It is possible for the observed distribution of events not to lead to this assumption [1]. The probability, where infinitely many possibilities come into consideration, must of course be treated as a limit. That is, if I divide the stretch AB into arbitrarily many parts of arbitrary lengths and regard it as equally likely that the event should occur in any one of these parts, we immediately have the simple case of dice before us. And now I can – arbitrarily – lay down a law for constructing parts of equal likelihood. For instance, the law that, if the lengths of the parts are equal, they are equally likely. But any other law is just as permissible.

Couldn't I, in the case of dice too, take, say, five faces together as one possibility, and oppose them to the sixth as the second possibility? And what, apart from experience, is there to prevent me from regarding these two possibilities as equally likely?

Let's imagine throwing, say, a red ball with just one very small green patch on it. Isn't it much more likely in this case for the red area to strike the ground than for the green? – But how would we support this proposition? Presumably by showing that when we throw the ball, the red strikes the ground much more often than the green. But that's got nothing to do with logic. – We may always project the red and green surfaces and what befalls them onto a surface in such a way that the projection of the green surface is greater than or equal to the red; so that the events, as seen in this projection, appear to have a quite different probability ratio from the one they had on the original surface.

If, e.g., I reflect the events in a suitably curved mirror and now imagine what I would have held to be the more probable event if I had only seen the image in the mirror.

The one thing the mirror can't alter is the number of clearly

---

1] In the manuscript, Wittgenstein writes this sentence in the form, 'Die beobachtete Verteilung von Ereignissen kann mich zu dieser Annahme führen.' ['The observed distribution of events can lead me to this assumption.'] In the typescript the 'mich' is changed to 'nicht'; this is the reading given in demarcated possibilities. So that if I have *n* coloured patches on my ball, the mirror will also show *n*, and if I have *decided* that these are to be regarded as equally likely, then I can stick to this decision for the mirror image too.

To make myself even clearer: if I carry out the experiment with a concave mirror, i.e., make the *observations* in a concave mirror, it will perhaps then look as if the ball falls more often on the small surface than on the much larger one; and it's clear that neither experiment – in the mirror or outside it – has a claim to precedence.

What now, does it really mean to decide that two possibilities are equally likely?

Doesn't it mean that, first, the natural laws known to us give no preference to either of the possibilities, and second, that under certain conditions the relative frequencies of the two events approach one another?

---

the German text and which we have followed. It is possible that the typescript reading is a misprint, but it does seem to make neatest sense in the context, provided one allows the slightly strained way of taking 'kann nicht', ['The observed distribution of events cannot lead to this assumption' appears not to fit the context at all.] [trans.]

APPENDIX 1

Written in 1931

The use of the words 'fact' and 'act'. – 'That was a noble act.' – 'But, that never happened.' –

It is natural to want to use the word 'act' so that it only corresponds to a *true* proposition. So that we then don't talk of an act which was never performed. But the proposition 'That was a noble act' must still have a sense even if I am mistaken in thinking that what I call an act occurred. And that of itself contains all that matters, and I can only make the stipulation that I will only use the words 'fact', 'act' (perhaps also 'event') in a proposition which, when complete, asserts that this fact obtains.

It would be better to drop the restriction on the use of these words, since it only leads to confusion, and say quite happily: 'This act was never performed', 'This fact does not obtain', 'This event did not occur'.

Complex is not like fact. For I can, e.g., say of a complex that it moves from one place to another, but not of a fact.
But that this complex is now situated here is a fact.

'This complex of buildings is coming down' is tantamount to: 'The buildings thus grouped together are coming down'.

I call a flower, a house, a constellation, complexes: moreover, complexes of petals, bricks, stars, etc.
That this constellation is located here, can of course be described by a proposition in which only its stars are mentioned and neither the word 'constellation' nor its name occurs.

But that is all there is to say about the relation between complex and fact. And a complex is a spatial object, composed of spatial objects. (The concept 'spatial' admitting of a certain extension.)

A complex is composed of its parts, the things of a kind which go to make it up. (This is of course a grammatical proposition concerning the words 'complex', 'part' and 'compose'.)

To say that a red circle is *composed* of redness and circularity, or is a complex with these component parts, is a misuse of these words and is misleading. (Frege was aware of this and told me.)

It is just as misleading to say the fact that this circle is red (that I am tired) is a complex whose component parts are a circle and redness (myself and tiredness).

Neither is a house a complex of bricks and their spatial relations; i.e. that too goes against the correct use of the word.

Now, you can of course point at a constellation and say: this constellation is composed entirely of objects with which I am already acquainted; but you can't 'point at a fact' and say this.

'To describe a fact', or 'the description of a fact', is also a misleading expression for the assertion stating that the fact obtains, since it sounds like: 'describing the animal that I saw'.

Of course we also say: 'to point out a fact', but that always means; 'to point out the fact that . . .'. Whereas 'to point at (or point out) a flower' doesn't mean to point out that this blossom is on this stalk; for we needn't be talking about this blossom and this stalk at all.

It's just as impossible for it to mean: to point out the fact that this flower is situated there.

To point out a fact means to assert something, to state something. 'To point out a flower' doesn't mean this.

A chain, too, is composed of its links, not of these and their spatial relations.

The fact that these links are so concatenated, isn't *'composed'* of anything at all.

The root of this muddle is the confusing use of the word 'object'.

The part is smaller than the whole: applied to fact and component part (constituent), that would yield an absurdity.

The following translations have been used throughout this discussion: *Tat,* act; *Tatsache,* fact; *Ereignis,* event; *hinweisen auf,* point out; *zeigen auf,* point at. The one nuance it seems impossible to pick up in English is the link between '*Diese Tatsache besteht*' = 'this fact obtains' and '*Dieser Komplex besteht aus . . .*' = 'this complex is composed of'; we have rendered the noun from *bestehen,* '*Bestandteil*', 'component part'; in translations of the *Tractatus* and other related discussions these last two are usually rendered 'consists of', 'constituent' (as Wittgenstein indicates in the last paragraph). [trans.]

The Concept of Infinity in Mathematics
(The end of 1931)

Infinitely Long

If you speak of the concept 'infinity', you must remember that this word has many different meanings and bear in mind which one we are going to speak of at this particular moment. Whether, e.g., of the infinity of a number series and of the cardinals in particular. If, for example, I say 'infinite' is a characteristic of a rule, I am referring to *one* particular meaning of the word. But we might perfectly well say a continuous transition of colour was a transition 'through infinitely many stages', provided we don't forget that here are defining the meaning of the phrase 'infinitely many stages' *anew* by means of the experience of a colour transition. (Even if by analogy with other ways of using the word 'infinite'.)

(If we say that this area of our subject is extraordinarily difficult, that isn't true in the sense that we are, say, talking about things which are extraordinarily complicated or difficult to imagine, but only in the sense that it is extraordinarily difficult to negotiate the countless pitfalls language puts in our path here.)

'I once said there was no extensional infinity. Ramsey replied: "Can't we imagine a man living for ever, that is simply, never dying, and isn't that extensional infinity?" I can surely imagine a wheel spinning and *never* coming to rest' [1]. What a peculiar

---

1] Cf. §145, p. 165, 166.

argument: 'I can imagine . . .'! Let's consider what experience we would regard as a confirmation or proof of the fact that the wheel will never stop spinning. And compare this experience with that which would tell us that the wheel spins for a day, for a year, for ten years, and we shall find it easy to see the difference in the grammar of the assertions '. . . never comes to rest' and '. . . comes to rest in 100 years'. Let's think of the kind of evidence we might adduce for the claim that two heavenly bodies will orbit around one another, without end. Or of the Law of Inertia and how it is confirmed.

'Suppose we travel out along a straight line into Euclidean space and that at 10m. intervals we encounter an iron sphere, *ad. inf.*' [1]. Again: What sort of experience would I regard as confirmation for this, and what on the other hand for there being 10,000 spheres in a row? – A confirmation of the first sort would be something like the following: I observe the pendulum movement of a body. Experiments have shown me that this body is attracted by iron spheres in accordance with a certain law; supposing there to be 100 such spheres in a series at a particular position with respect to the body under test would explain, on the assumption of this law of attraction, an approximation to the observed (or supposed) behaviour; but the more spheres we suppose there to be in the series, the more closely does the result calculated agree with the one observed. In that case, it makes sense to say experience confirms the supposition of an infinite series of spheres. But the difference between the sense of the statement of number and that of 'an infinite number' is as great as the difference between this experience and that of seeing a number of spheres.

'The merely negative description of not stopping cannot yield a positive infinity' [2]. With the phrase 'a positive infinity' I

1] See p. 166.
2] In the Manuscript, this sentence immediately follows the paragraph about the red spheres.

thought of course of a countable (= finite) set of things (chairs in this room) and wanted to say that the presence of a colossal number of such things can't be inferred from whatever it is that indicates to us that they don't stop. And so here in the form of my assertion I make the strange mistake of denying a fact, instead of denying that a particular proposition makes sense, or more strictly, of showing that two similar sounding remarks have different grammars.

What an odd question: 'Can we imagine an endless row of trees?'! If we speak of an 'endless row of trees', we will surely still link what we mean with the experiences we call 'seeing a row of trees', 'counting a row of trees', 'measuring a row of trees' etc. 'Can we imagine an endless row of trees?'! Certainly, once we have laid down what we are to understand by this; that is once we have brought this concept into relation with all these things, with the experiences which define for us the concept of a row of trees.

What in experience is the criterion for the row of trees being infinite? For that will show me how this assertion is to be understood. Or, if you give me no such criterion, what am I then supposed to do with the concept 'infinite row of trees'? What on earth has this concept to do with what I ordinarily call a row of trees? Or didn't you in the end only mean: an enormously long row of trees?

'But we are surely familiar with an experience, when we walk along a row of trees, which we can call the row coming to an end. Well, an endless row of trees is one such that we never have this experience.' – But what does 'never' mean here? I am familiar with an experience I describe by the words 'He never coughed during the whole hour', or 'He never laughed in his whole life'. We cannot speak of an analogous experience where the 'never' doesn't refer to a time interval. And so once again analogy leaves us in the lurch here and I must try to find out *ab initio* how the word 'never' can be used so as to make sense in this case. – Admittedly such uses can be found, but their rules are to be examined in their own right. For example, the proposition that a row of trees is infinitely long (or that we shall *never* come to its end), could be a natural law of the same sort as the Law of Inertia, which certainly says that under certain conditions a body moves in a straight line with constant velocity; and here it could indeed be said that under those conditions the movement will *never* end. But if we ask about the verification of such a proposition, the main thing to be said is that it is falsified if the movement (row of trees) comes to an end. There can be no talk of a verification here, and that means we are dealing with a fundamentally different kind of proposition (or with a proposition, in a different sense of that word). Naturally I don't want to say that this is the only significant use of the expression 'infinite row of trees' or of the word 'never' (in all eternity). But each such use must be described in its own right and has its own laws. It's no help to us that we find a way of speaking ready-made in our ordinary language, since this language uses each of its words with the most varied meanings, and understanding the use of the word in *one* context does not relieve us from investigating its grammar in another. Thus we think something like 'It is still surely possible to imagine an infinitely long life, for a man lives for an infinite length of time, if he simply never dies.' But the use of the word 'never' just isn't that simple.

Let's now discuss an endless life in the sense of an hypothesis (cf. the Law of Inertia), and the man living it choosing in succession an arbitrary fraction from the fractions between 1 and 2, 2 and 3, 3 and 4, etc. *ad inf.* and writing it down. Does this give us a 'selection from all those intervals'? No, . . ./see above, §146, p. 167.

'But now let's imagine a man who becomes more and more adept at choosing from intervals, so that he would take an hour for the first choice, half an hour for the second, a quarter for the third, etc. *ad inf.* In that case he would have done the whole job in two hours!' [1] Let's now imagine the process. The choice would consist, say, in his writing down a fraction, and so in moving his hand. This movement would get quicker and quicker; but however quick it becomes, there will always be a last interval that has been dealt with in a particular time. The consideration behind our objection depends on forming the sum $1 + \frac{1}{2} + \frac{1}{4} + \ldots$, but that is of course a *limit* of a series of sums, and not a sum in the sense in which, e.g., $1 + \frac{1}{2} + \frac{1}{4}$ is a sum. If I were to say 'He needs an hour for the first choice, half an hour for the second, a quarter for the third, etc. *ad. inf.*' then this remark only makes sense so long as I *don't* ask about the velocity of the choice at the time instant $t = 2$, since our reckoning gives *no* value for this (for there's no value $c = $ infinity here as far as we're concerned, since we haven't correlated any experience with it). My law gives me a velocity for any instant *before* $t = 2$, and so is to that extent applicable and in order. Thus the fallacy lies only in the sentence 'In that case he would have done the whole job in two hours'. (If we can call that a fallacy, since the sentence is in fact senseless in this context.)

Let's now consider the hypothesis that under certain conditions someone will throw the digits of π (say, expressed in a system to the base 6). This hypothesis is, then, a law according to which I can work out for any throw the number of spots showing. But what if we modified the hypothesis into one that under certain conditions someone would *not* throw the digits of π! Shouldn't that make sense too? But how could we ever know that this hypothesis was correct, since up to any given time he may have thrown in agreement with π, and yet this would not refute the hypothesis. But that surely just means that we have to do with a different *kind* of hypothesis; with a kind of proposition for which no *provision* is made in its grammar for a falsification. And it is open

---

1] An apparent reference to a remark of H. Hahn.

to me to call that a 'proposition' or 'hypothesis' or something quite different, as I like. (π is not a decimal fraction, but a *law* according to which decimal fractions are formed.)

The infinity of time is not a duration.

If we ask 'What constitutes the infinity of time?' the reply will be 'That no day is the last, that each day is followed by another'. But here we are misled again into seeing the situation in the light of a false analogy. For we are comparing the succession of days with the succession of events, such as the strokes of a clock. In such a case we sometimes experience a fifth stroke following four strokes. Now, does it also make sense to talk of the experience of a fifth day following four days? And could someone say 'See, I told you so: I said there would be another after the fourth'? (You might just as well say it's an experience that the fourth is followed by the fifth and no other.) But we aren't talking here about the prediction that the sun will continue to move after the fourth day as before, *that*'s a genuine prediction. No, in our case it's not a question of a prediction, no event is prophesied; what we're saying is something like this: that it makes sense, in respect of any sunrise or sunset, to talk of a next. For what is meant by designation of a period of time is of course bound up with something happening: the movement of the hand of a clock, of the earth, etc., etc.; but when we say 'each hour is succeeded by a next', having defined an hour by means of the revolution of a particular pointer (as a paradigm), we are still not using that assertion in order to prophesy that this pointer will go on in the same way for all eternity: – but we want to say: that it *'can* go on in the same way for ever'; and that is simply an assertion concerning the grammar of our determinations of time.

Let's compare the propositions 'I'm making my plans on the assumption that this situation will last for two years' and 'I'm making them on the assumption that this situation will last for ever'. – Does the proposition make sense 'I believe (or expect, or hope), that it will stay like that throughout infinite time'?

We may say: 'I am making arrangements for the next three days', or 10 years, etc., and also 'I'm making arrangements for an indefinite period'; – but also 'for an infinite time'? If I 'make arrangements for an indefinite period', it is surely possible to mention a time for which at any rate I am no longer making arrangements. That is, the proposition 'I am making arrangements for an indefinite period' does not imply every arbitrary proposition of the form 'I am making arrangements for n years'.

Just think of the proposition: 'I *suspect* this situation will continue like this without end'!

Or how comical this rebuttal sounds: 'You said this clockwork would run for ever – well, it's already stopped *now*'. We feel that surely every finite prediction of too long a run would also be refuted by the fact, and so in some sense or other the refutation is incommensurable with the claim. – For it is nonsense to say 'The clockwork didn't go on running for an infinite time, but stopped after 10 years' (or, even more comically: '... but stopped after only 10 years').

How odd, if someone were to say: 'You have to be very bold to predict something for 100 years; – but how bold you must be to predict something for infinite time, as Newton did with his Law of Inertia!'

'I believe it will go on like that for ever.' – 'Isn't it enough (for all practical purposes) to say you believe it will go on like that for 10,000 years?' – That is to say, we must ask: Can there be grounds for this belief? What are they? What are the grounds for assuming that it will go on for 1,000 more years; what for assuming it will go on for 10,000 more years; – and, now, what are the grounds for the infinite assumption?! – That's what makes the sentence 'I suspect it will go on without end' so comic; we want to ask, why do you suspect that? For we want to say it's senseless to say you suspect that: because it's senseless to talk of grounds for such a suspicion.

Let's consider the proposition 'This comet will move in a parabola with equation . . .'. How is this proposition used? It cannot be verified; that is to say: *we* have made no provision for a verification in its grammar (that doesn't of course mean we can't say it's true; for '*p* is true' says the same as '*p*'). The proposition can bring us to make certain observations. But for those a finite prediction would always have done equally well. It will also determine certain actions. For instance, it might dissuade us from looking for the comet in such and such a place. But for that too, a finite claim would have been enough. The infinity of the hypothesis doesn't consist of its *largeness*, but in its open-endedness.

'Eventually, the world will come to an end': an infinite hypothesis.

The proposition that eventually – in the infinite future – an event (e.g. the end of the world) will occur, has a certain formal similarity with what we call a tautology.

Infinite Possibility

Different use of the word 'can' in the propositions 'Three objects can lie in this direction' and 'Infinitely many objects can lie in this direction' [1]. What sense, that is to say, what grammar could such a way of talking possess? We might for example say: 'In the natural number series 1, 2, 3, 4 . . . infinitely many numerals can follow the "1"'; that is tantamount to: 'The operation | 1 may be applied ever again (or: without end)'. And so if, for example, someone writes the numeral 100 + 1 after the numeral 100, that rule gives him the right to do so. On the other hand, there is no

---

1] Cf. §142, p. 162.

sense here in saying: 'If it's permissible to write down infinitely many numerals, let's write infinitely many numerals (or try to)!' –

Analogously, if I say a division yields an infinite decimal fraction, then there isn't *one* result of the division called 'an infinite decimal', in the sense in which the number 0.142 is a result of $1 \div 7$. The division doesn't yield as its final result *one* decimal number, or a number of decimal numbers – but rather we can't talk of 'its final result': it endlessly yields decimal fractions; not 'an endless decimal fraction'. 'Endlessly' not 'endless'.

Let's now imagine the following case: I have constructed a particular kind of die, and am now going to predict: 'I shall throw the places of π with this die'. This claim is of a different form from the apparently similar 'I shall throw the first ten places of π with this die'. For in the second case there is a proposition 'I shall have thrown the first ten places of π within the hour', but this proposition becomes nonsense (not false), if I substitute 'the places' for 'the first ten places'. In the sentence 'Any arbitrary number of throws is possible', 'possible' may be equivalent to 'logically possible' ('conceivable'), and then it is a rule, not an empirical proposition, and is of a similar sort to that of the rule 'numerals can follow 1 without end'. But we might also construe it as a kind of empirical proposition, a kind of hypothesis: but then it would be the kind of hypothesis which has no verification provided for it, only a falsification, and so it would be a different kind of proposition (a 'proposition' in a different sense) from the empirical proposition: 'Three throws are possible with this die'. This – unlike the *rule* 'Three throws are conceivable' – would mean something like: 'The die will still be usable after three throws'; the hypothesis 'Infinitely many throws are possible with this die' would mean 'However often you throw it, this die will not wear out'. It's very clear that these propositions are different in kind, if you think of the nonsensical order 'Throw it infinitely often' or 'Throw *ad infinitum*', as opposed to the significant 'Throw it three times'. For it is essential to a command that we can check whether it has been carried out.

If we wish to say infinity is an attribute of possibility, not of reality, or: the word 'infinite' always goes with the word 'possible', and the like, – then this amounts to saying: the word 'infinite' is always a part of a *rule*.

Let's suppose we told someone: 'I bought a ruler yesterday with infinite curvature'. Here, however, the word 'infinite' surely occurs in the description of a reality. – But still, I can never have the experience which would justify me in saying that the ruler actually had an infinite radius of curvature, since a radius of 100^{100} km would surely do just as well. – Granted, but in that case I can't have the experience which would justify me in saying the ruler is *straight* either. And the words 'straight' (or in another context 'parallel') and 'infinite' are in the *same* boat. I mean: If the word 'straight', ('parallel', 'equally long', etc., etc.) may occur in a description of reality, then so may the word 'infinite' [1].

'All that's infinite is the possibility' means '"infinite" qualifies "etc.".' And so far as this is what it does, it belongs in a rule, a law. It's out of place in describing experience only when we mean by 'experience that corresponds to a law' an endless series of experiences. – The slogan 'all that's infinite is the possibility, not the reality' is misleading. We may say: '*In this case* all that's infinite is the possibility'. – And we justifiably ask: what is it that is infinite about this hypothesis (e.g. about the path of a comet)? Is there something huge about this assumption, this thought?

If we say 'The possibility of forming decimal places in the division $1 \div 3$ is infinite', we don't pin down a fact of nature, but give a rule of the system of calculation. But if I say: 'I give you infinite freedom to develop as many places as you like, I won't stop you', then this isn't enunciating the rule of the system of calculation, it's saying something about the future. 'Yes, but still only as the description of a possibility.' – No, of a reality! But *of*

1] Cf. §147, p. 169; §212, p. 265.

course not that of 'infinitely many places'; to say that would be to fall into the very grammatical trap we must avoid.

The fact that it permits the endless formation of numerals doesn't make grammar infinitely complicated.

To explain the infinite possibility, it must be sufficient to point out the features of the sign which lead us to assume this infinite possibility, or better: from which we read off this infinite possibility. That is, what is actually present in the sign must be sufficient, and the possibilities of the sign, which once more could only emerge from a description of signs, do not come into the discussion [1]. And so everything must be already contained in the sign '/1, x, $x + 1$/' – the expression for the rule of formation. In introducing infinite possibility, I mustn't reintroduce a mythical element into grammar. If we describe the process of division $1.0 \div 3 = 0.3$, which leads to the quotient 0.3 and remainder 1,

1

the infinite possibility of going on with always the same result must be contained in this description, since we certainly aren't given anything else, when we see 'that it must always go on in the same way'.

And when we 'see the infinite possibility of going on', we still can't see anything that isn't described when we simply describe the sign we see.

1] Cf. §139, p. 159; §144, p. 164.

APPENDIX 2

From F. Waismann's shorthand transcript of
Wittgenstein's talks and conversation between December
1929 and September 1931.

(From F. Waismann's notes for 25 December 1929.)

I once wrote: 'A proposition is laid like a yardstick against reality. Only the outermost tips of the graduation marks touch the object to be measured.' I should now prefer to say: a *system of propositions* is laid like a yardstick against reality. What I mean by this is: when I lay a yardstick against a spatial object, I apply *all the graduation marks simultaneously*. It's not the individual graduation marks that are applied, it's the whole scale. If I know that the object reaches up to the tenth graduation mark, I also know immediately that it doesn't reach the eleventh, twelfth, etc. The assertions telling me the length of an object form a system, a system of propositions. It's such a whole system which is compared with reality, not a single proposition. If, for instance, I say such and such a point in the visual field is *blue*, I not only know that, I also know that the point isn't green, isn't red, isn't yellow etc. I have simultaneously applied the whole colour scale. This is also the reason why a point can't have different colours simultaneously; why there is a syntactical rule against *fx* being true for more than one value of *x*. For if I apply a *system* of propositions to reality, that of itself already implies – as in the spatial case – that in every case only *one* state of affairs can obtain, never several.

When I was working on my book I was still unaware of all this and thought then that every inference depended on the form of a tautology. I hadn't seen then that an inference can also be of the form: A man is 6 ft tall, therefore he isn't 7 ft. This is bound up with my then believing that elementary propositions had to be independent of one another: from the fact that one state of affairs obtained you couldn't infer another did not. But if my present conception of a system of propositions is right, then it's even the rule that from the fact that one state of affairs obtains we can infer that all the others described by the system of propositions do not.

(Waismann's notes, Wednesday, 17 December, 1930, Neuwald-egg. Transcript of Wittgenstein's words, unless otherwise indicated.)

I've been reading a work by Hilbert on consistency. It strikes me that this whole question has been put wrongly. I should like to ask: *Can* mathematics be inconsistent at all? I should like to ask these people: Look, what are you really up to? Do you really believe there are contradictions hidden in mathematics?

Axioms have a twofold significance, as Frege saw.

1) The rules, *according to* which you play.
2) The opening positions of the game.

If you take the axioms in the second way, I can attach no sense to the claim that they are inconsistent. It would be very queer to say: this configuration (e.g. in the Hilbertian formula game, $0 \neq 0$) is a contradiction. And if I do call some configuration or other a contradiction, that has no essential significance, at least for the game *qua game*. If I arrange the rules so that this configuration can't arise, all I've done is made up a different game. But the game's a game, and I can't begin to understand why anyone should attach such great importance to the occurrence of this configuration: they behave as though this particular one were tabu. I then ask: and what is there to get excited about if this configuration does arise?

The situation is completely different if the axioms are taken as the rules *according to* which the game is played. The rules are – in a certain sense – statements. They say: you may do this or this, but not that. Two rules can be inconsistent. Suppose, e.g., that in chess one rule ran: under such and such circumstances the piece concerned must be taken. But another rule said: a knight may never be taken. If now the piece concerned happens to be a knight, the rules contradict one another: I don't know what I'm supposed to do. What do we do in such a case? Nothing easier: we introduce a new rule, and the conflict is resolved.

My point, then, is: if inconsistencies were to arise between the rules of the game of mathematics, it would be the easiest thing in the world to remedy. All we have to do is to make a new stipulation to cover the case in which the rules conflict, and the matter's resolved.

But here I must make an important point. A contradiction is only a contradiction *when it arises*. People have the idea that there might at the outset be a contradiction hidden away in the axioms which no-one has seen, like tuberculosis: a man doesn't suspect anything and then one day he's dead. That's how people think of this case too: one day the hidden contradiction might break out, and then the catastrophe would be upon us.

What I'm saying is: to ask whether the derivations might not eventually lead to a contradiction makes no sense at all as long as I'm given no method for discovering it.

While I can play, I can play, and everything's all right.

The truth of the matter is that the calculus *qua* calculus is all right. It doesn't make any sense whatever to talk about contradiction. What we call a contradiction arises when we step outside the calculus and say in prose: 'Therefore all numbers have this property, but the number 17 doesn't have it.'

In the calculus the contradiction can't be expressed at all.

I can play with the chessmen according to certain rules. But I can also invent a game in which I play with the rules themselves. The pieces in my game are now the rules of chess, and the rules of the game are, say, the laws of logic. *In that case I have yet another game and not a metagame.* What Hilbert does is mathematics and not metamathematics. It's another calculus, just like any other.

(Sunday, 28 December 1930, at Schlick's home.)
The problem of the consistency of mathematics stems from two

sources: (1) From the idea of non-Euclidean geometry where it was a matter of proving the axiom of parallels by means of the given paradigm of a *reductio ad absurdum*. (2) From the Burali–Forti and Russellian antinomies.

The impetus behind the present preoccupation with consistency came mainly from the antinomies. Now, it has to be said that these antinomies haven't got anything to do with consistency in mathematics, that there's no connection here at all. For the antinomies didn't in fact arise in the calculus, but in ordinary everyday speech, precisely because we use words ambiguously. So that resolving the antinomies consists in replacing the vague idiom by a precise one (by reflecting on the strict meaning of the words). And so the antinomies *vanish* by means of an *analysis*, not of a *proof*.

If the contradictions in mathematics arise through an unclarity, I can *never dispel this unclarity by a proof*. The proof only proves what it proves. But it can't lift the fog.

This of itself shows that there can be no such thing as a consistency proof (if we are thinking of the inconsistencies of mathematics as being of the same sort as the inconsistencies of set theory), that the proof can't begin to offer what we want of it. If I'm unclear about the nature of mathematics, no proof can help me. And if I'm clear about the nature of mathematics, the question of consistency can't arise at all.

Russell had the idea that his 5 'primitive propositions' were to be both the basic configurations and the rules for going on. But he was under an illusion here, and this came out in the fact that he himself had to add further rules (in words!).

So we must distinguish: the basic configurations of the calculus (the opening positions of the game) and the rules telling us how to get from one configuration to another. This was already made clear by Frege in his critique of the theories of Heine and Thomae: 'How surprising. What would someone say if he asked what the rules of chess were and instead of an answer was shown a group of chessmen on the chessboard? Presumably that he couldn't find a rule in this, since he didn't attach any sense at all to these pieces and their layout' (*Grundgesetze*, II, p. 113).

Now if I take the calculus as a calculus, the positions in the game can't represent contradictions (unless I arbitrarily call one of the positions that arise in the game a 'contradiction' and exclude it; all I'm doing in that case is declaring that I'm playing a *different* game).

The idea of inconsistency – this is what I'm insisting on – is contradiction [1], and this can only *arise in the true/false* game, i.e. only where we are making assertions.

That is to say: A contradiction can only occur among the *rules of the game*. I can for instance have one rule saying the white piece must jump over the black one.

Now if the black is at the edge of the board, the rule breaks down. So the situation can arise where I don't know what I'm meant to do. The rule doesn't tell me anything any more. What would I do in such a case? There's nothing simpler than removing the inconsistency: I must make a decision, i.e. introduce another rule.

By permission and prohibition, I can always only define a game, never *the game*. What Hilbert is trying to show by his proof is that the axioms of arithmetic have the properties of *the* game, and that's impossible. It's as if Hilbert would like to prove that a contradiction is inadmissible.

Incidentally, suppose two of the rules were to contradict one another. I have such a bad memory that I never notice this, but always forget one of the two rules or alternately follow one and then the other. Even in this case I would say everything's in order.

1] 'Die Idee des Widerspruchs ist die Kontradiktion'. The use of the ordinary German word for contradiction and the (practically synonymous) loan-word gives to this sentence overtones difficult to reproduce in English. The main point of the remark seems to be 'Look, by a contradiction we must mean a *contradiction*' (Everything's what it is and not another thing), where he goes on to spell out what is involved in the notion of contradiction, and what can be overlooked in talking of contradictions within calculi. But there are additional overtones introduced by the fact that the word *Kontradiktion* is the word used in the *Tractatus* as the converse of *Tautologie*. It would produce artificialities to translate *Widerspruch* and *Kontradiktion* by different words: in most contexts Wittgenstein uses them virtually interchangeably. Where this has seemed the most natural rendering (as in 'consistency proof') we have translated 'Widerspruch' by 'inconsistency'. We think that the force of Wittgenstein's remarks comes over clearly enough to render clumsy and unnecessary the use of different standard translations for the two words. [trans.]

The rules are instructions how to play, and as long as I can play they must be all right. They only cease to be all right the moment I *notice* that they are inconsistent, and the only sign for that is that I can't apply them any more. For the logical product of the two rules is a contradiction, and the contradiction no longer tells me what to do. And so the conflict only arises when I notice it. While I could play there was no problem.

In arithmetic, too, we arrive at 'the edge of the chessboard', e.g. with the problem $\frac{0}{0}$. (Were I to say $\frac{0}{0} = 1$, I could prove $3 = 5$ and thus would come into conflict with the other rules of the game.)

We see then that as long as we take the calculus as a calculus the question of consistency cannot arise as a serious question at all. And so is consistency perhaps connected with the *application* of the calculus? With this in mind, we must ask ourselves:

What does it mean, to apply a calculus?

It can mean two different things.

1) We apply the calculus in such a way as to provide the grammar of a language. For, what is permitted or forbidden by the rules then corresponds in the grammar to the words 'sense' and 'senseless'. For example: Euclidean geometry construed as a system of syntactical rules according to which we describe spatial objects. 'Through any 2 points, a straight line can be drawn' means: a claim mentioning the line determined by these 2 points makes sense whether it happens to be true or false.

A rule of syntax corresponds to the position in the game. (Can the rules of syntax contradict one another?) Syntax cannot be justified.

2) A calculus can be applied so that *true* and *false* propositions correspond to the configurations of the calculus. Then the calculus yields a theory, describing something.

Newton's three laws have a completely different significance from those of geometry. There is a verification for them – by experiments in physics. But there is no such thing as a justification for a game. That is highly important. You can construe geometry in this way too, by taking it as the description of actual measurements. Now we have claims before us, and claims can indeed be inconsistent.

Whether the theory *can* describe something depends on whether the logical product of the axioms is a contradiction. Either I see straight off that they form a contradiction, in which case the situation's clear; or I don't – what then? Then there's a *hidden* contradiction present. For instance: Euclid's axioms together with the axiom 'The sum of the angles of a triangle is 181°'. Here I can't see the contradiction straight off, since I can't see straight off that a sum of 180° follows from the axioms.

As long as we stay within the calculus, we don't have any contradiction. For $s = 180°$, $s = 181°$ don't contradict one another at all. We can simply make two different stipulations. All we can say is: the calculus is applicable to everything to which it is applicable. Indeed, even here an application might still be conceivable, e.g. in such a way that, measured by one method, the sum of the angles of a triangle comes to 180°, and by another to 181°. It's only a matter of finding a domain whose description requires the multiplicity possessed by the axioms.

Now if a contradiction occurs at this point in a *theory*, that would mean that the propositions of the theory couldn't be translated into statements about how a galvanometer needle is deflected, etc., any more. It might for instance come out that the needle stays still or is deflected, and so this theory couldn't be verified.

Unlike geometrical equations, Maxwell's equations don't represent a calculus, they are a fragment, a part of a calculus.

What does it mean, mathematics must be 'made secure' [1]? What would happen if mathematics weren't secure? For is it any kind of claim at all, to say that the axioms are consistent?

Can one look for a contradiction? Only if there is a method for looking. There can be no such question as whether we will *ever* come upon a contradiction by going on in accordance with the rules. I believe that's the crucial point, on which everything

---

1] Cf. D. Hilbert *Neubegründung der Mathematik,* Gesammelte Abhandlungen III, p. 74.

depends in the question of consistency.

WAISMANN ASKS: But doesn't it make sense to ask oneself questions about an axiom system? Let's consider, for instance, the propositional calculus which Russell derives from 5 axioms. Bernays has shown one of these axioms is redundant, and that just 4 will do. He has gone on to show that these axioms form a 'complete system', i.e. that adding another axiom which can't be derived from these 4 makes it possible to derive any proposition you write down whatever. *This* comes down to the same thing as saying that every proposition follows from a contradiction. Now, isn't that a *material insight* into the Russellian calculus? Or, to take another case, I choose 3 axioms. I can't derive the same set of propositions from *these* as I can from all 5. Isn't that a material insight? And so can't you look upon a consistency proof as the recognition of something substantial?

WITTGENSTEIN: If I first take 3 propositions and then 5 propositions, I can't compare the classes of consequences at all unless I form a *new system* in which both groups occur.

And so it isn't as if I have both systems – the one with 3 axioms and the one with 5 axioms – in front of me and now compare them from outside. I can't do that any more than I can compare, say, the integers and the rational numbers until I've brought them into *one* system. And I don't gain a material insight either; what I do is once more to construct a calculus. And in this calculus the proposition 'The one class includes more than the other' doesn't occur at all: that is the prose accompanying the calculus.

Can one ask: When have I applied the calculus? Is it possible for me not to know whether I have applied the calculus, and to have to wait until I have a consistency proof?

(Tuesday, 30 December, at Schlick's house)

WAISMANN reads out § 117 and § 118 of Frege's *Grundgesetze*.
WITTGENSTEIN comments:

If one looks at this naïvely, the chief thing that strikes one is that mathematicians are always afraid of only *one* thing, which is a sort of nightmare to them: contradiction. They're not at all worried, e.g. by the possibility of a proposition's being a tautology, even though a contradiction is surely no worse than a tautology. In logic, contradiction has precisely the same significance as tautology, and I could study logic just as well by means of contradictions. A contradiction and a tautology of course *say* nothing, they are only a method for demonstrating the logical interrelations between propositions.

It's always: 'the law [Satz] of contradiction'. I believe in fact that the fear of contradiction is bound up with its being construed as a *proposition* [Satz]: $\sim(p\cdot\sim p)$. There's no difficulty in construing the law of contradiction as a rule: I forbid the formation of the logical product $p\cdot\sim p$. But the contradiction $\sim(p\cdot\sim p)$ doesn't begin to express this prohibition. How could it? The contradiction doesn't say anything at all, but the rule says something.

WAISMANN REPEATS HIS QUESTION: You said that by prohibitions and permissions I can always only determine *a* game, but never *the* game. But is that right? Imagine for instance the case where I permit any move in chess and forbid nothing – would that still be a game? Mustn't the rules of a game then still have certain properties for them to define a game at all? Couldn't we then interpret the demand for consistency as one to exclude the 'tautological' game – the game in which anything is permissible? That is to say, if the formula 'o ≠ o' can be derived by a legitimate proof and if in addition with Hilbert we add the axiom 'o ≠ o → 𝔄', where 𝔄 stands for an arbitrary formula, then we can derive the formula 𝔄 from the inference pattern

$$\text{o} \neq \text{o}$$
$$\text{o} \neq \text{o} \rightarrow \mathfrak{A}$$
$$\overline{\qquad\mathfrak{A}\qquad}$$

and write it down, too. But that means that in this case *any* formula can be derived, and so the game loses its character and its interest.

WITTGENSTEIN: Not at all! There's a mistake here, i.e. a confusion between 'a rule of the game' and 'position in the game'. This is how it is: the game is tautological if the rules of the game are tautological (i.e. if they no longer forbid or permit anything); but that isn't the case here. This game, too, has its own particular rules: it's one game among many, and that the configuration 'o ≠ o' arises in it is neither here nor there. It's just a configuration which arises in *this* game, and if I exclude it, then I have a *different* game before me. It simply isn't the case that in the first instance I don't have a game before me but in the second I do. One class of rules and prohibitions borders on another class of rules and prohibitions, but *a game doesn't border on a non-game*. The 'tautological' game must arise as the limit case of games, as their natural limit. The system of games must be delimited from within, and this limit consists simply in the fact that the rules of the game vanish. I can't get this limit case by myself setting up particular rules and prohibitions; for that just gives me once more one game among many. So if I say: The configuration 'o ≠ o' is to be permitted, I am once more stating a rule, defining a game; merely a different one from the one where I exclude this configuration.

That is to say: by rules I can never define *the* game, always only *a* game.

WAISMANN ASKS: There's a theory of chess, isn't there? So we can surely use this theory to help us obtain information about the possibilities of the game – e.g. whether in a particular position I can force mate in 8, and the like. If, now, there is a theory of the game of chess, then I don't see why there shouldn't also be a theory of the game of arithmetic and why we shouldn't apply the propositions of this theory to obtain material information about the possibilities of this game. This theory is Hilbert's metamathematics.

WITTGENSTEIN: What is known as the 'theory of chess' isn't a theory describing something, it's a kind of geometry. It is of course in its turn a calculus and not a theory.

To make this clear I ask you whether, in your opinion, there is a difference between the following two propositions: 'I can force mate in 8' and 'By the theory I have proved I can force mate in 8'? No! For if in the theory I use a symbolism instead of a chessboard and chess set, the demonstration that I can mate in 8 consists in my actually doing it in the symbolism, and so, by now doing with signs what I do with pieces on the board. When I make the moves and when I prove their possibility – then I have surely done *the same thing* over again in the proof. I've made the moves with symbols, that's all. The only thing missing is in fact the actual movement; and of course we agree that moving the little piece of wood across the board is inessential.

I am doing in the proof what I do in the game, precisely as if I were to say: You, Herr Waismann, are to do a sum, but I am going to predict what digits will be your result: I then simply do the sum for my own part, only perhaps with different signs (or even with the same, which I construe differently). I can now work out the result of the sum all over again; I can't come to the same result by a totally different route. It isn't as if you are the calculator and I recognize the result of your calculation on the strength of a *theory*. And precisely the same situation obtains in the case of the 'theory of chess'.

And so if I establish in the 'theory' that such and such possibilities are present, I am again moving about within the game, not within a metagame. Every *step* in the calculus corresponds to a move in the game, and the whole difference consists only in the physical movement of a piece of wood.

Besides, it is highly important that I can't tell from looking at the pieces of wood whether they are pawns, bishops, rooks, etc.

I can't say: that is a pawn *and* such and such rules hold for this piece. No, it is the rules alone which *define* this piece: a pawn *is* the sum of the rules for its moves (a square is a piece too), just as in the case of language the rules define the logic of a word.

WAISMANN RAISES THE OBJECTION: Good, I can see all that. But so far we have only been dealing with the case that the theory says such and such a position is possible. But what if the theory proves the *impossibility* of a certain position – e.g. the 4 rooks in a straight line next to one another? And just this sort of case is dealt with by Hilbert. In this case the theory simply cannot reproduce the game. The steps in the calculus no longer correspond to moves in the game.

WITTGENSTEIN: Certainly they don't. But even in this case it must come out that the theory is a calculus, just a different one from the game. Here we have a *new* calculus before us, a calculus with a different multiplicity.

In the first instance: *If I prove that I cannot do such and such, I don't prove a proposition, I give an induction.*

I can *see* the induction *on the chessboard,* too. I'll explain in a moment what I mean by that. What I prove is that no matter how long I play I can't reach a particular position. A proof like that can only be made by induction. It is now essential for us to be quite clear about the nature of proof by induction.

In mathematics there are two sorts of proof:

1) A proof proving a particular formula. This formula appears in the proof itself as its last step.

2) Proof by induction. The most striking fact here is that the proposition to be proved doesn't itself occur in the proof at all. That is to say, induction isn't a procedure leading to a proposition. Instead, induction shows us an infinite possibility, and the essence of proof by induction consists in this alone.

We *subsequently* express what the proof by induction showed us as a proposition and in doing so use the word 'all'. But this proposition adds something to the proof, or better: the proposition stands to the proof as a sign does to what is designated. The proposition is a *name* for the induction. It goes proxy for it, it doesn't follow from it.

You can also render the induction visible on the chessboard itself, e.g., by my saying I can go there and back, there and back, etc. But the induction no longer corresponds to a move in the game.

So if I prove in the 'theory' that such and such a position cannot occur, I have given an induction which shows something but expresses nothing. And so there is also no proposition at all in the 'theory' which says 'such and such is impossible'.

Now it will be said that there must still be some connection between the actual game and the induction. And there is indeed such a connection – it consists in the fact that once I have been given the proof by induction I will no longer try to set up this position in the game. Before I might perhaps have tried and then finally given up. Now I don't try any more. It's exactly the same here as when I prove by induction that there are infinitely many primes or that $\sqrt{2}$ is irrational. The effect of these proofs on the actual *practice* of arithmetic is simply that people stop looking for a '*greatest* prime number', or for a fraction equal to $\sqrt{2}$. But here we must be even more precise than this. *Could* people previously search at all? What they did had, to be sure, a certain likeness to searching, but was something of an entirely different sort; they did something, expecting that as a result something else would occur. But that wasn't searching at all, any more than I can search for a way of waggling my ears. All I can do is move my eyebrows, my forehead and such parts of my body in the hope that my ears will move as well. But I can't *know* whether they will, and thus I can't *search* for a way of making them.

Within *the* system in which I tell that a number is prime, I can't even ask what the number of primes is. The question only arises when you apply the substantival form to it. And if you have discovered the induction, that's also something different from computing a number.

The inductions correspond to the formulae of algebra (calculation with letters) – for the reason that the internal relations between the inductions are the same as the internal relations between the formulae. The system of calculating with letters is a new calculus; but it isn't related to ordinary numerical calculation as a metacalculus to a calculus. *Calculation with letters isn't a theory.* That's the crucial point. The 'theory' of chess – when it investigates the impossibility of certain positions – is like algebra in relation to numerical calculation. In the same way, Hilbert's 'meta-mathematics' must reveal itself to be mathematics in disguise.

Hilbert's proof: ('Neubegründung der Mathematik', 1922)

'But if our formalism is to provide a complete substitute for the earlier theory which actually consists of inferences and statements, then material contradiction must find its formal equivalent' [1] $a = b$ *and* $a \neq b$ are never to be simultaneously provable formulae.

The demonstration of consistency on Hilbert's simple model does in fact turn out to be inductive: the proof shows us by induction the possibility that signs must continue to occur on and on →.

The proof lets us see something. But what it shows can't be expressed by a proposition. And so we also can't say: 'The axioms are consistent'. (Any more than you can say there are infinitely many primes. That is prose.)

I believe giving a proof of consistency can mean only one thing: looking through the rules. There's nothing else for me to do. Imagine I give someone a long list of errands to run in the town. The list is so long that perhaps I have forgotten one errand and given another instead, or I have put together different people's errands. What am I to do to convince myself that the errands can be

---

1] D. Hilbert: Gesammelte Abhandlungen III, p. 170.

carried out? I have to run through the list. But I can't 'prove' anything. (We mustn't forget that we are only dealing here with the *rules* of the game and not with its configurations. In the case of geometry, it's perfectly conceivable that when I go through the axioms I don't notice the contradiction.) If I say: I want to check whether the logical product is a contradiction, this comes to the same thing. *Writing it out* in the form of a contradiction only makes the matter *easier*. If you now choose to call that a 'proof', you are welcome to do so: even then it is just a method of making it easier to check. But it must be said: in and of itself even such a proof cannot guarantee that I don't overlook something.

No calculation can do what checking does.

But suppose I search systematically through the rules of the game? The moment I work within a system, I have a calculus once more; but then the question of consistency arises anew. And so in fact there is nothing for me to do but inspect one rule after another.

What would it mean if a calculus were to yield 'o $\neq$ o'? It's clear we wouldn't then be dealing with a sort of modified arithmetic, but with a totally different kind of arithmetic, one without the slightest similarity to cardinal arithmetic. We couldn't then say: in such and such respects it still accords with our arithmetic (as non-Euclidean geometry does with Euclidean – here the modification of an axiom doesn't have such radical implications); no, there wouldn't be the slightest trace of similarity left at all. Whether I can apply such a calculus is another matter.

Besides, there are various difficulties here. In the first instance, one thing isn't clear to me: $a = b$ surely only expresses the substitutability of b for a. And so the equation is a rule for signs, a rule of the game. Then how can it be an axiom, i.e. a position in the game? From this angle a formula such as o $\neq$ o is utterly unintelligible.

For it would in fact mean: you can't substitute o for o – am I then supposed to inspect whether perhaps the one o has a flourish which the other doesn't? What on earth does such a prohibition mean? It's the same story as if I say $a = a$. That too is rubbish, no matter how often it gets written down. Schoolmasters are perfectly right to teach their children that $2 + 2 = 4$, but not that $2 = 2$. The way children learn to do sums in school is already in perfect order and there's no reason to wish it any stricter. In fact it's also evident that $a = a$ means nothing from the fact that this formula is never used.

If, when I was working with a calculus, I arrive at the formula $o \neq o$, do you think that as a result the calculus would lose all interest?

SCHLICK: Yes, a mathematician would say such a thing was of no interest to him.

WITTGENSTEIN: But *excuse* me! It would be enormously interesting that precisely this came out! In the calculus, we are always interested in the result. How strange! This comes out here – and that there! Who would have thought it? Then how interesting if it were a contradiction which came out! Indeed, even at this stage I predict a time when there will be mathematical investigations of calculi containing contradictions, and people will actually be proud of having emancipated themselves even from consistency.

But suppose I want to apply such a calculus? Would I apply it with an uneasy conscience if I hadn't already proved there was no contradiction? But how can I ask such a question? If I can apply a calculus, I have simply applied it; there's no subsequent correction. What I can do, I can do. I can't undo the application by saying: strictly speaking that wasn't an application.

Need I first wait for a consistency proof before applying a calculus? Have all the calculations people have done so far been really – *sub specie aeterni* – a hostage against fortune? And is it conceivable that a time will come when it will all be shown to be illegitimate? Don't I know what I'm doing? It in fact amounts to a wish to prove that certain propositions are not nonsense.

So the question is this: I have a series of propositions, e.g. p, q, r ... and a series of rules governing operations, e.g. '·', 'v', '~', and someone asks: if you apply these rules concerning the operations to the given propositions, can you ever arrive at nonsense? The question would be justified if by 'nonsense' I mean contradiction or tautology. I must then make the rules for forming statements in such a way that these forms do not occur.

(1 January 1931, at Schlick's house)

Is one justified in raising the question of consistency? The strange thing here is that we are looking for something and have no idea what it really is we are looking for. How, for example, can I ask whether Euclidean geometry is consistent when I can't begin to imagine what it would be for it to contain a contradiction? What would it be like for there to be a contradiction in it? This question has first to be answered before we investigate such questions.

One thing is clear: I can only understand a contradiction [Widerspruch], if it is a contradiction [Kontradiktion] [1]. So I put forward the case in which I have a series of propositions, let's say p, q, r ..., and form their logical product. I can now check whether this logical product is a contradiction. Is *that* all the question of consistency amounts to? That would take five minutes to settle. Surely in this sense, no one can *doubt* whether the Euclidean axioms are consistent.

But what else could the question mean? Perhaps: if we go on drawing inferences sooner or later we will arrive at a contradiction? To that we must say: Have we a method for discovering the contradiction? If not, then there isn't a question here at all. For we cannot search to infinity.

WAISMANN: Perhaps we can still imagine something – namely the schema for indirect proof. By analogy, we transfer that to an axiom system. We must distinguish two things: a problem which can be formulated *within* mathematics, which therefore also already possesses a method of solution; and the idea which pre-

---

1] Cf. Footnote on p. 321 above.

cedes and guides the construction of mathematics. Mathematicians do in fact have such guiding ideas even in the case of Fermat's Last Theorem. I'm inclined to think that the question of consistency belongs to this complex of pre-mathematical questioning.

WITTGENSTEIN: What's meant by analogy? E.g. analogy with indirect proof? Here it's like the trisection of an angle. I can't look for a way to trisect an angle. What really happens when a mathematician concerns himself with this question? Two things are possible: (1) He imagines the angle divided into 3 parts (a drawing); (2) He thinks of the construction for dividing an angle into 2 parts, into 4 parts. And this is where the mistake occurs: people think, since we can talk of dividing into 2, into 4 parts, we can also talk of dividing into 3 parts, just as we can count 2, 3 and 4 apples. But trisection – if there were such a thing – would in fact belong to a completely different category, a completely different system, from bisection, quadrisection. In the system in which I talk of dividing into 2 and 4 parts I can't talk of dividing into 3 parts. These are completely different logical structures. I can't group dividing into 2, 3, 4 parts together since they are completely different forms. You can't count forms as though they were actual things. You can't bring them under one *concept*.

It's like waggling your ears. The mathematician naturally lets himself be led by associations, by certain analogies with the previous system. I'm certainly not saying: if anyone concerns himself with Fermat's Last Theorem, that's wrong or illegitimate. Not at all! If, for instance, I have a method for looking for whole numbers satisfying the equation $x^2 + y^2 = z^2$, the formula $x^n + y^n = z^n$ can intrigue me. I can allow myself to be intrigued by a formula. And so I shall say: there's a *fascination* here but not a *question*. Mathematical 'problems' always fascinate like this. This kind of fascination is in no way the preparation of a calculus.

WAISMANN: But what then is the significance of the proof of the consistency of non-Euclidean geometry? Let's think of the simplest case, that we give a model, say, of two-dimensional Riemannian geometry on a sphere. We then have a translation: every concept (theorem) of the one geometry corresponds to a concept (theorem) of the other. If now the theorems in the one case were to include a contradiction, this contradiction would also have to be detectable in the other geometry. And so we may say: the Riemannian axiom system is consistent provided the Euclidean one is. We have then demonstrated consistency relative to Euclidean geometry.

WITTGENSTEIN: Consistency 'relative to Euclidean geometry' is altogether nonsense. What happens here is this: a rule corresponds to another rule (a configuration in the game to a configuration in the game). We have a *mapping*. Full stop! Whatever else is said is prose. One says: *Therefore* the system is consistent. But there is no 'therefore', any more than in the case of induction. This is once more connected with the proof being misconstrued, with something being read into it which it doesn't contain. The proof is the proof. *The internal relations in which the rules (configurations) of one group stand to one another are similar to those in which the rules (configurations) of the other group stand. That's what the proof shows and no more.*

On *Independence*: Let's suppose we have 5 axioms. We now make the discovery that one of these axioms can be derived from the other four, and so was redundant. I now ask: What's the significance of such a discovery? I believe that the situation here is exactly as it is in the case of Sheffer's discovery that we can get by with one logical constant.

Above all, let's be clear: the axioms define – when taken with the rules for development of the calculus – a group of propositions. This domain of propositions isn't also given to us in some other way, but *only* by the 5 axioms. So we can't ask: Is *the same* domain perhaps also defined by 4 axioms alone? For the domain isn't detachable from the 5 axioms. These 5 axioms and whatever derives from them are – so to speak – my whole world. I can't get outside of this world.

Now how about the question: are these 5 axioms independent?

I would reply: is there a method for settling this question? Here various cases can arise.

1) There is no such method. Then the situation is as I've described it: All that I have are the 5 axioms and the rules of development. In that case I can't seek to find out whether one of these axioms will perhaps *ever* emerge as a consequence of the others. And so I can't raise the question of independence at all.

2) But suppose now that one of the axioms does come out as the result of a proof, then we haven't at all proved that only 4 axioms are sufficient, that one is redundant. No, I can't come to this insight through a logical inference, I must *see* it, just as Sheffer *saw* that he could get by with one logical constant. I must see the new system in the system within which I am working and in which I perform the proof.

It's a matter of seeing, not of proving. No proposition corresponds to what I see – to the possibility of the system. Nothing is claimed, and so neither is there anything I can prove. So if in this case I give 5 axioms where 4 would do, I have simply been guilty of an oversight. For I should certainly have been in a position to know at the outset that one of these 5 axioms was redundant, and if I have written it down all the same, that was simply a mistake. Granted, it isn't enough in this case simply to set up the axioms, we must also prove that they really are independent.

Now Hilbert appears to adopt this last course in the case of geometry. However, one important point remains unclear here: is the use of models a *method*? Can I look for a model systematically, or do I have to depend on a happy accident? What if I can't find a model which fits?

To summarize: The question whether an axiom system is independent only makes sense if there is a method for deciding the question. Otherwise we can't raise this question at all. And if, e.g., someone discovers one axiom to be redundant, then he hasn't proved a proposition, he has read a new system into the old one.

And the same goes for consistency.

Hilbert's axioms:

I.1 and I.2: 'Any two distinct points A, B define a straight line *a*'

'Any two distinct points on a straight line define that line.'

I already don't know how these axioms are to be construed, what their logical form is.

WAISMANN: You can of course write them as truth functions by saying, e.g.: 'for all *x*, if *x* is a point, then . . .', I believe, however, that we miss the real sense of the axioms in this way. We mustn't introduce the points one after another. It seems much more correct to me to introduce the points, lines, planes by means of co-ordinates as it were at one fell swoop.

WITTGENSTEIN: That's my view too. But one thing I don't understand: What would it mean to say that these axioms form a contradiction? The position is that as they stand they can't yield a contradiction, unless I determine by a rule that their logical product is a contradiction. That is, the situation with contradiction here is just as it is with the incompatibility of the propositions: 'This patch is green' and 'This patch is red'. As they stand, these propositions don't contradict one another at all. They only contradict one another once we introduce a further rule of syntax forbidding treating both propositions as true. Only then does a contradiction arise. (Cf. above p. 323: the example with 'the sum of the angles of a triangle = 180°'.)

(September 1931)

WAISMANN ASKS: (You said earlier) there was no contradiction at all in the calculus. I now don't understand how that fits in with the nature of indirect proof, for this proof of course depends precisely on producing a contradiction in the calculus.

WITTGENSTEIN: What I mean has nothing at all to do with indirect proof. There's a confusion here. Of course there are contradictions in the calculus; all I mean is this: it makes no sense to talk of a *hidden* contradiction. For what would a hidden contradiction be? I can, e.g., say: the divisibility of 357,567 by 7 is hidden, that is, as long as I have not applied the criterion – say the rule for division. In order to turn the divisibility from a hidden one into an open one, I need only apply the criterion. Now, is it like that with contradiction? Obviously not. For I can't bring the contradiction into the light of day by applying a criterion. Now I say: then all this talk of a hidden contradiction makes no sense, and the danger mathematicians talk about is pure imagination.

You might now ask: But what if one day a method were discovered for establishing the presence or absence of a contradiction? This proposition is very queer. It makes it look as if you could look at mathematics on an assumption, namely the assumption that a method is found. Now I can, e.g., ask whether a red-haired man has been found in this room, and this question makes perfect sense, for I can describe the man even if he isn't there. Whereas I can't ask after a method for establishing a contradiction, for I can only describe it (the method) once it's there. If it hasn't yet been discovered, I'm in no position to describe it, and what I say are empty words. And so I can't even begin to ask the question what would happen if a method were discovered.

The situation with the method for demonstrating a contradiction is precisely like that with Goldbach's conjecture: what is going on is a random attempt at constructing a calculus. If the attempt succeeds I have a calculus before me again, only a different one from that which I have used till now. But I still haven't proved the calculus is a calculus, nor can that be proved at all.

If someone were to describe the introduction of irrational

numbers by saying he had discovered that between the rational points on a line there were yet more points, we would reply: 'Of course you haven't discovered new points between the old ones: you have constructed new points. So you have a new calculus before you.' That's what we must say to Hilbert when he believes it to be a discovery that mathematics is consistent. In reality the situation is that Hilbert doesn't establish something, he lays it down. When Hilbert says: $0 \neq 0$ is not to occur as a provable formula, he defines a calculus by permission and prohibition.

WAISMANN ASKS: But still you said a contradiction can't occur in the calculus itself, only in the rules. The configurations can't represent a contradiction. Is that still your view now?

WITTGENSTEIN: I would say that the rules, too, form a calculus, but a different one. The crucial point is for us to come to an understanding on what we mean by the term contradiction. For if you mean one thing by it and I mean another, we can't reach any agreement.

The word 'contradiction' is taken in the first instance from where we all use it, namely from the truth functions, and mean, say, $p \cdot \sim p$. So in the first instance we can only talk of a contradiction where it's a matter of assertions. Since the formulae of a calculus are not assertions, there can't be contradictions in the calculus either. But of course you can stipulate that a particular configuration of the calculus, e.g. $0 \neq 0$, is to be called a contradiction. Only then there is always the danger of your thinking of contradiction in logic and so confounding 'contradictory' and 'forbidden'. For if I call a particular configuration of signs in the *calculus* a contradiction, then that only means that the formation of this configuration is forbidden: if in a proof you stumble upon such a formula, something must be done about it, e.g. the opening formula must be struck out.

In order to avoid this confusion, I should like to propose that in place of the word 'contradiction' we use a completely new sign which has no associations for us except what we have explicitly laid down: let's say the sign S. *In the calculus, don't take anything for granted*. If the formula S occurs, as yet that has no significance at all. We have first to make further stipulations.

WAISMANN ASKS: An equation in arithmetic has a twofold significance: it is a configuration and it is a substitution rule. Now what would happen if in arithmetic or analysis a proof of the formula $o \neq o$ were to be found? Then arithmetic would have to be given a completely different meaning, since we wouldn't any longer be entitled to interpret an equation as a substitution rule. 'You cannot substitute o for o' certainly doesn't mean anything. A disciple of Hilbert could now say: there you see what the consistency proof really achieves. Namely this proof is intended to show us that we are entitled to interpret an equation as a substitution rule.

WITTGENSTEIN: That, of course, is something it can't mean. Firstly: how does it come about that we may interpret an equation as a substitution rule? Well, simply, because the grammar of the word 'substitute' is the same as the grammar of an equation. That is why there is from the outset a parallelism between substitution rules and equations. (Both, e.g., are transitive.) Imagine I were to say to you 'You cannot substitute a for a'. What would you do?

WAISMANN: I wouldn't know what to think, since this claim is incompatible with the grammar of the word 'substitute'.

WITTGENSTEIN: Good, you wouldn't know what to think, and quite right too, for in fact you have a new calculus in front of you, one with which you're unfamiliar. If I now explain the calculus to you by giving the grammatical rules and the application, then you will also understand the claim 'You cannot substitute a for a'. You can't understand this claim while you remain at the standpoint of the old calculus. Now, if say the formula $o \neq o$ could be proved, that would only mean we have two different calculi before us: one calculus which is the grammar of the verb 'substitute', and another in which the formula $o \neq o$ can be proved. These two calculi would then exist alongside one another.

If someone now wanted to ask whether it wouldn't be possible to prove that the grammar of the word 'substitute' is the same as the grammar of an equation, i.e. that an equation can be interpreted as a substitution rule, we should have to reply: there can be no question of a proof here. For how is the claim supposed to run which is to be proved? That I apply the calculus, after all, only means that I set up rules telling me what to do when this or that comes out in the calculus. Am I then supposed to prove that I have set up rules? For surely that's the only sense the question whether I have applied the calculus can have. I once wrote: the calculus is not a concept of mathematics.

WAISMANN: You said on one occasion that no contradictions can occur in the calculus. If, e.g., we take the axioms of Euclidean geometry and add in the further axiom: 'The sum of the angles of a triangle is 181°', even this would not give rise to a contradiction. For it could of course be that the sum of the angles has two values, just as does $\sqrt{4}$. Now if you put it like that, I no longer understand what an indirect proof achieves. For indirect proof rests precisely on the fact that a contradiction is derived in the calculus. Now what happens if I lay down as an axiom an assumption which has been refuted by an indirect proof? Doesn't the system of axioms thus extended present a contradiction? For instance: in Euclidean geometry it is proved that you can only drop *one* perpendicular from a point onto a straight line, what's more by an indirect proof. For suppose there are two perpendiculars, then these would form a triangle with two right angles, the sum of whose angles would be greater than 180°, contradicting the well known theorem about the sum of the angles. If I now lay down the proposition 'there are two perpendiculars' as an axiom and add the rest of the axioms of Euclidean geometry – don't I now obtain a contradiction?

WITTGENSTEIN: Not at all. What is indirect proof? Manipulating signs. But that surely isn't everything. A further rule now comes in, too, telling me what to do when an indirect proof is performed. (The rule, e.g., might run: if an indirect proof has been performed, all the assumptions from which the proof proceeds may not be struck out.) *Nothing is to be taken for granted here. Everything must be explicitly spelt out.* That this is so easily left undone is bound up with the fact that we can't break away from what the words 'contradiction' etc. mean in ordinary speech.

If I now lay down the axiom 'Two perpendiculars can be dropped from one point onto a straight line', the sign picture of an indirect proof is certainly contained in this calculus. But we don't use it as such.

What then would happen if we laid down such an axiom? 'I'd reach a point where I wouldn't know how to go on.' Quite right, you don't know how to go on because you have a new calculus before you with which you are unfamiliar. A further stipulation needs making.

WAISMANN: But you could always do that when an indirect proof is given in a normal calculus. You could retain the refuted proposition by altering the stipulation governing the use of indirect proof, and then the proposition simply wouldn't be refuted any more.

WITTGENSTEIN: Of course we could do that. We have then simply destroyed the character of indirect proof, and what is left of the indirect proof is the mere sign picture.

(December 1931)

WAISMANN formulates the problem of consistency:

The significance of the problem of consistency is as follows: How do I know that a proposition I have proved by transfinite methods cannot be refuted by a finite numerical calculation? If, e.g., a mathematician finds a proof of Fermat's Last Theorem which uses essentially transfinite methods – say the Axiom of Choice, or the Law of the Excluded Middle in the form: either Goldbach's conjecture holds for all numbers, or there is a number for which it doesn't hold – how do I know that such a theorem can't be refuted by a counter-example? That is not in the least self-evident. And yet it is remarkable that mathematicians place so much trust in the transfinite modes of inference that, once such a proof is known, no one would any longer try to discover a counter example. The question now arises: Is this trust justifiable? That is, are we sure that a proposition which has been proved by transfinite methods can never be refuted by a concrete numerical calculation? That's the mathematical problem of consistency.

I will at the same time show how the matter seems to stand to me by raising the analogous question for ordinary algebra. How do I know, when I have proved a theorem by calculating with letters, that it can't be refuted by a numerical example? Suppose, e.g., I've proved that $1 + 2 + 3 + \ldots + n = \frac{n(n+1)}{2}$ – how do I know this formula can survive the test of numerical calculation? Here we have precisely the same situation. I believe we have to say the following: the reason why a calculation made with letters and a numerical calculation lead to the same result, i.e., the reason why calculating with letters can be applied to concrete numbers, lies in the fact that the axioms of the letter calculus – the commutative, associative laws of addition etc. – are chosen from the outset so as to permit such an application. This is connected with the fact that we choose axioms in accordance with a definite recipe. That is, an axiom corresponds to an induction, and this correspondence is possible because the formulae possess the same multiplicity as the induction, so that we can project the system of induction onto the system of formulae. And so there is no problem in this case, and we can't raise the question at all whether a calculation with letters can even come into conflict with a numerical calculation. But what about analysis? Here there really seems at first sight to be a problem.

WITTGENSTEIN: First of all: what are we really talking about? If by 'trust' is meant a disposition, I would say: that is of no interest to me. That has to do with the psychology of mathematicians. And so presumably something else is meant by 'trust'. Then it can only be something which can be written down in symbols. What we have to ask about seems to be the reason why two calculations tally. Let's take a quite simple example:

$$2 + (3 + 4) = 2 + 7 = 9$$
$$(2 + 3) + 4 = 5 + 4 = 9$$

I have here performed two independent calculations and arrived on both occasions at the same result. 'Independent' here means: the one calculation isn't a copy of the other. I have two different processes.

And what if they didn't agree? Then there's simply nothing I can do about it. The symbols would then just have a different grammar. The associative and commutative laws of addition hold on the basis of grammar. But in group theory it's no longer the case that $AB = BA$; and so, e.g., we couldn't calculate in two ways, and yet we still have a calculus.

This is how things are: I must have previously laid down when a calculation is to be correct. That is, I must state in what circumstances I will say a formula is proved. Now if the case arose that a formula counted as having been proved on the basis of one method, but as refuted on the basis of another, then that wouldn't in the least imply we now have a contradiction and are hopelessly lost; on the contrary we can say: the formula simply means different things. It belongs to two different calculi. In the one calculus it's proved, in the other refuted. And so we really have two different formulae in front of us which by mere accident have their signs in common.

A whole series of confusions has arisen around the question of consistency.

Firstly, we have to ask where the contradiction is supposed to arise: in the rules or in the configurations of the game.

What is a rule? If, e.g., I say 'Do this and don't do this', the other doesn't know what he is meant to do; that is, we don't allow a contradiction to count as a rule. We just don't call a contradiction a rule – or more simply the grammar of the word 'rule' is such that a contradiction isn't designated as a rule. Now if a contradiction occurs among my rules, I could say: these aren't rules in the sense I normally speak of rules. What do we do in such a case? Nothing could be more simple: we give a new rule and the matter's resolved.

An example here would be a board game. Suppose there is one rule here saying 'black must jump over white'. Now if the white piece is at the edge of the board, the rule can't be applied any more. We then simply make a new stipulation to cover this case, and with that the difficulty is wiped off the face of the earth.

But here we must be even more precise. We have here a contradiction (namely between the rules 'white must jump over black' and 'you may not jump over the edge of the board'). I now ask: Did we possess a method for discovering the contradiction at the outset? There are two possibilities here:

1) In the board game this possibility was undoubtedly present. For the rule runs: 'In general . . .' If this means 'in this position and in this position . . .' then I obviously had the possibility right at the beginning of discovering the contradiction – and if I haven't seen it, that's my fault. Perhaps I've been too lazy to run through all the cases, or I have forgotten one. There's no serious problem present in this case at all. Once the contradiction arises, I simply make a new stipulation and so remove it. We can always wipe the contradiction off the face of the earth.

But whether there is a contradiction can always be settled by inspecting the list of rules. That is, e.g., in the case of Euclidean geometry a matter of five minutes. The rules of Euclidean geometry don't contradict one another, i.e., no rule occurs which cancels out an earlier one (p and $\sim p$), and with that I'm satisfied.

2) But now let's take the second case, that we have no such method. My list of rules is therefore in order. I can't see any contradiction. Now I ask: Is there now still any danger? It's out of the question. What are we supposed to be afraid of? A contradiction? But a contradiction is only given me with the method for discovering it. As long as the contradiction hasn't arisen, it's no concern of mine. So I can quite happily go on calculating. Would

the calculations mathematicians have made through the centuries suddenly come to an end because a contradiction had been found in mathematics ? Would we say they weren't calculations ? Certainly not. If a contradiction does arise, we will simply deal with it. But we don't need to worry our heads about it *now*.

What people are really after is something quite different. A certain paradigm hovers before their mind's eye, and they want to bring the calculus *into line with this paradigm*.

EDITOR'S NOTE

Our text is a typescript that G. E. Moore gave us soon after Wittgenstein's death: evidently the one which Wittgenstein left with Bertrand Russell in May, 1930, and which Russell sent to the Council of Trinity College, Cambridge, with his report in favour of a renewal of Wittgenstein's research grant. [1] All the passages in it were written in manuscript volumes between February 2nd, 1929, and the last week of April, 1930. The latest manuscript entry typed and included here is dated April 24th, 1930. On May 5th, 1930, Russell wrote to Moore that he had 'had a second visit from Wittgenstein . . . . He left me a large quantity of typescript which I am to forward to Littlewood as soon as I have read it.' [J. E. Littlewood, F.R.S., Fellow of Trinity College.] In his report to the Council, dated May 8th, Russell says he spent five days in discussion with Wittgenstein, 'while he explained his ideas, and he left with me a bulky typescript, *Philosophische Bemerkungen*, of which I have read about a third. The typescript, which consists merely of rough notes, would have been very difficult to understand without the help of the conversations'. The Council had authorized Moore to ask Russell for a report, and I suppose they asked Moore to return the typescript to Wittgenstein. Wittgenstein asked Moore to take care of it. Apparently he did not keep a copy himself.

Wittgenstein had made an earlier visit to Russell, in March, 1930, and Russell wrote to Moore then that 'he intends while in Austria to make a synopsis of his work which would make it much easier for me to report adequately. . . . He intends to visit me again in Cornwall just before the beginning of the May term, with his synopsis'. Wittgenstein can hardly have called the *Bemerkungen* a synopsis when he gave it to Russell; nor did Russell when he wrote to Moore and then to the Council about it. On the other hand it

---

1] *The Autobiography of Bertrand Russell,* Volume II, pp. 196–200. London, 1968.

is a selection and a rearrangement of passages from what he had in manuscript and in typescript at the time. It was made from slips cut from a typescript and pasted into a blank ledger in a new order. The 'continuous' typescript was made from Wittgenstein's manuscript volumes I, II, III and the first half of IV. In the typing Wittgenstein left out many of the manuscript passages – more from I and II than from the others. In this typing he changed the order of some large blocks of material. This was nothing like his rearrangement of the slips he cut from it for the *Philosophische Bemerkungen* as Moore gave it to us.

It was not 'merely rough notes'. But it was not easy to read, and Wittgenstein would not have published it without polishing. No spacing showed where a group of remarks hang closely together and where a new topic begins. Paragraphs were not numbered. And it was hard to see the arrangement and unity of the work until one had read it a number of times. (Russell did not have time to read it through once.) If he had thought of making this type-script more *übersichtlich* Wittgenstein might have introduced numbers for paragraphs, as he did in the *Brown Book* and in the *Investigations*. He might have divided into chapters, as he did with the typescript of 1932/33 (No. 213) – although he never did this again. (See Part II of *Philosophische Grammatik*.) The 1932/33 typescript was the only one for which he made a table of contents. We cannot guess whether he would have tried to do this for the *Philosophische Bemerkungen*. For the *Blue Book* he gave neither numbers nor chapter divisions. If he did at first think of the *Bemerkungen* which he left with Russell as a *'synopsis'* of his writing over the past 18 months, he might have thought of some system of numbering (I am thinking of the *Tractatus*) which would show the arrangement. But I have found no reference or note in this sense.

He went on writing directly after he had seen Russell – from the entries in the manuscript volume you would think there had not been a break. He had kept a copy of the typescript he had cut into slips to form the *Philosophische Bemerkungen*. (The top copy, in fact – and the least legible, for the first 60 pages of it: his type-writer ribbon was exhausted and hardly left ink marks. Later he used to dictate to a professional typist.) In a number of places he added to what he had typed or revised it – writing in pencil or ink on the back of the typed sheets or between the lines or in the margins. And in certain places he took pages from this copy and cut sections from it – pasting them into manuscript books or clipping them together with slips from other typescripts to form the 1932/33 typescript. In one or two places I have quoted a pencilled revision in a footnote here. But I do not think generally that the revisions he made there can be counted as revisions of the typescript (with its title page and motto) which he had left with Russell. They belonged to a far-reaching change and development in Wittgenstein's thinking, and a different book.

He had arrived in Cambridge sometime in January, 1929, and began his first manuscript volume on February 2nd. (Manuscript 'volume', as distinct from 'notebook': it was generally a hard covered notebook, often a large ledger. Such a volume is never rough notes, as the paper-covered and pocket notebooks often are.) Volumes I and II cannot be separated, for he wrote at first on the right-hand pages only; when he reached the end of volume II in this way he continued what he was writing on the *left*-hand pages of volume II, and when he came to the end of the volume on this side he continued on the left-hand pages of volume I – and on to the end of I. Volume III begins where this leaves off. He started III at the end of August or the beginning of September, 1929. (After the first week he did not date his entries in I and II. The first date in III comes on page 87 of the manuscript. It is: 11.9.29.)

He wrote *Some Remarks on Logical Form* to read to the Aristotelian Society and Mind Association Joint Session in July, 1929 – but he disliked the paper and when the time came he ignored it and talked about infinity in mathematics. In volumes I and II there are discussions of suggestions he makes in the *Logical Form* paper. The *Philosophische Bemerkungen* has a few of these; but many – those central to the paper, I think – are left out. Some remarks about 'phenomenological language' may refer to the earlier view in that paper. And the first sentence in §46 may refer to the example using coordinates there.

In Appendix I: Wittgenstein's typescript of 'Complex and Fact'

(*Komplex und Tatsache*) is taken from manuscript volume VI, in an entry dated 30.6.31. – more than a year after the last passage in the *Bemerkungen*. It is the first of three sections of what he had put together as a single typescript (now printed together in *Philosophische Grammatik*). These are numbered consecutively as forming a single essay, although they do not come close to one another in the manuscripts. 'Infinitely Long' and 'Infinite Possibility' are numbered consecutively, as though forming one essay, as well. Both groups seem to have been typed along with the 1932/33 typescript and Wittgenstein kept them together with it, but they do not form part of it.

Of the two sections that *follow* 'Complex and Fact' in the typescript, about two-thirds of the remarks are here in *Philosophische Bemerkungen*, especially §93 to the end of §98. In the manuscript (volume VI) the discussion of 'complex ≠ fact' grows out of 'I describe the fact which would be the fulfilment' of an order or of an expectation – and the apparent difficulty that this description is 'general in character', whereas the 'fulfilment' when it arrives is something you can point to. As though I had painted the apple that was going to grow on this branch, and now the apple itself is there: as though the grown apple was the event I was expecting. But the apple is not an event at all. 'The fact (or event) is described in general terms.' But then the fact is treated as though it were on all fours with a house or some other sort of complex. I expected the man, and my expectation is fulfilled. But *the man I expected* is not the fulfilment; but *that he has come*. This leads directly to 'complex ≠ fact'. And this was important for the understanding of '*describing*'.

Expectation and fulfilment have a different role in mathematics – not like their role in experience. And in mathematics there is *not* this distinction.

'In mathematics description and object are equivalent. "The fifth number in this series of numbers has these properties" says the *same* as "5 has these properties". The properties of a house do not *follow* from its position in a row of houses; but the properties of a number are the properties of a position.'

You cannot *describe* what you expect to happen in the development of a decimal fraction, except by writing out the calculation in which it comes. Wittgenstein used to put this by saying 'the description of a calculation accomplishes the same as the calculation; the description of a language accomplishes the same as the language'.

The passage I have quoted comes just before the discussion of 'Infinitely Long' in the manuscript (volume IX). Revising his account of 'description' brought with it a revision of the account of the *application* of mathematics, and especially of the use of expressions like 'infinity' in the mathematical sense for the description of physical happenings.

RUSH RHEES

TRANSLATORS' NOTE

This note, like the translation itself, runs the risk of overlying and obscuring the original. Yet we very much wish to express our thanks for help received, and we also feel we should mention one or two significant areas where we are conscious of having only half-resolved the difficulties of translation.

Wittgenstein's style often depends on repeating certain words or groups of words in order to create a series of sometimes unexpected interrelations and back-references within the discussion. Some of these terms, e.g. *Raum* [space], have a straightforward English equivalent, whereas others prove less tractable. In such cases to use the same word in English throughout would unduly strain against the natural bent of English usage, whilst varying the English equivalents blunts the point of Wittgenstein's remarks. One term important enough to single out is *Bild*: 'picture' covers much the same area as this term in Wittgenstein's usage, but various phrases, e.g. *Erinnerungsbild* [memory image] are beyond its natural scope. For *Maßstab* we have usually said 'yardstick', since like *Maßstab* it can be used to convey a general notion of measure or standard whilst retaining, to some degree, its characteristics as a measure of length. At times these characteristics come into their own, for instance when Wittgenstein says someone shows his understanding of the notion of height in that he knows it is measured by a *Maßstab* and not by a weighing machine. At another point he reflects that the yardstick [*Maßstab*] needn't of course be a yardstick, it could equally well be a dial or scale with a needle. And, of course, it isn't strictly correct to say that the application is what makes a stick into a yardstick, it makes a stick (of any length) into a measuring stick, or a rod into a measuring rod [*Maßstab*]. Occasionally, we felt that 'ruler' or 'measure' would be more natural – neither of us thought people would keep yardsticks in their pockets – and that such mild variation in equivalents might possibly emphasize the unity of the underlying principle: they are all standards of measurement. A word curiously difficult to translate is *suchen*: 'seek', 'search (for)' and 'look (for)' all create difficulties, the first because it has the wrong kind of resonance, the others because of the occurrence of such sentences as 'Tell me how you *suchen*, and I will tell you what you *suchen*'. 'Tell me how you are searching and I will tell you what you are searching for' throws unwanted emphasis on 'for', and it is obvious that 'looking' and 'looking for' don't fit in with this pattern of syntax. We have generally said 'proposition' for *Satz*, but some contexts ask for 'sentence' in English and others for 'theorem'. In such cases important links are lost, and wherever it seemed appropriate we have indicated this fact. The word *Übersichtlichkeit*, which occurs at the beginning of the book, must have given trouble to all translators, who have variously rendered it as 'perspicuity', 'surveyability' and 'synoptic view', whereas we have rendered it freely as 'bird's-eye view'. The idea at stake here is that a range of phenomena is made *übersichtlich* or *übersehbar* when presented in such a way that we can simultaneously grasp the phenomena individually and as a whole, i.e. if their interrelations can be seen or surveyed in their entirety (you could say in *RFM* that a proof is *übersehbar* if it may be taken in as a single proof). Although differing from the German in that it suggests the elimination of the less important elements, 'bird's-eye view' seems to work well enough in our context. However, in view of the use Wittgenstein later makes of this concept, we felt we should signal its presence in the German text and express the hope that 'bird's-eye view' has something of its immediacy and simplicity.

In preparing this translation we have received help and encouragement from a number of people, especially members of the Philosophy Department in the University of Leeds, and also members of the German Department. We are indebted to Mrs Inge Hudson for some suggestions about German usage and particularly to Peter Long for suggesting apt and pleasing ways of catching the force of the original at a number of points. Finally, we owe a special debt of gratitude to Rush Rhees for allowing us a completely free hand with the translation and for making considered and valuable suggestions on virtually every paragraph. We hope that these remarks indicate in some degree the extent to which we have benefited from his generosity.

This is a translation of the German edition of *Philosophische Bemerkungen*, edited by Rush Rhees, published Oxford 1964. The only divergences are a few additional footnotes requested by Rush Rhees. The following list of *Corrigenda* to the German edition was prepared by Rush Rhees and ourselves.

As far as practicable the pagination of the translation follows that of the German edition.

CORRIGENDA FOR GERMAN TEXT

p. 41, 8 lines up: for 'Nun, wenn festgelegt wird' read 'Nur, ...'

p. 51, 9 lines up: for 'als' read 'also'

p. 68, 19 lines down: for 'in einem erwarteten Zustand' read: 'in einem erwartenden Zustand'

p. 80, 13 lines down: for 'heraussehen' read 'heraussehnen'

p. 81, line 19: for 'Vieleicht' read 'Vielleicht'

p. 92, line 15: for 'indem' read 'in dem'
line 16: for 'in dem Zahn eines andern' read 'in dem Zahn in eines andern ...'

p. 93, line 3: for 'und kann es' read 'und es kann'
line 5: for '?' read '.'

p. 95, 9 lines up: for 'M' read 'N'

p. 99, Lower Diagram as in E.T.

p. 115, 12 lines up: insert 'es' before 'offenbar'

p. 116, line 7: for 'Gesichtsfeld' read 'Gesichtsbild'
6 lines up: for 'ein' read 'mein'

p. 118, 2 lines up: for 'in der zweiten' read 'in die zweite'

p. 121, line 20: insert comma after 'gesprochen'

p. 122, 13 lines up: for '(F(x)' read 'F(x)'
5 lines up: for 'drei' read 'zwei'

In Section X quantifiers should be as in English text. For an explanation see E.T. page 126, footnote.

p. 124, lines 6 and 7: for 'F' and 'G' read 'φ' and 'ψ'

p. 139, line 9: for 'A,B,C, A,C,B,' read 'ABC, ACB,'

p. 144, 5 and 7 lines up: for 'Chr n)' read 'Chr n'

p. 150, line 1: insert 'nicht' before 'weh'

p. 153, lines 9 and 16: for 'Ahne' read 'Ahn'

p. 159, 6 lines up: italicise 'Struktur'

p. 169, line 8: italicise 'Struktur'

p. 174, 3 lines up: '(ist das aber wahr?).⟨': i.e. insert closing quotation mark

p. 177 *et seq.*: replace '$\sin x = 1 - \frac{x^3}{3!} + \ldots$' by '$\sin x = x - \frac{x^3}{3!} + \ldots$'

p. 178, 13 lines up: for 'synthetischen' read 'syntaktischen'

p. 179, 10 lines up: for 'zwei der ersten analogen Systeme' read 'zwei den ersten analoge Systeme'

p. 180, 2 lines up: delete 'sich'

p. 182, line 14: for 'Operationen' read 'Iterationen'

p. 193, last line: for 'Interpertation' read 'Interpretation'

p. 200, line 11: for 'eigentliche' read 'Eigentliche'

p. 206, 9 lines up: for 'R⚹' substitute 'R*':

p. 207, line 6: for 'einen Leiter' read 'eine Leiter'

p. 210, 5 lines up: for 'als' read 'also'

p. 212, line 11: for '(x)$\cdot$ φx = ψx' read '(x)$\cdot$f$_1$x = f$_2$x'

p. 214, line 13: for 'Menschen, den . . .' read 'Menschen den'
  line 16: for 'x = $\{^0_2\}$' read 'x = $\{^0_2\}$'

p. 215, 6 lines up: for 'm $\rangle$ n' read 'm > n'

p. 219, 6 lines up: replace comma by question mark after 'Grenzen-losigkeit'

p. 223, line 9: for 'dazu käme' read 'dazukäme'

p. 225, 8 lines up: for '0,142837' read '0,142837'

p. 229, line 12: for 'daß ich' read 'daß, wenn ich'

p. 232, 4 lines up: for 'derer' read 'deren'

p. 233, line 7: for Kpirale' read 'Spirale'
  15 lines up: for 'eines unendliches Gesetzes' read 'eines unendlichen Gesetzes'

p. 237, for footnote: '1] Siehe unten, S.240' read
  '1] Siehe oben, S.232, §189, ersten Neben-satz'

p. 240, 12 lines up: for 'P = 0,1110101001' read
  'P = 0,0110101001'
  4 lines up: for '1,1414' read '1,414'

p. 241, 3 lines up: 'Zahl? « –': i.e. insert closing quotation mark

p. 243, Diagram as in E.T.

p. 253, 7 lines up: for 'rot, kreisförmig' read 'rot und kreisförmig'

p. 255, line 10: for 'Zweidrittelkreis' read 'Kreis'

p. 263, 2 lines up: for 'etwas' read 'etwa'

p. 266, 7 lines up: for 'Keis' read 'Kreis'

p. 272, line 11: for 'Unsinn,' read 'Unsinn),'

p. 275, line 6: throughout this discussion Wittgenstein talks of '45 Grad'. It appears this is a slip and that the discussion would make clearer sense with '90 Grad' passim.

p. 276, line 4: for 'Blau – Rot' read 'Blau-Rot'

p. 279, 10 lines up: for 'Zwischen' read '*Zwischen*'
  8 and 5 lines up: for 'orangefarbenen' read 'orangefarbigen'

p. 280, 10 lines up: for 'ankennt' read 'anerkennt'

p. 284, line 13: for 'mir' read 'mit'

p. 287, line 18: for 'Jede' read 'Jene'

p. 295, Diagram at top of page as in E.T.

p. 296, line 6: for 'nicht' read 'mich': Cf. footnote to E.T.

p. 304, 8 lines up: for 'Fällen' read 'Fallen'

p. 333, line 20: 'p, q r' read 'p, q, r'

p. 343, line 14: for '$\frac{2}{n(n+1)}$' read '$\frac{n(n+1)}{2}$'